RURAL ENGLAND
OUR COUNTRYSIDE AT THE CROSSROADS

RURAL ENGLAND
OUR COUNTRYSIDE AT THE CROSSROADS
DERRIK MERCER & DAVID PUTTNAM

with photographs by
DERRY BRABBS

Macdonald
Queen Anne Press

A Queen Anne Press Book

Concept and Compilation © CPRE 1988
Text © Derrik Mercer 1988
Photographs © Derry Brabbs 1988

First published in Great Britain in 1988 by
Queen Anne Press, a division of
Macdonald & Co (Publishers) Ltd
3rd Floor
Greater London House
Hampstead Road
London NW1 7QX

A Pergamon Press plc Company

Title page photograph: Farmland near Harrogate, North Yorkshire

British Library Cataloguing in Publication Data

Puttnam, David
    Rural England Our countryside at the crossroad.
    1. England. Countryside. Conservation
    I Title II. Mercer, Derrik
    333. 76'16'0942

    ISBN 0–356–12761–3

Typeset by Butler & Tanner Ltd, Frome and London
Printed and bound in Great Britain by
Purnell Book Production Ltd, Paulton
Member of BPCC plc

CONTENTS

ACKNOWLEDGMENTS

The preparation of this book coincided with a period of intense debate about the future of the English countryside. Reports poured forth from official and unofficial sources about the crisis in agriculture, forestry, planning, energy exploration and recreation policies. Helping to guide me through the complexities and acronyms were many individuals and organisations. Of these, the Council for the Protection of Rural England (CPRE) bore the brunt of my questions and I am indebted to CPRE staff for their patience and time as well as their expertise.

Nationally, Robin Grove-White, then CPRE's director, helped to get the book under way and somehow found time to read the manuscript in draft form while speeding round the country between speaking engagements. Richard Bate, David Conder and Fiona Reynolds of CPRE's national staff also provided invaluable help during the preparation of the book plus constructive comments on the draft text. To them especially, but to all of CPRE's staff at its London headquarters, I pay particular thanks.

I was anxious that the book should reflect grass-roots concerns as well as a metropolitan perspective. To this end, I contacted all forty-three CPRE branches and associations (excluding that based in London), and virtually all of them supplied me with copies of their journals and annual reports. I managed to meet representatives of twenty-three county branches during my travels and spoke on the telephone or corresponded with eleven others. Any project which takes one to every county of England has to be enjoyable, but my travels were made even more rewarding by the friendly help which I received from these local organisations. The individuals are too numerous to name, so I hope they will accept that this collective note of gratitude is no less sincere for its anonymity.

Although this book has been prepared in collaboration with the CPRE, it is by no means the only organisation which I have consulted during its preparation. I would therefore like to acknowledge the assistance of the Countryside Commission, Nature Conservancy Council, Ministry of Agriculture, Department of the Environment, Forestry Commission, Ramblers' Association, Council for National Parks, Open Spaces Society, Agriculture Development and Advisory Service and the National Farmers' Union. A number of individuals gave generously of their time during my visits to their areas or organisations and, in several cases, read sections of the text to check for accuracy. From national park authorities there were Terry Carroll (Northumberland), John Baker (Yorkshire Dales), Ken Parker (Peak District) and Nick Pennington (North York Moors); from local authorities David Brewster (Norfolk Broads Authority), Melinda Appleby (Suffolk County Council), Vernon Hazel (Hampshire), Mike Shepherd (Dorset), Ken Brown (Somerset), Bill Lanning and

BELOW LEFT: *Poppy field in Lincolnshire*

BELOW: *The Quantocks near Broomfield, Somerset*

David Saunders (East Sussex); from other organisations Dr Brian Johnson (Nature Conservancy Council) and Kate Ashbrook (Open Spaces Society). I am grateful to John Tabor in Essex and Tony Norman in Herefordshire for showing me round their farms; to Conoco and St Albans Sand and Gravel Company for access to their mineral sites; and to Bill Wilder, then chairman of the Farming and Wildlife Advisory Group, for talking so fully about how the Group sees the future of farming and conservation.

A general book of this kind draws upon many more specialist works; two in particular I would like to acknowledge are *The History of the Countryside* by Oliver Rackham (Dent), and *The Changing Countryside*, edited by John Blunden and Nigel Curry (Croom Helm). The 'Countryside Heritage' series of reports published by Hampshire County Council were also helpful as well as impressive. I am grateful, too, to Dorset County Council for making available two unpublished studies: *The Conservation of the Dorset Heaths* by Brian Rippey (1973) and *The Conservation of Chalk Downland in Dorset* by Carys James (also 1973).

If any errors have survived the process of research and triple-checking, the fault rests with the author rather than those whom I consulted. It is in any case difficult to satisfy everyone. One day's post brought a comment that the text was perhaps a little unfair to farmers and another that it was too kind to them. I have tried throughout to adopt as positive a tone as is warranted by what I found. Where there are schemes that provide grounds for optimism, these are reported. I have also tried to avoid a shrill, anatagonistic tone; castigating farmers in general is too simplistic given regional variations and forty years of official incentives to intensify production. If agriculture is a recurring theme, it is

7

because four fifths of England is a farmed landscape. Whatever happens in farming inevitably affects landscape and wildlife. And it is necessary to understand how our countryside has evolved if we are fully to appreciate why it now faces a crisis.

All of these issues are illuminated by the magnificent photographs of Derry Brabbs, whose work alone explains why the Council for the Protection of Rural England is fighting to ensure that the English countryside remains the source of enjoyment and inspiration that it is today. I hope that this book will make more people aware of what is at stake.

Derrik Mercer
Autumn 1987

FOREWORD AND
GLOSSARY

It may help readers to understand how the book is organised. After David Puttnam's introduction, it is divided into six regional chapters. Government and other bodies vary in how they allocate counties to regions, so it is virtually impossible to please all local interests. Parts of Gloucestershire, for instance, look south towards Bristol and the West Country, while northern sections of the county gravitate more naturally to Birmingham. A few counties – Cheshire, Essex and Oxfordshire – are therefore mentioned in more than one chapter, but the division used here seems more valid than any alternative.

Some issues also recur in more than one chapter – green belts and hedgerow loss, for instance. But each issue is described in detail only once, so that Northern England focuses in some detail on policies for the uplands, forestry, mineral extraction and areas of outstanding natural beauty; the Pennine Shires on national parks, moorland, hay meadows and the urban fringe; the Midlands on agriculture and recreation in the wider countryside; the West Country on the coast, wetlands and military use of national parks; Eastern England on heathland, environmentally sensitive areas and hedgerows; and south-east England on ancient woodland, downland and development pressures, including green belts.

Organisations

There are dozens of national and local organisations with interests in the countryside. Some have roles which are more or less self-explanatory, such as the Ramblers' Association, Royal Society for the Protection of Birds (RSPB) and National Farmers' Union (NFU). But confusion sometimes arises about the differing responsibilities of the government-appointed bodies with interests in the countryside and those of some of the large voluntary bodies. Of these, the organisations which feature most frequently in this book are:

Council for the Protection of Rural England (CPRE): Founded in 1926 as the Council for the Preservation of Rural England, the CPRE is a national organisation lobbying at Westminster, and increasingly in Europe, for measures to protect and enhance the countryside. It has forty-three regional branches or associations which monitor changes in their areas as well as contributing to the formation of CPRE's national policy. Similar, but separate, organisations exist in Wales and Scotland. The distinctive role of CPRE is explained more fully in the introduction by David Puttnam, CPRE's President.

Countryside Commission: A government-appointed and -funded body with responsibilities for conserving the natural beauty of the countryside and for promoting improved access and facilities for countryside recreation. An advisory and promotional body, rather than an executive one, it is also responsible for advising governments on all countryside matters, including national parks. The Commission covers England and Wales; Scotland has a similar but separate organisation.

Development Commission: Originally set up in 1909 by Lloyd George, the Development Commission seeks to promote the economic and social life of rural areas by building small factories and workshops, supporting rural services and providing assistance to small businesses — principally through its main agency, the Council for Small Industries in Rural Areas (CoSIRA). Separate agencies cover England, Wales and Scotland. Like the Countryside Commission, it has an advisory role to the Department of the Environment.

Farming and Wildlife Advisory Group (FWAG): A voluntary organisation which grew out of a conference held in 1969 between conservation and farming groups. Now backed by organisations as diverse as the RSPB and National Farmers' Union, FWAG has sixty-four county associations throughout Britain and over thirty full-time farm conservation advisers. These advisers help farmers prepare conservation plans and offer guidance on matters such as trees, hedgerows and ponds.

Forestry Commission: Established in 1919 with a duty to promote timber production, the Forestry Commission had its responsibilities amended in 1985 to incorporate a new duty to achieve a 'reasonable balance' between the interests of forestry and those of the environment. The Commission has a dual role, managing nearly 3 million acres of woodland in Britain and also acting as the government's adviser on forestry policy with responsibilities for grants and tree-felling control.

National Trust: A charity founded in 1895 to protect places of historic interest or natural beauty. In 1987 the Trust had around 1.4 million members and owned 189 historic houses open to the public, 111 gardens, 470 miles of unspoiled coastline and 500,000 acres of open countryside. One trust covers England, Wales and Northern Ireland; another covers Scotland.

Nature Conservancy Council (NCC): A body appointed and funded by the government to promote nature conservation with a specialist scientific interest in safeguarding wildlife and

10

Biddenden, Kent

geological sites and conducting research. The NCC has a direct executive role in managing national nature reserves and scheduling sites of special scientific interest (SSSIs).

Royal Society for Nature Conservation: This acts as the national association of forty-seven county naturalist trusts and is the major voluntary national body concerned with all aspects of nature conservation in Britain. Many county trusts run local nature reserves.

Designated countryside

Area of outstanding natural beauty (AONB): This designation covers thirty-eight areas of England and Wales, with four more awaiting designation. The areas vary greatly in size and character. While falling short of national park status (being generally smaller, less wild or with more limited recreation possibilities), the areas nonetheless possess a quality of landscape judged in the national interest worthy to maintain. AONBs are designated by the Countryside Commission, subject to government confirmation. Although it does not confer the executive authority enjoyed by national parks, designation is intended to strengthen the hand of local authorities in discouraging unsuitable development. In 1987 AONBs covered over 12 per cent of England and Wales.

Country park: An area of open country or woodland, usually within easy reach of towns, offering recreation of a variety between that encountered in the wilder landscapes of national parks and that of suburban parks. In England and Wales more than 200 country parks have been established by local authorities and others since 1970, usually with assistance from the Countryside Commission. Many offer trails, picnic sites and visitor centres.

Environmentally sensitive area (ESA): An area designated by the Ministry of Agriculture (in consultation with the Countryside Commission and NCC) in which farmers are offered annual payments to pursue methods which will maintain traditional landscapes, wildlife and historic features. Nine areas came into force in 1987, with more to follow in 1988. Although farmers' participation in the payment scheme is voluntary, three quarters of all land included in the first group of ESAs is covered by it.

Green belt: An area of land outside a city to limit the outward spread of urban development. The inner boundary of a green belt provides a break between town and country. The prime objective of this 'cordon sanitaire' is to prevent urban sprawl and the coalescence of settlements. Once established, green belts offer encouragement to agriculture, recreation and amenity. First proposed for London in 1944, the principle of green belts was extended to the rest of Britain in 1955. A government circular said then that only developments associated with farming, forestry, low-intensity recreation or other rural uses would normally be allowed inside green belts. The policy was strengthened in 1984 when the government recognised that green belts also provided a spur to urban regeneration.

Heritage coast: An area of attractive coastline in England and Wales, designated by the Countryside Commission, for which the Commission encourages and assists local authorities to prepare management plans to conserve the coast and enhance recreation possibilities. Thirty-nine sections of coast had been defined by 1987, covering 851 miles of shore, or 31 per cent of the coastline. Five more potential heritage coasts await designation.

Landscape Conservation Order (LCO): Long sought by conservation groups such as the CPRE as a power of last resort, comparable to Tree Preservation Orders (see below). The CPRE would like all local authorities and national park authorities to have the power to issue LCOs in order to prevent landscape features or areas being significantly damaged by agricultural or other developments. Landowners would have rights of appeal to the Department of the Environment upon refusal of consent. In 1987 the government issued proposals for LCOs, but suggested restricting them to *parts* of national parks.

National nature reserve: An area designated by the NCC as outstanding for its wildlife habitats and natural features. Reserves are not always fully open to the public, but are managed for scientific study and protection of rare flora and

12

fauna. Some reserves are managed under lease by organisations such as local naturalists' trusts. More than 200 national nature reserves had been designated by 1986, covering nearly 400,000 acres of Britain, of which roughly a quarter are owned by the NCC.

National park: Ten national parks were established in the 1950s covering approximately 9 per cent of England and Wales. Land is not nationally owned, but each park has its own authority, whose prime duties are to conserve and enhance the natural beauty of the landscape and to promote public enjoyment of the park. The Countryside Commission is responsible for advising governments on policy for national parks. A Broads Bill was introduced in 1987 providing comparable (if differently executed) status for the Norfolk and Suffolk Broads.

Ramsar sites: These are wetlands of international importance for waterfowl and other birds. They take their name from an international convention held at Ramsar, Iran, in 1971. This drew up criteria for establishing the importance of wetland sites and called upon signatories to protect these wetlands. Subsequent conferences have refined the definition of sites still further; a European Community 'birds directive' fulfils a similar role. Britain is among forty-three signatories to the convention, but although over 200 wetland sites meet the Ramsar criteria, only thirty-one had been formally designated by the government up to 1987.

13

Site of special scientific interest (SSSI): An area designated by the NCC to provide protection for wildlife and natural features. Around 6000 sites have been identified (although not all have yet been formally notified) and these cover roughly 8 per cent of Britain's total land area. Many are within national parks or other designated countryside. Landowners with SSSIs on their land must notify the NCC of any proposed actions which would affect the land; if the NCC objects, it must offer compensation as part of management agreements for the land.

Tree Preservation Order (TPO): Under the 1971 Town and Country Planning Act, local authorities can stop the felling of trees in the interests of amenity. Anyone may object to the making of a TPO. If there are objections, the ultimate decision passes to the Department of the Environment (DoE) which may arrange a local inquiry. In practice, more TPOs have been issued over trees in towns than those in the countryside.

INTRODUCTION

BY DAVID PUTTNAM

There is no escaping the fact that I am fundamentally an urban being – born and raised in north London and working in that most metropolitan of businesses, the film industry.

Yet my home is now in deepest Wiltshire and my heart set firmly in the English countryside. I am also President of the Council for the Protection of Rural England (CPRE).

Does that combination of commitments, urban and rural, seem strange? I don't believe it should.

This book is part of an attempt to show why it makes very good sense for all of us, wherever we live, to be concerned about the future of our countryside. In the late twentieth century, our complicated 'post-industrial' society is posing new problems for the cultural and natural heritage. It also offers the possibility of new accommodations.

England's countryside presents one huge paradox.

On the one hand, it is what it appears – a wonderful tapestry of landscapes and communities, intimate, varied, and an ever-present source of interest and refreshment; an inspiration to the vast number of us who visit or work in it. Almost all of us subscribe to an English tradition that views the countryside as the provider of simple, natural pleasures.

Yet beneath that surface is a harder-edged reality. Many of the landscapes we value are *creations*, artificial creations in a sense – emanating from political and economic forces, and struggles between interest groups, an endless series of compromises and battles. In other words, behind the pastoral scenes, there has constantly been tension and debate.

That conundrum lies at the centre of this book. It is clear in the interplay between Derry Brabbs's probing photographs and the incisiveness of Derrik Mercer's text.

We all need a beautiful countryside. But securing it

Allerford, Somerset

demands noisy dispute about the way in which our land is to be used. My own organisation, the CPRE, is, I am proud to say, at the centre of much of that argument.

True conservation of the natural heritage can never succeed unless it is grounded in a tough understanding of present realities – there is no place for wishful thinking. The uses to which land has been put have always been primarily determined by economic and political issues. In recent years, local historians have shown us how powerfully past events – the Dissolution of the Monasteries, the eighteenth-century Enclosure movement, the Industrial Revolution, the nineteenth-century railway boom, and so on – have shaped landscapes most of us regarded as 'natural'.

What was true in the past is even truer today.

In the late 1980s, everything about the countryside – its prosperity, its wildlife richness, its appearance, its accessibility – depends upon decisions made by ordinary men and women. And many of those decisions can be influenced by the rest of us, for good or ill. What distinguishes today's countryside from that of past ages is that the speed and scale of change and potential change is now *far* greater than anything our ancestors faced.

As we near the end of the century, new pressures threaten further transformation of the face of rural England. Give a thought to just three of the looming problems.

First, more and more people, myself included, want to live in the countryside. But what are the implications for our cities of huge outflows of population? Won't their alarming deterioration be accelerated? And can extensive new housing be accommodated within and around villages and market towns of rural England without destroying their charm completely?

Or take the new high-tech industries, more footloose than ever before. They too are eroding the old distinctions between town and country. Will it be possible to square *this* change, the need to find space for dynamic new enterprises that can create wealth for us all, with the need to protect and pass on our rural heritage?

Or consider agriculture itself, overwhelmingly the dominant use of rural land. Thirty years ago, farming and conservation went hand in hand. In fact, for the countryside, farming *was* conservation. Now, all too often, the two are at odds. Many recent farming techniques – vast fields, massive use of fertilisers and pesticides, intense specialisation – have been brutally damaging to wildlife and landscapes. Of course, in narrow (and important) terms of increased food production, they have succeeded. But this success is itself now penalising farmers. In Britain and other EEC countries, there are increasing demands to reduce subsidies to farmers, so that they will grow *less* food.

What will this mean for the way that land is used in future? What are the implications for conservation? Surely, farmers in difficulty will sell off land for housing development? If millions of acres rapidly become uneconomic to farm by present methods in England and Wales, as some experts predict, we may face a nightmare prospect. The scale of development sprawl on the green fields of the shires could be immense.

All these forces – new trends in housing and industrial development and the new situation in agriculture – are already re-shaping rural England. We have to face them, guide them and where necessary resist and transform them, if we are to have any chance of retaining our natural heritage. That is what conservation means for the countryside in the late twentieth century.

The CPRE has always been a *realistic* environmental body. As a membership organisation, we have been leaders in the conservation movement since our foundation in 1926 – and we have fought many battles over the years. Many of these have been local, as the chapters that follow show. But some of the most important have been national and even international, in Westminster, Whitehall and Brussels. That is why, even though as a charity we have to raise every penny we spend, I attach such importance to our expert research and campaigning staff in London. We have achieved a great deal in recent years – winning battles for the green belts, for the wider countryside, for new conservation subsidies for farmers, for the protection of our rivers – and we have rescued many attractive areas under threat. Every controversy poses the same fundamental question: how can the beauty, cultural importance and accessibility of our countryside be secured, while at the same time ensuring that the needs of those who live and work in it and of the wider community are fulfilled?

The past five years have seen a blossoming of environmental awareness in Britain – in the public at large, in the media and among many politicians. The CPRE has been at the centre of raising this 'green' conscience, in tandem with

16

bodies as diverse as the Friends of the Earth, Royal Society for the Protection of Birds, World Wildlife Fund, Countryside Commission and Greenpeace.

Our role is a distinctive one, at grass roots in the shires and nationally in the political vanguard. The experience we have gained will be tested over the next year or so. The government intends to 'reform' much of the town and country planning system. And its plans for privatising the water and electricity industries will pose acute environmental dilemmas.

It is inevitable that in our small sophisticated nation there will be recurring tensions between rival claims of conservation and development. However sensitive the developers, large-scale projects such as the Channel Tunnel or the new M40 motorway between Oxford and Birmingham bring with them enormous development pressures in peaceful rural areas.

I have one advantage, as a fundamentally urban person who is now completely committed to the countryside. I am in a position to understand how increasing numbers of English people like myself feel about it. We have now to protect and enhance every last scrap of countryside that exists, because, quite simply, there isn't any more. This will not be achieved without many further struggles, involving bodies such as the CPRE, in the face of powerful political and economic interests. We will have to plot, persuade, cajole and pull strings.

I should love to have been part of a civilisation like that of the Italians in the Renaissance, who left behind such a wonderful cultural legacy. Probably, we cannot quite emulate that in contemporary Britain, but at least we can leave behind the model of a society which cared genuinely for its cultural and natural heritage.

The acid test for how well we succeed will be how things turn out in our countryside. Our children and our grand-children will be both judges and victims of our vision and our commitment.

17

1

NORTHERN ENGLAND

'Barren and frightful' was the writer Daniel Defoe's eighteenth-century dismissal of the Lake District, far less appealing to him than Preston or Carlisle. He was not alone in regarding mountains and moors as places of danger rather than of beauty.

Derwentwater

18

Over the last 200 years concepts of beauty have so changed that the Lake District has now been proposed as a world heritage site: a region whose natural features are regarded as among the finest in the world.

Lakeland has a unique place in the history of man's relationship with the countryside. It was here, where England's highest mountains soared above our largest lakes, that romantic poets such as Wordsworth and Southey wrote of a new affinity with the natural world. It was here that sports such as rock climbing and fell walking began, as man discovered physical as well as aesthetic pleasures in wild places. Here, visions of national parks were first nurtured and in 1895 the National Trust was conceived, partly to conserve a landscape increasingly perceived to be as threatened as it was revered. Many twentieth-century battles over access, forestry, reservoirs and recreation had their origins here, with implications for the countryside far beyond. No part of Britain has done more to alter public perception of the countryside from a place of work to a place also of pleasure than this small corner of north-west England. Nor, in any other region of comparable size, do such diverse landscapes blend together more intoxicatingly. Fells and lakes, mountains and meadows, rivers and mires, waterfalls and woods are compressed into an area barely thirty miles wide. There is even a stretch of coast, which does not enjoy the renown it deserves.

The fame of the lakes has tended to distract attention from the rest of northern England. Yet here are to be found the greatest Roman monument in Britain, the most southerly outpost of arctic vegetation lingering from the aftermath of the last Ice Age, the most dramatic combination of coast and castles. The moors and dales of the northern Pennines and Cheviots are relatively remote from the cities of the northeast coast and so less crowded than those further south. Indeed, the border country of the Cheviots in Northumberland is the least populated part of England, offering solitude but also temptation. With so few people to complain,

the Cheviots have been deemed suitable for massive affor-estation, military training, reservoirs and nuclear-waste dumping. Elsewhere in these northern counties the rugged landscapes conceal valuable minerals, so that from coast to coast there have been struggles between mineral companies and environmentalists. Sometimes these struggles take place literally on the beaches, with controversies over nuclear discharges at Sellafield in Cumbria and coal tips in County Durham.

In theory, large tracts of northern England have gained some measure of protection in the last forty years, either as national parks (which are explored more fully in chapter 2) or as areas of outstanding natural beauty (AONBs). Yet neither of these designations entails control over agriculture, the dominant force in shaping the landscape beneath the 2500-foot contour. Large-scale afforestation also lies outside planning control and threatens to increase as private com-panies move in to take advantage of falling land prices and enforced sales. In the Lake District, development for housing or tourism is another pressure, jeopardising or tarnishing the scenery which lures so many people to northern England.

Such scenery may seem immutable, transcending the foibles of mankind. This may be fundamental to its appeal, yet it is an illusion. The uplands bear the imprint of our forebears as well as the natural forces of geology and climate. To survive they must continue to be worked: picture the dales without stone walls or the fells and moors with scrub where sheep now graze on heather and rough grassland. It is essentially a farmed landscape that we admire in areas such as the lakes and northern dales. Occasionally, man may need to intervene in order to maintain landscapes which have lost

20

BELOW LEFT: *The border country of the Cheviots is the least populated part of England*

BELOW CENTRE: *Pike of Stickle, Langdale*

BELOW RIGHT: *Stone circle at Castlerigg, near Keswick*

their original working purpose but which are valuable for wildlife; the broad-leaved woodland of the Lake District is one such case. But generally the future of landforms cannot be divorced from the future of rural communities. The uplands are not countryside museums to be preserved for the delectation of visitors; they are still being shaped by man, just as they have been since the first stone axe was carved from the Langdale Pikes some 5000 years ago.

A thin line of scree below the crags of Pike of Stickle marks the site of a Neolithic axe factory. Langdale axes helped to transform the face of more than just the Lake District; they have been found as far south as Hampshire and Norfolk. Previously man had lived a nomadic existence, hunting for food and moving on. With stone axes, he could chop down trees and settle in one place to farm the land. Bronze and iron tools later supplanted the stone axes, but the process of woodland clearances had begun. Pollen analysis of the lake muds and peat bogs of the Lake District suggest that some clearances were aided by burning. Livestock grazing then inhibited any return to the trees which had once clothed all but the highest fells.

Many generations and cultures have left their marks on the Lake District. From prehistoric times there are hill forts and stone circles such as Castlerigg near Keswick; from the Roman occupation there is Hardknott Fort, perched gloriously over Eskdale; from the Vikings there are valley settlements whose origins are betrayed by a rich legacy of Danish placenames (such as 'beck' for stream and 'thwaite' for clearing or meadow); from the Normans there are ruined abbeys such as Furness, from where Cistercian monks operated vast sheep-runs. Royal hunting forests, medieval quarrying and early

21

industry all helped to shape the Lake District long before it was ever considered a place of recreation. Not that man should have too exalted an idea of his significance: in the calendar of geological time, the first prehistoric settlements do not even rate as yesterday.

Most of the rocks in the Lake District are between 400 and 500 million years old, among the oldest in England. The variety of scenery — rocky crags, smooth fells and deep valleys — stems in part from its geological diversity, with volcanic rocks, slates, clays, sandstone and limestone variously exposed. A huge earth movement about 400 million years ago created a dome around what is now Scafell from which rivers still radiate in all directions. But it was the Ice Age which turned a mountainous district into a lake district. Glaciers flowed outwards from the dome, deepening existing valleys to leave steep cliffs, as at Great Langdale, and, when the ice retreated, waterfalls and streams tumbled from tributary valleys above the main valley floor. Just below the mountain peaks, ice accumulated in basins known as 'corries', which today are often filled by small lakes or tarns. Corries are sometimes separated by sharp ridges known as 'aretes', of which Helvellyn's Striding Edge is the most famous. The main lakes formed in the deepened valleys, partly because troughs were created where the glaciation was most powerful and partly because the valleys were later dammed by rocky debris from the melting glaciers. Other debris lay on the ground, sometimes to be used for field walls.

After the ice retreated, some 13,000 years ago, the warmer, wetter climate enabled trees to conquer most of England. Only sand dunes, salt marshes and the highest mountains

ABOVE: *Hardknott Fort, Eskdale*

LEFT: *Helvellyn's Striding Edge*

resisted the encroaching woodland. Although the height at which trees could grow varied around Britain, it was still high by present standards – often above 2000 feet and occasionally as high as 3000 feet, according to analysis of pollen deposited by trees and plants. So virtually all the Pennines and all but the rockiest crags of the Lake District were covered by trees. Oak and hazel were the dominant trees in northern England, with small-leaved lime in warmer parts of Lakeland and some elm and pine in Durham. Prehistoric man's clearance of this primeval wildwood was an astonishing achievement. It might seem an unrewarding labour, given the infertile soils which were laid bare. However, the uplands were not always so inhospitable.

Until the Iron Age, man settled and farmed this higher land. Why he shifted to the lowlands is not altogether understood. The cause may have been a worsening climate, which made it difficult to grow crops at high altitudes (and which would account for today's lower 'tree line'). It may have been the creation of better tools, which made possible the removal of the more firmly rooted lowland trees. It may have been the accumulation of peat, which reduced soil fertility. It may have been a declining need for defensible settlements. Whatever the combination of factors, the uplands ceased to be areas of extensive settlement and cultivation. To this day, they have remained poorer than their lowland neighbours. Now we face a new dilemma: how to sustain local communities without harming landscapes acclaimed for their national importance?

Most of the problems of the uplands – and many of the attempted solutions – can be seen in northern England. The uplands are generally taken to mean land above the 800-feet (240-metre) contour. Four-fifths of this land in England is either a national park or area of outstanding natural beauty. Many sites of special scientific interest (SSSIs) for wildlife are also found in the uplands; 14 per cent of the Lake District national park, for instance, are SSSIs. Thus, the uplands have an importance for wildlife as well as an attraction as places for tourism or recreation. In the Lake District, tourism is now the main source of income, providing work for a third of the resident population. Lakeland has many different characters and appeals to diverse interests. But whether visitors come to potter or to climb, to sail or to watch birds, the survival of this unique combination of landscapes is crucial to the prosperity of the district.

However, 12 million people a year cannot visit an area barely thirty miles wide by forty miles long without themselves posing an occasional threat. Wordsworth worried about this in the nineteenth century with the coming of the railways, but it was the motor car which really opened up the Lake District to mass tourism. Nowadays there are queues not only on the roads but on some of the fells: even in winter several hundred people reach the top of Helvellyn each Sunday. Tarn Hows may be a site of special scientific interest but it is also a source of intense public interest: on average half a million people a year visit the wooded lakeside, turning a narrow country lane into a one-way system. Heavily used paths have eroded fell slopes and fragile lake shores, destroying habitats and scarring the countryside. Power boats and water-skiing have shattered the calm of several lakes, provoking disputes with rival leisure interests such as anglers and windsurfers.

A bank holiday weekend in Bowness-on-Windermere is a time to share Wordsworth's anxieties rather than his enchantment. Yet his 'sublime landscape' is rarely impaired by crowds in the quieter western lakes and northern fells. More importantly, recreation is one area where a national park authority can act. Controls have been imposed on water sports and caravans; where possible, car parks have been screened, lakeside development curbed, remote dales protected; and the footpath network has been improved to complement the tradition of public access to the fells. Securing the right to roam over mountain and moorland was one of the aims of the national park movement in the 1930s. Although the eventual legislation decreed no such right, it largely exists in the Lake District. Whether through common land or the extensive holdings of the National Trust and the national

Haystacks, Buttermere, showing footpath erosion

park, there are few restraints on public access to the open fells. Nowadays the national park authority is more concerned about the consequences of access, such as litter, sheep worrying and damage to walls. The Friends of the Lake District, the Cumbrian association of the Council for the Protection of Rural England (CPRE), has some worries about tourism, such as proposals for lakeside chalets near Keswick or leisure centres overlooking Windermere. Large-scale tourist amenities could undermine the ability of the national park authority to contain recreation pressures. As a planning authority, the national park can seek to combat potentially damaging development. It is less well equipped for environmental battles.

Only recently has farming emerged as a problem. A century ago it was mining and quarrying which perturbed the embryonic conservationists. Railways enabled local quarries to send roofing slate all over the country, greatly expanding production. Iron ore, lead, graphite, limestone, tungsten and copper have also been mined, in some cases since the sixteenth century. Only slate is now mined commercially in central Lakeland, with eight quarries in the mid-1980s employing 200 people and enjoying a revival after years of decline. In 1987 there were applications pending to extend three of the sites. The national park authority aims to restrict development to existing sites so that its impact is localised. No similar powers exist to curb the environmental side-effects of modern agriculture.

Sheep and cattle rearing dominate the central fells and are essential to maintain the valley meadows and rough grazing of moor and grasslands. At lower levels, and around the fringes of the national park, there is a declining but still sizeable dairy sector and some horticulture. Despite a trend towards farm amalgamations, farms are still small — 70 per cent were under 125 acres in 1984, with a third officially regarded as part-time enterprises, demanding fewer than 250 working days a year. For some farmers, bed and breakfast has become a staple element in the family income. Outside the Lake District, hill farmers do not always have such an opportunity to diversify, which is why governments have sought to assist upland farming against the vagaries of climate and infertility.

Virtually the entire Lake District national park is classified as a 'less favoured area' under Europe's common agricultural policy. So are most of the other national parks, as well as upland areas such as the North Pennines (AONB). Designation as a less favoured area involves government payments for numbers of livestock and a higher rate of capital grant for new buildings, drainage and grassland improvement. Hill farmers have received special assistance since 1946 and, in bad years, government grants can amount to almost their entire income. But the EEC policy directive for less favoured areas implies social and environmental aims in seeking to 'ensure the continuation of farming, *thereby* maintaining a minimum population level and conserving the countryside', (author's emphasis). Is not the 'continuation of farming' the

25

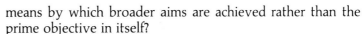

means by which broader aims are achieved rather than the prime objective in itself?

Groups such as the CPRE and the Council for National Parks have urged the government to interpret rural development more broadly than simply as agricultural output. Some grants are now given for tourist or craft-related farm enterprises, but the Ministry of Agriculture maintains that anything more than this would not be sanctioned by Britain's European partners. The dispute might seem arcane if the limited interpretation of the less favoured area policy was not priming changes which threaten traditional landscapes. In the Lake District the effects of agricultural change may appear less dramatic than the loss of moorland in the North York Moors or meadows in the Yorkshire Dales, described in chapter 2. Nevertheless, one survey of four areas commissioned by the Friends of the Lake District reported in 1986 that in the last forty years 38 per cent of hedgerows and 13 per cent of stone walls had been lost, while fencing had increased from 20.5 to 169 miles. Mostly, the hedgerows and stone walls are dying of neglect; they are not being grubbed out or removed, but simply left to decay. Changes in the nature of farming have serious consequences for a landscape where the contrast between valley grasslands and open fell is an integral part of its appeal. In 1986, the park authority said:

Changes in farming methods over many years and a great reduction in the farming workforce have led to examples of collapsed walls, derelict hedgerows and the invasion of improved land by bracken and rushes, giving an air of neglect to parts of the farming landscape. On the other hand, and often alongside the former, are the signs of mechanisation: new larger buildings, drainage schemes, and agricultural improvement of rough grazing as farmers attempt to increase the stock-carrying capacity of their farms and hence their income. These same pressures are also seen in the heavily grazed woodlands and occasionally in the clearance of areas of trees.

Some of the most damaging government grants have been withdrawn, notably those for ploughing, draining or reseeding moorland. Since 1980 farmers in national parks seeking government grants have been obliged to notify park authorities of their proposals. But as explained more fully in chapter 2, if a minister dismisses the park authority's objection – or if the farmer goes ahead without a grant – there is little that the national park can do.

In the Lake District, pioneering schemes for upland management and the design of farm buildings established a dialogue between the park authority and farmers which has not always existed elsewhere. An uplands management scheme has been run since 1969, involving the Ministry of Agriculture as well as the Countryside Commission. It has helped farmers manage small woodlands, repair stone walls and cope with visitors. Conservation grants have been paid to maintain wildlife habitats such as ponds and encourage tree planting.

Tarn Hows has half a million visitors annually

27

28

Controls over the design of farm buildings (recently extended to their siting) have also proved successful, with only eight buildings out of 342 eliciting objections between 1979 and 1984. But the successes have been modest, like the money available to the national park. It would help if the park were designated an environmentally sensitive area (ESA), because the scheme enables farmers to receive Ministry of Agriculture grants if they pursue methods which maintain traditional landscapes. (The background to ESAs is explained fully in chapter 5, pages 177–80, although they arise in each regional study of this book.) In the uplands, even ESA designation could be insufficient if other agricultural grants remain unchanged.

Headage payments, known as hill livestock compensatory allowances, are the bedrock of upland farming. Farmers are paid for each head of livestock they keep, which implicitly encourages them to increase numbers. However, part-time farmers are ineligible for such support, thereby making them vulnerable to takeovers by larger neighbours. Some small farms have found it difficult to raise the capital required to handle higher stock numbers. Throughout the uplands, therefore, the number of farms has shrunk – in the Lake District by no fewer than a quarter between 1963 and 1975. Almost equally great has been the loss of labour – a fifth in the Lake District in the same twelve-year period. Losses elsewhere have been even higher. So much for maintaining populations, which is one aim of the EEC policy for less favoured areas. But what of the second objective: conserving the countryside?

Larger farms mean less need for boundary walls, even if there were the farmworkers to maintain them, and more

abandoned buildings to fall derelict. Increased stocking can be detrimental to the landscape and wildlife. On Exmoor and North York Moors farmers have reseeded the moorland and 'improved' the rough grassland. Some improvement and fencing of open fells have occurred in the Lake District, but a far wider problem is the overgrazing encouraged by headage payments. This can cause serious erosion of soil and vegetation with consequent effects on wildlife. Common land, where many people have grazing rights, is particularly vulnerable to overgrazing. With 60 per cent of the Lake District's enclosed fell land classified as common land – a tenth of the commons of England and Wales – the national park authority impatiently awaits implementation of proposals put forward by the Common Land Forum. In 1986 this panel, representing landowners and conservationists, suggested a management scheme which would allow some controls over grazing levels. (It also urged greater public access in return for sanctions against trespass and damage by the public; in Lakeland this, at least, is not an issue.)

The proposals of the Common Land Forum have been accepted in principle by the government, which has promised legislation. Pleas for a more flexible approach to agricultural grants have met a less favourable response. Flat-rate headage payments take no account of any variation in the land, enabling farmers with better land to graze it more intensively, thereby earning increased headage payments. No ceilings are imposed to prevent overgrazing, no strings attached to keep farmworkers on the payroll. In the Lake District, the effects of such a system are partially disguised by the extra income generated through tourism and by the role of the National Trust, the park's largest landowner. More than eighty-five fell farms, large tracts of woodland and lake shore are among the 23 per cent of the Lake District national park owned by the Trust. Here conservation does come first – in principle. In practice, the Trust has been criticised by some of its members for failing to spend sufficient money to maintain the stone walls and hedgerows of its estates.

Among the lakes owned by the National Trust is Wastwater, the deepest lake of all and the wildest. If you approach by road, the Wasdale screes rise precipitously from the opposite bank, while ahead is the majestic outline of Great Gable flanked by Kirkfell, Lingmell and Scafell Pike, England's highest mountain at 3206 feet. The lake's beauty (and a concerted campaign by local and national conservation groups) saved it in 1980 when British Nuclear Fuels sought to take more water from Wastwater for its plant at Sellafield (*née* Windscale) on the Cumbrian coast. At the same time the North West Water Authority applied to take more water from Ennerdale by artificially raising water levels.

With up to 150 inches of rain a year, the Lake District is not short of water and its hard rocks have long been used as a water-catchment area for north-west England. In all, the water authority draws from twenty-four lakes and reservoirs, including Windermere and Ullswater. Increased use of the lakes has been resisted because of the impact of building on

29

ABOVE LEFT: Bowness-on-Windermere – one of many Lake District towns and villages under intense visitor pressure

ABOVE: Wastwater – the deepest lake and the wildest – and Great Gable

the landscape and wildlife. At Ennerdale, the water level would have been raised by 4 feet, drowning trees and agricultural land. New weirs and embankments would have changed still further the outline of what is the only major lake without a road to the top on at least one side. Ennerdale and Wastwater are dead-end lakes – except for fell walkers – and so less visited than central Lakeland. This remoteness allied to their grandeur was sufficient to win a public inquiry: both schemes were rejected on the grounds that unacceptable damage would be done to the appearance of the two lakes. 'If it is right that any places in England should be inviolate,' said the government inspector, 'surely Wastwater is one of them.'

Thus the wild heart of Lakeland was preserved and with it some truly wild wildlife. Rocky crags, high tarns, peatland bogs and basin mires all harbour rare plants. Above them can be seen our rarest birds of prey, including the world's densest population of peregrine falcon and England's only breeding site for golden eagles. Several of the lakes are habitats for rare species of fish, although Esthwaite is now polluted by sewage and fertilisers. Acid rain is also emerging as an increasing problem, according to surveys of lichens in the internationally important Borrowdale woodlands south of Keswick. Five per cent of the national park comprises broad-leaved woodland, adding yet further diversity to landscape, wildlife and recreation. A greater number of trees, however, are now conifers. Massive afforestation in areas such as Ennerdale in the 1920s and 1930s aroused fierce opposition, but not because trees were in any way alien to the Lake

30

ABOVE: Plans to raise the water level at Ennerdale would have drowned trees and agricultural land

RIGHT: Esthwaite Water is polluted by sewage and fertilisers

District. Although the Domesday Book had little to say about what is now Cumbria (and nothing at all about Northumberland and Durham), it is known that woods used to play an important part in the Lakeland economy. They provided charcoal for early industry before rivers such as the Kent were harnessed for their water power. Bobbins and tanning were among other woodland industries which ensured that the woods were not only managed but also protected from agricultural 'reclamation'. These woodlands bear little relation to the twentieth-century plantations of the Forestry Commission. For fifty years conservationists have been fighting a rearguard battle to defend the fells from forestry. At first they were motivated by distaste for the regimented lines of the new forests and the loss of public access. Now, as concern grows over the effect on wildlife, the battleground is no longer confined to the Lake District.

Indeed, the ability of the Lakeland to marshal its defences has increased pressures elsewhere. In 1936, after years of controversy which culminated in the formation of the Friends of the Lake District in 1934, a voluntary agreement was reached between the CPRE and the Forestry Commission. This declared that 'there is in the Lake District a central block, which by reason of its unusual beauty and seclusion and remoteness, should be ruled out altogether from afforestation'. Some 300 square miles of the central fells were thus protected, although the agreement has not prevented sporadic battles as foresters eyed the lower fells. Botanically rich bogs, moors and limestone pavements have all been lost. In the 1980s Forestry Commission proposals to extend their plantation at Grassguards in the Duddon Valley provoked bitter opposition until a smaller scheme provided the basis for an uneasy truce in one of Lakeland's loveliest dales.

Uncertainty in agriculture, as prices tumble and surpluses soar, will ensure that other struggles will ensue between conservationists and foresters. The significance of two recent disputes, concerning Ashtead Fell and Dent Fell, reached beyond Cumbria. First, the battlegrounds were strategically sited at the fringes of the Lake District national park, where opposition would be weaker. Second, the plantations were proposed by private forestry firms rather than the publicly owned Forestry Commission. However, the private schemes were aided by grants from the Forestry Commission — very little forestry takes place without such grants. A similar pattern can be detected in recent forestry pressure on the Northumberland national park, which spans the lonely countryside between Hadrian's Wall and the Scottish border. The contrast here with the Lake District is acute: Northumberland has fewer residents (2000 people scattered over 398 square miles) and fewer visitors (1 million a year) than any other national park. And, without attracting anything like the attention engendered in the lakes, its coniferous forest has doubled in thirty years to 20 per cent of the park.

Oddly, for a country that was once largely covered by trees, the conflict over afforestation stems from a lack of woodland. The First World War shattered previous govern-

BELOW: Surveys of lichens in the Borrowdale woodlands have highlighted the damage caused by acid rain

BELOW RIGHT: The 1920s and 1930s saw massive conifer plantations in areas such as Ennerdale Forest

ment policy of relying upon cheap timber imports. A fifth of the private woodlands were felled, many to provide pit props for mines which supplied the iron and steel industry. Never again, said the politicians, and the Forestry Commission was set up in 1919 charged with increasing the supply of native timber. In 1924 the Commission estimated that only 5 per cent of Britain was forested; sixty years later, the proportion had doubled. Britain is still Europe's least wooded country, so the Forestry Commission argues that continued expansion is in the national interest. Between 1976 and 1985, an area roughly the size of Cheshire was newly forested, with further increases envisaged as farmland becomes redundant. Yet the industry has long outlived its original justification.

In 1957, with national defence committed to a nuclear deterrent, it was accepted that there was no longer any need for a long-term strategic reserve of timber. Social objectives, notably the provision of upland jobs, were touted for a time as a reason for maintaining high levels of production, until research showed that afforestation provided fewer jobs than the farming it replaced. Import saving is another benefit put forward to justify a continuing expansion of forestry; but it is questionable whether subsidising native timber production is more cost-effective than buying cheaper timber from abroad. None of this might matter if the twentieth-century forests were an unblemished asset to the countryside. Despite the excellence (and popularity) of many recreation facilities provided by the Forestry Commission, this is not so.

The Forestry Commission concedes that many of its early plantations imposed a blanket uniformity over landscapes. 'On a bright landscape they are so much blotting paper,' sneered an early critic in the Lake District. Later forests have

33

been more sensitively designed, with a greater regard for contours, valleys and wildlife. But the worries of the Countryside Commission and Nature Conservancy Council (NCC) will not be stilled by cosmetic changes to tree lines; they stem from the character of the forests themselves – and that of the land lost to conifers.

Afforestation means planting bare land with trees; these are not forests or woods in which trees grow and regenerate naturally. Because of financial pressures, the Forestry Commission sought land where farming profits were marginal and prices therefore cheap. It found some such land on the heaths of lowland England in Breckland and Dorset, but overwhelmingly the quest for marginal land led the foresters to the uplands. Here, they found that the only species that prospered in the infertile soils, high rainfall, low temperatures and strong winds were coniferous. No matter, these were just what the foresters wanted; the faster growth of conifers was as essential to the economics of commercial forestry as cheap land. Several species were planted, including Scots pine, the only native conifer. By far the most successful was sitka spruce, from coastal British Columbia. In the 1970s this accounted for 60 per cent of all Forestry Commission plantings, with lodgepole pine second at 14 per cent, mostly in the waterlogged, peaty soils of the far north of Scotland.

The effects of afforestation are swift, although they vary at different stages of a forest's life. A study of nature conservation and afforestation published by the NCC in 1986 acknowledged that for the first ten years a young forest provides a good wildlife habitat. Freed from grazing or burning, shrubs and grasses can grow taller, mosses and lichens deeper. Songbirds such as the whinchat and stonechat are found when an area is mainly open ground, tree pipits and willow warblers when trees are young. Then, says the NCC study:

As the young trees expand and coalesce, their dense growth increasingly suppresses all other vegetation. By the time the young plantation closes to form thicket, at 10–15 years, other plant life has almost totally disappeared within the planted area and much of the previous animal community with it. Tree density is all important because it determines light penetration, which in turn affects the development of vegetation under the trees and hence the associated animal communities ... Spruce gives especially deep shade, but even larch and Scots pine grown in dense canopy can virtually eliminate the ground flora.

Thinning the trees allows some ground vegetation to return, although the flora of coniferous plantations remains limited, apart from a few species associated with Scots pine. Thinning also enables birds such as woodcocks and tawny owls to penetrate the forest. Otherwise songbirds are confined to the fringes or rides of the forest, where the cones attract crossbills and siskins. But what have been lost? Lapwing, wheatear, skylark, golden plover, dunlin, snipe, greenshank, redshank, curlew, red grouse and meadow pipit disappear almost immediately their open-ground habitats have been disturbed. So do ravens. Other birds of prey, such as merlins and kestrels,

34

Dent Fell – the site of a recent battle between conservationists and foresters

depart once the forests close in and the animal population dwindles. Plant life also has its casualties: wet-loving plants such as sundew and butterwort are effectively killed by the drainage effects of pre-plantation ploughing. Rainfall drainage, soil chemistry, water acidity are also changed by using techniques of arable farming – ploughing, fertilisers and herbicides – on land which, for the most part, has never been cultivated before. Some 2.6 million acres of the uplands, including habitats rated as internationally important for wild-life, have been converted to forests, mainly of alien conifers. The NCC says:

The crucial point is that the new forests are quite different from the heaths, grasslands, peat bogs and sand dune communities which they replace. However good they may become as wildlife habitats in their own right, these forests are not and never can be a compensatory substitute for such open ground ecosystems which are highly valued in their existing condition. The mountains and moorlands of the north and west, where nearly all new planting is taking place, are the last substantial areas of wild land in Britain, where both scenic beauty and wildlife can be studied and enjoyed as an inter-related whole in settings free from the grosser intrusions of human activity.

The NCC paid due tribute in their study to the efforts made by the Forestry Commission to improve plantations for wildlife, and the Countryside Commission has welcomed provision by the foresters of well-designed recreation facilities. Judicious felling and restocking enable forests to sustain trees of varying ages and accordingly more diverse wildlife. The design of new forests, such as planting patterns near streams and the creation of more open rides, reflects not only greater empathy for conservation but also the results of research into the effects of older plantations on wildlife and water supply. Broad-leaved trees are increasingly an element in plantations, albeit generally a minor one confined to the forest fringes. Since 1985 the Forestry Commission has had a duty (among others) 'to protect and enhance the environment'. In the past, concern for conservation did not influence the choice of area. And because cheapness of land remains crucial for the industry's viability, the uplands are likely to remain the foresters' prime hunting ground, despite the agricultural uncertainties of the 1980s.

Foresters would love to come down the hills to the more fertile soils of the lowlands. The NCC would be in favour of this since, if appropriately selected, the land to be planted would tend to be less valuable for wildlife. In Britain as a whole, 30 per cent of the upland grass areas, heaths and blanket bogs have been lost or significantly damaged since 1950, mostly through afforestation or reclamation. Lowland plantings will undoubtedly increase, as farmers convert (or, more likely, sell) their marginal land, but this will not preclude further conflict between forestry and conservation. Forestry operates on small profit margins and likes large plantations, which spread the costs of investment and management. Such sites are found more readily in the uplands where, although wildlife and scenic beauty are more highly prized, farming and settlement are less intensive.

Agriculture's difficulties are increasing the attractions of England to foresters. Until now Scotland and Wales have borne the brunt of new plantations – and the conservationists' anger, most recently over massive afforestation in the 'flow country' of Sutherland and Caithness. Only 3 per cent of the Forestry Commission's plantations are in England, and broad-leaved woodlands still cover more ground than conifers. But the upland area alone that is technically plantable for new forests would more than quadruple the existing coniferous acreage. Falling land values are heightening the pressure on the Cheviots and northern Pennines; most of it, ominously, comes from private companies with little of the Forestry Commission's new concern for conservation. Roger Carr, the chairman of the Countryside Commission for Scotland, has urged greater controls over forestry. Launching the Commission's annual report in 1987, he said, 'We do not believe that freedom to plant conifer forests, partly at our expense, at the expense of wildlife, wherever a landowner wishes, is reasonable. Increased planting targets and the new encouragement to farmers to enter into forestry increases our concern.

ABOVE: Wark Forest exemplifies the gloomy kingdom of the sitka spruce

Whether many private companies would be quite so keen to plant forests without tax 'incentives' is doubtful. These have acted, in effect, as a subsidy for the wealthy, offering not only tax relief of up to 60 per cent of the cost of plantations on top of grants but also exemption from capital gains tax when the land is sold after ten years. The existence of what is effectively a tax dodge, the absence of planning controls over new plantations, the lack of any obligation upon private companies to follow a conservation plan or provide public access, the compensation for not planting sites of special scientific interest and the low rate of profit despite hefty subsidies have all focused almost as much attention on the fiscal aspects of forestry as on its effects on flora and fauna.

Government-appointed organisations such as the NCC and the Countryside Commission habitually take a balanced approach. The trenchant conclusions of the NCC report therefore shook government officials, besides the Forestry Commission. Although Whitehall's attempts to soften the allegedly 'shrill and assertive' tone of the draft report were resisted by the NCC, both the Council and the Countryside Commission stress that they are not against forestry as such; the argument is about what kind of trees are planted, how they are planted and where they are planted. Increasingly, they back the view of the CPRE, among others, that forestry subsidies, like those for agriculture, should be recast to promote conservation and the rural economy rather than increased production regardless of cost. More specifically, both countryside watchdogs are now against further blanket afforestation in most of the uplands − 'nature's last stronghold', in the words of the NCC − and for greater planning control over an industry overwhelmingly dependent upon public money. With four-fifths of the English uplands given some form of recognition for their natural beauty, should not public interest in their conservation carry more weight than private interest in their exploitation?

Anyone tempted to disagree should go to northern England. Admire Yeavering Bell, a moorland covered with archaeological sites and of substantial wildlife interest west of Wooler in Northumberland, where the national park decided to buy the land to thwart afforestation. Compare conifer-clad Ennerdale with leafy Borrowdale or awesome Wasdale. Wark Forest, north of Haltwhistle in Northumberland, exhibits the worst features of the old plantations, with wall-like edges to rectangular blocks of trees planted in rigid lines. In the gloomy kingdom of sitka spruce, colours never change with the seasons and you are more likely to hear chain-saws than bird-songs.

In Northumberland national park, designated as a park for its wild grassy and heather moorland, a fifth of the land under alien conifers is surely enough. The Forestry Commission appears, tacitly, to agree. Several proposed private afforestation schemes have been refused Forestry Commission grants after objections by the Northumberland national park authority. Relations between the two bodies have been

BELOW: *Yeavering Bell*

38

further improved by the Commission's efforts to diversify its existing forests through more sensitive replanting and by its emphasis on recreation. Although much of this recreation takes place in the Kielder Forest, just outside the park boundaries, nature trails, forest drives, picnic areas, camp sites and Kielder Water itself have encouraged far greater public use of the area than occurred hitherto. This harmony could be jeopardised by an agricultural crisis which is tempting farmers to sell their land to forestry companies. 'You can get three times the value from land being forested than farmed,' explained a national park official, as he pointed to locations ringing the park where moorland was coming on the market. 'If the process of afforestation continues at past rates, you won't have the national park you started out with.'

So much moorland has been lost to forestry that the national park authority now regards the extensive military presence in the area with relative equanimity. At least it has prevented reclamation for forestry or agriculture. Roughly a fifth of the park is used for military training, much of it farmed under conservation guidelines dictated by the Ministry of Defence. Important woodlands, such as the alder carr at Grasslees Burn, have been declared local nature reserves, and archaeological sites from prehistoric and Roman times have been marked and protected. The ethos of a national park as a place of natural beauty to be enjoyed by the public is nonetheless difficult to reconcile with military training; firing live shells may do less damage than ploughing, but it effectively bars the public from large tracts of moorland for anything up to 300 days a year. In practice, as the army was at Otterburn long before the national park was created, the park authority concentrates its attention on warding off any expansion or intensification of the military presence. Plans for a mock airstrip for bombing training were successfully resisted and improved access has been negotiated to the upper valley of the River Coquet.

Coquetdale, in the heart of the Cheviots, epitomises the appeal of the Northumberland national park: an isolated valley winding past lonely farmsteads with nothing to disrupt the solitude except the moorland sheep. The grassy Cheviots and the heathery Simonside Hills are superb hill-walking country and their appeal extends beyond a rugged appreciation of wide open spaces. SSSIs cover almost a sixth of the national park, including upland mires and woods as well as moors. The remoteness of the national park has helped to safeguard these sites and saved it from major development. There is just one active quarry and no major settlements. With only five people per square mile against the national average of 436, the granite of the Cheviots seemed just the place to dump nuclear waste. But if the park lacks residents, it does not lack friends, and the proposal to drill test boreholes was dropped after a public inquiry in 1980.

Recreation pressures are slight, with one exception. Seventeen miles of the 73-mile-long Hadrian's Wall run through the southern reaches of the national park. Here the wall

ABOVE RIGHT: Open moorland near Otterburn which is often closed to the public for army artillery practice

RIGHT: Negotiations with the army have resulted in improved public access to the upper valley of the River Coquet

dramatically exploits the contours and crags as it marches across the open countryside. Many of the stones were plundered by later generations – the wall was once between 15 and 20 feet high – but enough remain in the wall and in forts such as Housesteads to provide an imposing echo of Roman Britain. In the 1970s, the large number of visitors began to clog the most popular sites and threatened to undermine foundations, which had lasted the best part of 2000 years. Numbers have since declined, partly because of economic recession in the north, which has generally curbed day trips, and possibly also because country parks have been provided closer to the cities. The idea of a footpath along the length of the wall is now being investigated by the Countryside Commission as part of an overall strategy to disperse visitors along what it describes as 'the finest ancient monument this side of the Alps'.

The importance of Hadrian's Wall has persuaded the Northumberland national park to allocate a good proportion of its meagre conservation budget to the surrounding farmland. Enclosed farmland such as this is confined to the moorland fringe and valleys. Statistically, it occupies less than a tenth of the park, but it adds a variety to the landscape which the national park seeks to retain through conservation grants which help farmers maintain (and plant) small woodlands, manage hay meadows and repair stone walls. Apart from some overgrazing, agriculture has not been a significant threat to landscape, wildlife or archaeological sites. Most of the farms are large holdings, with sheep grazing dominating the open moorland and some cattle on the fringes.

Cumbria and Northumberland are predominantly rural counties, with livestock rearing in the hills and mixed farming in the valleys and plains; County Durham follows a similar pattern, despite its image as a bastion of mining and industry. Agricultural change has been less contentious here than further south, but hedgerows have nevertheless been lost, grassland ploughed or 'improved' and woodlands destroyed. Just over half of Northumberland's semi-natural ancient woodland and two-fifths of Cumbria's have gone in the last fifty years. Hedgerow loss has been greatest in the Eden Valley and Northumberland Plain, although overall losses since 1947 have been fewer in these northern counties than any other region of England. For the most part, stone walls have faced problems of decay and dereliction rather than destruction, with fencing proving an unappealing, if economic, substitute.

Only in the two national parks have farmers encountered any constraints – from the obligation to notify park authorities of any projects for which they seek government grants. No equivalent obligation applies to AONBs. Despite this, the National Farmers' Union (NFU) was among the opponents of plans to create a new AONB in the North Pennines, plugging the gap between the Yorkshire Dales and the Northumberland national parks along the Pennine chain. As long ago as 1929, the CPRE urged some recognition and protection for the North Pennines. In 1986, this was finally

ABOVE: *The Simonside Hills*

bestowed, although not before an unprecedented public inquiry had examined the Countryside Commission's proposals.

The inquiry proved an instructive exercise. Apart from the county councils, many local people joined the NFU in opposing the area's designation as an AONB. They feared it would stifle jobs, curb farming and increase bureaucracy. In seeking to rebut these fears, the Countryside Commission and the inquiry inspector laid bare the frailty of AONB designation. Despite public fears, said the inspector, the practical effect would be very limited. Designation conveys no power to interfere with farming, no right to increase public access to private land, no diminution of local council powers, no addition to planning procedures for mineral extraction and no veto over forestry. The Commission would like AONB designation to involve something like the system of prior notification which exists for farmers in national parks, but so far the government has rejected such an idea – just as it has rejected pleas for planning controls over forestry. Until thinking in Whitehall changes, the Countryside Commission remains strictly an advisory body and AONBs will depend for their effectiveness on cooperation rather than statutory gunpower.

41

ABOVE RIGHT: Hadrian's Wall marches across open countryside in the Northumberland national park

LEFT: The North Pennines, where many local people joined farmers in opposing the area's designation as an AONB

One of the few points of agreement in the North Pennines inquiry was that the area was indeed supremely beautiful — so beautiful that, in the 1940s, it had been held in reserve as a possible national park. Otherwise it would have been designated an AONB long ago. The inspector thought the landscape compared favourably with national parks: it contains the wildest and highest Pennine hills, with twenty peaks over 2000 feet and, in Alston, the highest market town in England. River valleys, with their meadows, woods and whitewashed farmhouses, soften the wild moors, although the Tees crashing down the waterfalls of Cauldron Snout and High Force is anything but gentle. The Wear, South Tyne and Allen also rise from these hills; but no part of the North Pennines can compare with Upper Teesdale. In addition to its natural beauty, Upper Teesdale has unparalleled botanical importance as the last refuge of arctic flora which covered Britain immediately after the last Ice Age. A crumbly rock known as sugar limestone prevented woodland colonising the area as occurred elsewhere. The result is an undisturbed

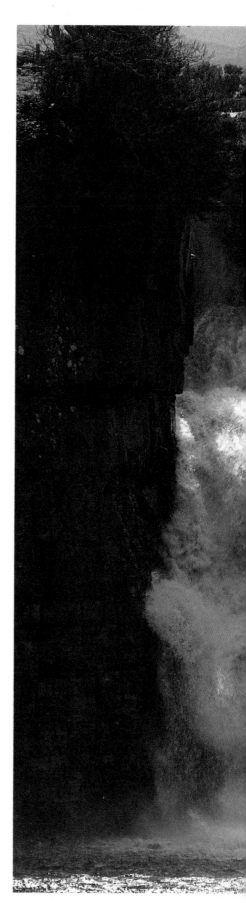

community of alpine and arctic flowers unique in western Europe. More rare plants grow here than in any other comparable region in Britain, illuminating the moorland grasses each spring with their pink, white, yellow and blue flowers.

At 860 square miles, the North Pennines would have been far larger than any of the thirty-six AONBs previously designated – and larger it is, even with roughly 15 per cent of the proposed area lopped off its south-eastern fringes by

the inspector. Tangible gains of designation are modest: £540,000 of Countryside Commission grants over five years, promises of consultation over forestry and hopes for voluntary agreements with farmers. The second-class status of AONBs is all too apparent, yet designation does provide a veneer of protection, which was implicitly acknowledged by the involvement in the inquiry of powerful opposing interest groups.

'The paradox is that the effect of designation is very limited, but its importance is very great,' claimed the Countryside Commission. Government and public bodies would be less likely to propose major developments in an AONB; plans for private developments would be assessed partly by their impact on the environment of an area accorded national recognition for its natural beauty. It was precisely this which worried some objectors at the North Pennines inquiry, despite assurances from the Countryside Commission that it backed efforts by the Development Commission to encourage small-scale rural industry.

For the Forestry Commission, the North Pennines is the largest remaining area of potentially plantable land in England ('a daunting prospect,' said an alarmed inspector about the possibility of widespread afforestation). For British Coal, the

43

FAR LEFT: In addition to its natural beauty, Upper Teesdale sustains an undisturbed community of alpine and arctic flowers unique in western Europe

LEFT: The Tees at High Force

ABOVE: Gentians at Upper Teesdale

AONB includes actual and potential sites for opencast mining. The Northern Pennines have been a centre for mineral extraction since Roman times; the moors around Nenthead have evocative remains of eighteenth-century lead mining. Although the revised boundaries of the AONB removed some of the mines and quarries from the designated area, mining remains an important source of employment in a part of the country where jobs have declined by almost a third since 1960. AONB designation gives conservationists an additional weapon which has more political weight than legislative small print might imply. Mining and forestry are most vulnerable. Mining is subject to planning controls, while afforestation is ultimately the responsibility of a minister, if proposals have been opposed by bodies such as local authorities and the Countryside Commission yet approved by the Forestry Commission's regional advisory committees. In national parks and AONBs, the Forestry Commission has to inform — but not consult — the Countryside Commission of proposed schemes covering more than twenty-five acres. But the mandate of AONBs to 'conserve and enhance natural beauty' entails no specific machinery to control the activities of the greatest influence on landscape — farming.

In the North Pennines, the Countryside Commission expressed concern about the reseeding of hay meadows and overgrazing of the moors. The proposals of the Common Land Forum (see page 29) offer some hope of tackling overgrazing (as well as improving public access to places such as Mickle Fell) on the moors. More immediately effective would have been designation as one of the Ministry of Agriculture's ESAs, where farmers are paid grants to maintain traditional landscapes. The Countryside Commission wanted the entire North Pennines to be made an ESA, along with both northern national parks. In the event, only Teesdale and Weardale were given such status by the ministry, along with seven valleys from the Yorkshire Dales.

The South Solway AONB was another rejected candidate for ESA status, a remote shoreline of empty beaches, salt marsh and shingle overlooking the Solway Firth. The Solway is also a SSSI with international importance for birds. According to the Royal Society for the Protection of Birds (RSPB), the estuary is used by more than 80,000 waders and 40,000 wildfowl. Yet it is threatened by a barrage scheme similar to that proposed at Morecambe Bay, the most important estuary for birdlife in Britain (see chapter 2, page 80). The RSPB is also concerned about plans for industrial development of the Tees estuary and for a holiday complex at Budle Bay, part of the Lindisfarne nature reserve on the Northumberland coast. A proposed nuclear-power station at Druridge Bay in Northumberland represents another threat to one of the most unspoiled coastlines in England, much of it rightly designated both as an AONB and as a heritage coast.

Within the Northumberland Coast AONB, roads rarely follow the shore, so the coast retains its natural appeal, with farmland culminating in a shore of great variety: sand dunes, springy turf, dark cobbles, marshes and columnar cliffs.

44

RIGHT: The Solway Firth, an SSSI with international importance for birds, is threatened by a barrage scheme

ABOVE: Druridge Bay, the site of a proposed nuclear-power station

Sweeping bays are separated by headlands of volcanic rock, sometimes topped by castles, as at restored Bamburgh and ruined Dunstanburgh. Offshore, the same volcanic rock forms the twenty-eight islands of the Farnes, an internationally renowned haunt of seabirds, where seventeen species breed. Closer to land – indeed, attached to land at low tide via a causeway – is romantic Holy Island or Lindisfarne with its ruined eleventh-century priory and a castle restored by Sir Edward Lutyens as the ultimate place in the country for a twentieth-century millionaire.

What a contrast to the scene 60 miles to the south, where for years colliery waste and sewage have been dumped on the beaches of Durham. Until the recent pit closures, between 2 and 2.5 million tonnes of waste was dumped on the beaches each year, far more than could ever be removed by the sea. So much waste was dumped that the shoreline moved 400 feet out to sea. As if this was not bad enough, untreated sewage added to the stench and filth on what were once sandy shores. Eight of the county's 11 miles of coast have been desecrated by pollution. Local councils have launched a plan to clean up the beaches, a task which will be made easier by the closure of the pits. Two small areas, which belie the pervading industrialisation, have found other benefactors:

Marsden Cliffs, limestone rocks pitted with caverns and inhabited by seabirds near South Shields, are to be managed by the National Trust; Castle Eden Deane, coastal valley woods south of Peterlee, is a national nature reserve run by the NCC.

The west coast of northern England offers a similar, if less dramatic, mixture of the good and ghastly: a nature reserve among the sand dunes of Ravenglass, abandoned steel works at Workington; cliffs at St Bees, the nuclear-reprocessing plant at Sellafield. Sellafield casts a wide shadow over the area, providing jobs for a region where industry has declined yet fanning fears about radioactive fallout over the fells and beaches. The Chernobyl disaster in 1986, hard on the heels of well-publicised scares about leaks at Sellafield, was blamed for deterring tourists from the Lake District. Restrictions on sheep sales as a result of Chernobyl have reinforced local worries about the long-term implications of having Sellafield as a neighbour.

ABOVE: Dunstanburgh Castle

BELOW: Bamburgh Castle

Sellafield lies outside the Lake District national park, but there is nothing to prevent such a plant being built, or existing, within a national park or AONB. When it comes to energy or minerals, national commercial interest invariably trumps national environmental interest, whatever politicians say about strict operating controls or subsequent site restoration. But countryside lacking any designation or protection is inevitably more vulnerable to development. One such area is the Derwent Valley in County Durham, an area of gentle hills and wooded valleys which is beset by

47

applications for opencast coal mining. What began in 1942 as an emergency response to the wartime need for extra coal is now the greatest single theat to the countryside of Durham and, increasingly, to Cumbria and Northumberland. Beyond these northern counties, opencast mining has also blighted Lancashire, West and South Yorkshire and Staffordshire. Nowhere is under more intense attack, however, than Durham, where opencast sites now outnumber the dwindling number of deep mines.

Opencast mining is effectively quarrying – a gigantic earth-moving operation to extract coal which is either too near the surface or in too thin a layer to be exploited through conventional deep mining. Modern opencast sites are both deeper and larger than they used to be, anything up to 600 feet deep and a mile wide. Compared with a modern deep mine, such as Asfordby in the Vale of Belvoir, opencast mining can require over a hundred times as much land per tonne of coal extracted. (The land to be devoured depends on the thickness of the coal seams; in Durham, the seams are mostly thin, requiring more land to be taken.) If opencast production continued at the rate of the mid-1980s – around 15 million tonnes a year – it would consume an area the size of Bedfordshire before the year 2000, according to evidence submitted to the Department of Energy by the CPRE. In fact, there is pressure to increase opencast production by 3 million tonnes annually.

That opencast sites are supremely ugly is hardly in dispute. Deeper and bigger sites generate more noise, more dust and more traffic, as well as despoiling larger areas of countryside. And it is open countryside, such as Durham's Derwent Valley and Plenmeller Common in the North Pennines AONB, that increasingly is under siege. Applications for opencast mining on sites affected by earlier industry or deep mining are rarely contentious; subsequent restoration can improve a landscape already derelict. No such claims can be supported when green-field sites are plundered for their coal. A superficial glance may suggest otherwise; grass and crops certainly grow

BELOW: Cleaned-up beaches near Seaham, County Durham

RIGHT: Cliffs at St Bees, Cumbria

and the original contours appear to have been restored, but look more closely and you notice that trees and hedgerows are stunted – clues betraying an overall loss of soil fertility which even heavy dosages of fertilisers cannot offset.

One study of crop yields suggests that restored sites lose at least 20 per cent of their original fertility, while in wildlife terms the loss may be even greater. John Atkinson, a former senior surveyor for the Ministry of Agriculture with responsibilities for opencast reclamation, told a conference in 1985 that on one site in Northumberland proposed for opencast development he identified 151 species of plant. Nearby, on a former opencast site restored ten years earlier, there were thirty species. Despite improvements in reclamation, it is impossible to recreate the soil conditions which existed before the ground was quarried. Soils lose some of their nutrients as they are stripped and stacked while mining proceeds. Then, too, the bed rock, which determines drainage patterns, is broken up into rubble. When these sterile soils are eventually returned to the site, they are compacted together, destroying much of the soil aeration crucial for subsequent fertility. Drainage systems are added, but waterlogged areas are common, eroding the topsoil and effectively limiting the range of crops which can eventually be grown. Restored fields are usually confined to silage, cereals or grazing, although grazing can compact still further the fragile surface soil. 'Restored opencast land,' said the Ministry of Agriculture in a leaflet to farmers, 'needs more care in management, more fertilisers and, when put down to grass, heavier seed rates than for normal, undisturbed land.'

Heftier application of fertilisers increases the risk of water pollution if the fertilisers are washed off the fields into streams or rivers. Nitrate pollution caused by fertilisers is a national

ABOVE: The nuclear-processing plant at Sellafield casts a wide shadow

BELOW: The Derwent Valley — beset by applications for opencast coal mining

problem, but the damage to underground soil structures of reclaimed opencast sites potentially magnifies the problem, says Desmond Napier, a Durham businessman and member of the CPRE, who has been a leading opponent of opencast mining for some years. He says, 'Surplus fertilisers, penetrating through the crushed and freshly exposed rock, leach out heavy metals that were stable over millions of years but which are now carried down into the ground water reserves, presenting a long-term, insidious and irreversible threat to our water reserves. This factor has been recognised by the EEC (in its proposals to protect water supplies) but not by the UK water authorities. They should carry out sample boring for monitoring after reclamation. Although this is not experienced, felt or seen by the individual concerned, it is just one more load, one more threat, to the local and national ecological balance.'

Environmentally, apart from cleaning up already derelict sites, opencast mining is therefore a disaster: short-term devastation compounded by long-term agricultural and wildlife decline. Economically, the coal should be nationally essential to warrant such destruction. The 1981 Flowers Report, the

LEFT: Langley opencast mine, County Durham

findings of a government-appointed independent commission on energy and the environment, is the most recent comprehensive study of opencast mining. It favoured a reduction of opencast production, which had grown from about 5 per cent of total output in the 1960s to between 12.5 and 15 per cent in the 1980s. The Flowers Report also proposed guidelines that would confine production to sites which either would be environmentally improved by restoration or could produce types of coal unavailable from deep mines. In principle, the government accepted the broad conclusions of the Flowers Report; in reality, it has allowed opencast production to be determined by market forces, and key guidelines were weakened or neutered. In 1987 the all-party House of Commons Energy Committee criticised the guidelines available to local planning authorities as vague and ineffective. Opencast production should be reduced, said the committee. Undaunted by such criticism, British Coal's Opencast Executive would like to increase annual production to 18 million tonnes – 20 per cent more than the maximum recommended by the Flowers Commission.

Unshackled by national constraints, British Coal and private operators have stepped up their proposals for new opencast pits. Five were lodged in Durham in one six-month period of 1986 alone. Piecemeal applications can disguise the scale of the assault; north of Whittonstall, supposedly separate sites would have resulted in nearly 6 miles of continuous workings. This plan was exposed by the spirited opposition of people such as Desmond Napier. With mining engineer Malcolm Brocklesby and law lecturer Leslie Rutherford, Napier has led effective counter-attacks against many opencast proposals in Durham and Northumberland. Their arguments are detailed and complex dissections of mining economics, challenging assertions that opencast coal is cheaper than coal from modern deep mines and arguing that it destroys more jobs than it creates. 'In spite of claims to the contrary, there is no economic justification for the majority of opencast extraction,' says Malcolm Brocklesby. 'Far from contributing to the profits of British Coal, current opencast policy is tending to increase energy costs.'

The pressure for opencast mining is greatest on the wider countryside beyond the designated national parks and AONBs. This unprotected countryside is also more propitious territory for gravel workings and forestry. Here, too, are the greatest pressures for housing and shopping developments, notably around cities such as Newcastle and Teesside conurbation. Yet none of the north's industrial centres is exactly lacking in derelict land within the cities. A few imaginative schemes show what can be done. Tyne Riverside country park, a few miles upstream from Newcastle, combines industrial archaeology and open countryside; Castle Eden Walkway in Cleveland and Derwent Walk in County Durham are popular footpaths along the tracks of abandoned railway lines; and Beamish open-air museum incorporates everything from trams to farms.

ABOVE: At Whittonstall, applications for supposedly separate opencast sites would have resulted in nearly 6 miles of continuous workings

ABOVE RIGHT: Quarry near Kirkby Stephen, Cumbria

Cumbria, despite pockets of industrial decay along the coast and around Carlisle, is overwhelmingly rural. Much of it has some degree of protection from unsightly development, with two national parks – 12 per cent of the Yorkshire Dales national park is in Cumbria – and parts of three AONBs in the county. But some fine countryside lies outside these areas: the northern Howgill Fells and the valleys of the Eden, Lune and Lyvennet, for instance. Much of it is under pressure in some form. It may be the encroachment of forestry or the Ministry of Defence's voracious appetite for more land, as seen in its attempts to acquire more training land at North Stainmore. The pressure may be as general as intensive agriculture or as specific as intrusive telecommunications masts or radar domes. Throughout northern England, the greatest underlying concern is the need to support rural populations through times of profound economic change.

In these largely upland counties, life has long been hard and uncertain. Working the land rarely earns a living in itself and for forty years governments have subsidised hill farmers, increasing production yet indirectly encouraging farm amalgamations and a decline in jobs. Rural development areas have been created to encourage small industries in the countryside, but they have failed to arrest the steady drift of people from the uplands. Population in the Durham dales fell by a quarter in the fifteen years up to 1987, with forecasts in a county council report of further job losses taking unemployment to 25 per cent by 1996. In the Northumberland national park, population has fallen by 10 per cent since the park was designated in 1956. In the Lake District, depopulation has been halted only as a result of inward migration by retired people, which can cause its own problems.

Tourism has become the only growth industry for many upland regions, earning Cumbria an estimated £150 million a year in the mid-1980s. In addition to creating many full-time jobs, it enables farmers to diversify. Where once hill farmers combined sheep rearing with mining, they now offer bed and breakfast. Yet tourism creates problems as well as jobs. Development proposals for new housing or large-scale tourist projects are among the greatest pressures on the Lake District. And it's not just the buildings themselves, but who owns them. A sixth of the houses in the Lake District are holiday homes, mostly bought at prices which local people cannot afford. In Langdale, the proportion was 37.5 per cent in the 1981 census. With fewer jobs and higher house prices, many rural areas enter into a spiral of decline, as a result of which schools, shops and hospitals close, buses cease to call. With unemployment also high in the towns, rural areas can easily be forgotten; the Durham dales, for instance, cover 42 per cent of the county but have only 2.5 per cent of its population.

So far governments have failed to devise a coherent strategy for the uplands beyond piecemeal help or ad hoc grants from the Development Commission. Through agencies such as the Council for Small Industries in Rural Areas (CoSIRA), the Development Commission builds small factories and assists rural councils to improve community services. Grants also exist to convert redundant buildings for village halls or workshops. In 1986 CoSIRA estimated that, in the previous decade, it had helped launch 40,000 businesses employing more than 200,000 people. However, proposals for a more integrated approach to national and local policies for conservation, farming, forestry, rural development, recreation and public services gather dust in Whitehall.

This failure to adopt an overall policy for the uplands will ultimately jeopardise what is probably their greatest asset — natural beauty. The future of England's uplands is dependent upon the economic health of the rural communities. Without people to maintain stone walls or hedgerows, without help to manage woodlands, without conservation of moorlands and meadows, the landscape and habitats of these northern counties will lose their lustre. Conservation should be part of

ABOVE: Limestone in the Lyvennet Valley

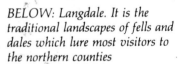

BELOW: Langdale. It is the traditional landscapes of fells and dales which lure most visitors to the northern counties

a new future for the uplands – directly as a source of income in grants to manage landscapes, and indirectly in offering an attractive environment to woo businessmen also being tempted by a variety of other development packages. If the countryside is not conserved, tourism will ultimately suffer, for it is the traditional landscapes of fells and dales which lure most visitors to the northern counties.

For 5000 years man has helped to shape the wildest landscapes in England; for 200 years, these areas have been widely regarded as our most dramatic countryside. Today, as much as when Neolithic farmers first cleared the trees, man has the capacity to influence the fate of this unique inheritance. We cannot preserve it exactly as it is now but we can nurture it, resisting or modifying changes which might be harmful and encouraging those which may enhance landscapes we have come to cherish. If we neglect such countryside, future generations will rue this century's contribution to the continuing evolution of England's uplands.

ABOVE RIGHT: Howgill Fells – unprotected countryside

2

THE PENNINE SHIRES

The moors and dales of Yorkshire and Lancashire are the quintessential upland scenery of England. Not so romantic as the Lakeland further north, yet with a ruggedness more emblematic of the northern character.

Not high enough to be classed as mountains, nor remote enough to be wilderness, yet every year walkers here require rescue as clouds or storms envelop the boggy moorland summits. These same, potentially inhospitable moors exert a powerful magnetism. For writers and artists, such as Emily Brontë and Henry Moore, the moors were an inspiration; for workers toiling in textile mills they provided an escape from cramped houses and the ceaseless clatter of machinery.

The untrammelled openness of the moors has always been more potent for their proximity to the great cities of the industrial revolution. Nowhere in southern England is there so close a bond between town and country as in the Pennine counties of Yorkshire and Lancashire. The countryside on our doorsteps is as much a part of our heritage as the wilder landscapes of the national parks. It is an integral ingredient of our lives, not just a pleasure to be savoured occasionally on high days and holidays. Knowledge of one form of countryside breeds respect and affection for others, so that first steps taken on family walks can lead to back-packing across the moors – or simply to another one-hour stroll and picnic next weekend.

Today these Pennine shires beckon visitors from further afield. Coach parties tour the dales and moors in search of 'Herriot's Yorkshire'; naturalists admire some of the world's finest limestone landscapes around Malham; walkers trek the Pennine Way and other paths in such numbers that matting or wooden boards now protect certain eroded hilltops. More controversial arrivals have been quarrymen digging for min-

Neglected outbuildings at Farndale

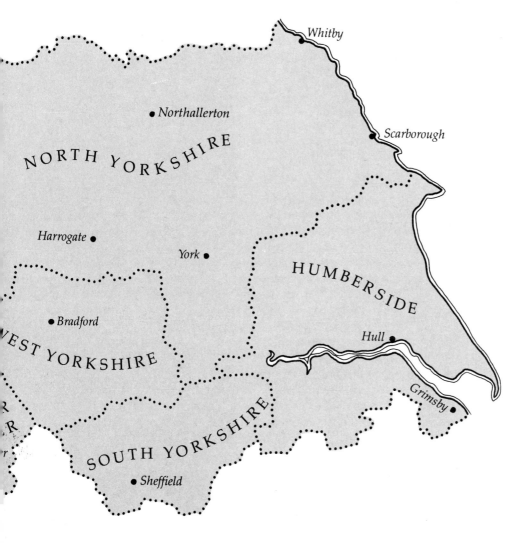

erals, foresters submerging almost a fifth of the North York Moors under conifers and second-home owners pushing house prices beyond the reach of local people. The wildness of the moors, as valued as it is rare in our crowded island, is now under attack.

Two national parks have been created in this region, each with a mandate not only to protect the landscape but also to promote public enjoyment of the moors and dales. In all, ten national parks have been established in England and Wales since a government white paper issued in 1945 spelled out a new vision for our most dramatic countryside. The parks were to be:

extensive areas of beautiful and relatively wild country in which, for the nation's benefit and by appropriate national decision and action, the characteristic beauty is strictly preserved; access and facilities for open air enjoyment are amply provided; wildlife and buildings and places of architectural and historic interest are suitably protected, while established farming use is effectively maintained.

What national parks have not had is any ability to control agriculture. Below the 2500-foot contour, most moors are semi-natural landscapes, reflecting 3500 years of man's endeavours to clear the ancient wildwood and tame the uplands. The imprint of man is more evident in the stone-walled fields of the Yorkshire Dales than on the moors. Here, closer inspection reveals a dramatically decreasing number of meadows along with the rich array of herbs and flowers for which the dales were once renowned. From the valley floor to the moorland plateau, new agricultural methods are transforming countryside which took centuries to evolve. Outside the national parks, the coastal marshes of Lancashire and the chalk downland of the Yorkshire Wolds have proved equally vulnerable to agricultural change.

Most of these Pennine shires (and neighbouring Humberside) comprise farmed landscapes, but the influence of so many towns and cities cannot be discounted. Cars have brought more people than ever before within reach of once-remote areas of the Pennines; 8 million people are within ninety minutes' drive of the Yorkshire Dales national park. To ease the burden on the national parks, country parks have been provided closer to the cities, often also to clear up the dereliction of abandoned industrial sites. The countryside of this urban fringe is heavily used — and increasingly in demand by house-builders and other developers. Yet too many green-field sites for factories or houses will create new conurbations, just as surely as Manchester and Leeds engulfed village neighbours a century ago.

In those days it was on the local moorland that factory workers sought some relief from the tyranny of the loom or the heat of the furnace. Bus services would terminate not at housing estates but on the moors. Moorland is by no means confined to the Pennines — it is found as far apart as Bodmin and Caithness — and its character (and wildlife) can vary

58

Urra Moor, North Yorkshire

greatly, even within North Yorkshire. Although the term 'moorland' is widely used in the sense of uncultivated rough-land, some moors are wet and boggy, some drier and covered by heather or bracken; many combine wet and dry areas. Despite such differences, moorland is regarded by some writers as 'the most distinctively British kind of vegetation'.

Nobody knows exactly how moorland was formed. It seems likely that the moors in the far north of Scotland are natural arctic tundra, while in England most moors were once covered by trees. Oliver Rackham, a Cambridge botanist who is acknowledged as the leading expert on British woodland, believes that more trees fell down of their own accord than were ever cleared by prehistoric man. He also doubts whether many trees would now grow on moorland unaided by the drainage and fertilisers employed by the Forestry Commission. Moorland's characteristic feature is a layer of peat accumulated from the remains of dead plants; this is a poor foundation for trees, particularly where rainfall of more than 70 inches a year keeps the ground permanently wet. Where man did clear the wildwood, peat tended to become thicker more quickly, making it even less possible for trees to regenerate naturally. Tree growth has been further inhibited by grazing, helping to create the moors we know today.

In prehistoric times many moors were cultivated and became centres of settlement before the lowland woods were cleared. The North York Moors are less well known and more compact then Dartmoor, but just as rich archaeologically. In *A Guide to the Prehistoric and Roman Monuments in England and Wales*, archaeologist Jacquetta Hawkes writes:

There are still ten thousand round barrows and cairns up here among the heather and coarse moorland grass, Bronze and Iron Age hut clusters, dykes and defences of all kinds, standing stones and stone circles, long barrows. The North York Moors are a single monument to prehistoric man, one of those small areas where his handiwork is often still dominant over that of his descendants.

One reason why so many ancient monuments survived, long after the focus of settlement shifted to the lowlands, is that the moorland surface remains intact. In Yorkshire its owners included Cistercian monks who grazed sheep from great abbeys such as Rievaulx and Fountains, kings who proclaimed Pickering a royal hunting reserve, and farmers who used common land on the moors as summer grazing for their livestock. A distinctive vegetation evolved of heather, moor-land grasses and blanket bog, varying with the depth of peat and degree of wetness. Nibbled and gnawed by sheep, deer and cattle, heather moorland is the ideal — indeed only — breeding ground for the red grouse.

One of the ironies of conservation is that some of our most prized landscapes owe their origin or survival in part to the slaughter of wildlife. There would be fewer copses without pheasant shooting, fewer ponds or 'unimproved' streams without angling. So it has been with grouse. The moors were regularly burned so that new heather could grow

ABOVE: *Rievaulx Abbey*

to provide better food and cover in which grouse could breed. So popular did grouse shooting become that large tracts of moorland were maintained as grouse moors, posing problems for public access, yet maintaining the heather in mint condition.

For 3000 years the moors were rarely ploughed – and then never at any depth: until the twentieth century. First it was the foresters, more recently the farmers, as modern technology conquered land previously dismissed as too wet or too infertile to warrant either afforestation or agricultural improvement. Even so, reclamation of the moors has been dependent upon subsidies from public funds to render it economic.

The extent of change is starkly evident in the North York Moors national park. Between 1950 and 1983, according to the park authority, 18.2 per cent of this moorland – some 48 square miles – has been planted for forestry and 7.3 per cent 'improved' for agriculture. Lower rainfall, peat of varying thickness or acidity and younger underlying rocks make the North York Moors more fertile than the more westerly Pennine moors, and accordingly more vulnerable. But these conditions have also produced England's largest expanse of heather-covered moorland. Few sights are more arresting in late summer than the sea of deep-purple ling heather stretching either side of the Pickering to Whitby road. Part of this area, known as Lockton High Moor, has come under acute

BELOW: Lockton High Moor has come under acute pressure from farming

61

pressure from farming. Had the national park authority not intervened, two thirds of Lockton High Moor could now be reseeded grassland or even fields of barley.

In the early years of the national park's existence, forestry posed the greatest threat to the moorland. However, the Forestry Commission has agreed not to extend its holdings substantially within the national park and has cooperated with the park authority in promoting footpaths and picnic

ABOVE: The Forestry Commission has promoted footpaths and picnic sites in areas such as Dalby Forest

sites in places such as Dalby Forest. In 1987 the Forestry Commission bowed to park authority protests and refused grant aid for a private large-scale afforestation scheme near Boultby. This strengthened the good relations between the two public bodies, but national park officers remain uneasy about the future. Forestry is being encouraged by the government as an alternative use for land no longer needed for agriculture and this will renew demands on the national park. More than 90 per cent of the moorland is technically plantable, given modern forestry techniques, and already there have been proposals not only for new plantations but also to convert existing woodlands to conifers. For the past fifteen years — initially fuelled by the now-abandoned ploughing grants — pressure has come more from farming than forestry. Over 900 acres of Lockton High Moor were bought by the park authority to retain it as moorland. But unless land is designated as a site of special scientific interest (SSSI), public bodies have few sanctions against a determined farmer or forester, if he forsakes the possibility of government grants.

Conversion of moorland to agriculture generally requires high capital investment and sustained fertiliser input. It can also entail enclosing open moorland with fencing and increasing the density of livestock. New strains of rye grass may be sown, which help to increase yields. The end result is that grass pasture, little different from that which can be found in many parts of England, replaces a heather moorland regarded as unique. Rare habitats harbour rare species so, as the moorland shrinks, there will be fewer birds of prey such as the merlin, buzzard and hen harrier hunting for meadow pipits, wheatears and voles in the heather. Nor are these the only consequences of agricultural conversion, as the national park authority makes plain: 'It transforms the landscape, reduces its ecological value (part of which is its scale), can destroy archaeological interest and removes most of its recreational potential.'

Its purchase of parts of Lockton High Moor and 1800 acres of neighbouring Levisham Moor, including the spectacular natural amphitheatre of the Hole of Horcum, symbolises the park's determination to resist any further losses of moorland.

63

RIGHT: The Hole of Horcum — a spectacular natural amphitheatre

These sites are also proving useful test-beds for ways to manage the moors. Here, as on Dartmoor, there are management programmes to combat the spread of bracken, to establish levels of grazing which allow the heather and moor grasses to flourish, and to minimise problems such as erosion caused by visitors. Bracken is a virulent menace, smothering between 15 and 40 per cent of the heather at Levisham Moor, for example, in the last thirty years. This forces sheep to crowd onto the remaining area of heather, which then becomes overgrazed. Spraying is expensive – £30 an acre in the mid-1980s – and never totally successful. Heather moorland also has to be burned regularly, if new heather is to replace the old plants and damaging, spontaneous fires are to be avoided. As the extent of the grouse moors and grazing have shrunk, traditional skills of moor management have declined. The park authority's experiments at Levisham and Lockton therefore have a value beyond their boundaries, yet outright purchase offers no general solution to the problem of the vanishing moors.

As is the case in all other national parks in Britain, the majority of the land in the North York Moors national park is privately owned. Less than 2 per cent of the moorland is owned by the national park, with another 7 per cent enjoying a degree of protection as either a SSSI or through National Trust ownership. Half the moorland is common land, yet this neither guarantees that it is managed properly nor increases the power of the national park authority. The proposals of the Common Land Forum (see page 29), if adopted, would make it more likely that problems of over-grazing (and restricted access) could be tackled. This still leaves two fifths of the moorland unprotected and, although the most important, the moors are not the only landform which the North York Moors national park authority seeks to conserve.

There are broad-leaved woodlands in valleys and around the moorland fringe; these woods of ash, oak and other deciduous species are often rich in wild flowers, but many are not regenerating. There is the farmed land, which now makes up two-fifths of the national park, a higher proportion than the moorland for which the park won its designation. Around the edges of the moors, in valleys and along the coast, there is some mixed farming, producing wheat, barley and potatoes as well as livestock. On higher land, sheep predominate. Valleys such as Farndale and Bransdale, draining south off the moors to the Vale of Pickering, have come under strong pressure for agricultural improvement. Local surveys suggest that, between 1953 and 1979, approximately a quarter of the hedgerows and a tenth of the stone walls were destroyed, adding to the transformation of the traditional moorland fringe. Fences have been erected along some moorland roads to prevent sheep being killed, sadly destroying the traditional openness of the higher moors.

Moorland, woodland and farmland, therefore, have all been transformed, with the national park authority unable to fulfil its conservation role. There will always be change in the countryside; nature, let alone man's ingenuity, is never static.

ABOVE: Farndale – a target for agricultural 'improvement'

ABOVE RIGHT: Fylingdales radar station in the North York Moors national park

RIGHT: Limestone pavement above Malham Cove

65

What national parks are supposed to do is ensure that change does not impair the quality or character of what, by designation, are accepted as special areas. This is no easy task, especially when, as in two Yorkshire national parks, agriculture is not merely the major influence over the landscape but also a major employer of local people. The North York Moors national park has introduced constructive schemes to foster greater understanding of conservation among farmers. Management programmes for moorland, uplands and woodlands have shown what can be done to maintain and enhance the land; but such successes are modest and do not dispel doubts over the capability of national parks, as now constituted and financed, to realise the vision of those who campaigned for their creation.

The Yorkshire Dales national park has faced different threats from those afflicting the North York Moors: no substantial military presence (while the Moors park has Fylingdales radar station) and minimal afforestation (only 2 per cent of the park, although half the park is technically capable of being planted), but far more intrusive mineral extraction. The most extensive quarrying involves that which gives the park its greatest distinction – limestone. For some, this means the dramatic gorges and cliffs around Malham; for others, woodlands such as the national nature reserve of Ling Gill; for yet others, a world of caves formed as rainwater dissolves elaborate networks of underground passages. Over half of England's limestone pavements are within the park. These are areas of exposed limestone where rainwater has opened up cracks in the rock, known as 'grikes', which form a sheltered habitat for rare and delicate lime-loving plants. According to the Nature Conservancy Council (NCC), 45 per cent of

Britain's limestone pavements have been damaged or destroyed since 1945, often scavenged for rockeries.

The limestone (and, to a greater extent, the millstone grit and sandstone also found in the Pennines) has been used more sympathetically to build the stone walls and field barns which characterise the homely patchwork of small fields for which the Yorkshire Dales are also known. The peat of the Pennine moors is generally thicker and soggier than that of the North York Moors, encouraging plants such as bog asphodel and the insect-eating sundew. As the Pennine moors are wetter and less accessible — heathery Swaledale is among the exceptions — agriculture has focused more on the valleys (or dales) than the boggy moorland plateaux. Yet 13 per cent of rough grazing was lost between 1974 and 1981 alone, says the Council for National Parks, largely as a result of moorland improvement and enclosure. In the valleys, many stone walls and field barns are being allowed to fall derelict, while what is happening to the fields themselves is equally alarming. Nationally, according to the NCC, no fewer than 95 per cent of herb-rich meadows have lost their wildlife value since the Second World War. Only two types of meadows remain in any numbers: water meadows, of which the best are to be found along the Thames Valley; and upland hay meadows, of which the Yorkshire Dales are the last stronghold in England — alas, they are imperilled here, too.

Life has rarely been easy for farmers in these hills, although the Cistercian monks prospered for a time. They left a legacy of stone walls, built to stake out their territories, and 'green lanes', along which they had driven their sheep from summer to winter pastures — Mastiles Lane between Malham and Kilnsey is the most famous. The dissolution of the monasteries led to the fragmentation of the great estates. Farms became smaller, although this did not deter landowners from the heroic construction of stone walls high onto the moors following the Enclosure Acts of the late eighteenth and early nineteenth centuries. The heather-covered millstone-grit moors in the north and east were grazed by sheep and often maintained for grouse, but from Tudor times the valleys became the preserve of dairy cattle. Wensleydale cheese was made in the farmhouse centuries before Lymeswold was a gleam in a marketing man's balance sheet. Dairy farming shaped both the landscape and the wildlife now under threat.

Hay was grown in the valley meadows while cattle grazed on the higher summer pastures; it was then mown and stored in field barns as fodder for the cattle who lived in the valleys in winter. The farms were small — even as recently as 1981 a third were under 50 acres. In this basic pastoral system hay was consumed where it was grown, manure deposited on or near the meadows which it could most benefit. The result, on the lime-enriched soil, were meadows ablaze with colour. With up to 120 species of grasses, herbs and flowers, the flora might vary from field to field. The fact that the hay meadows of the dales were not grazed in early summer was what distinguished them from pasture and enabled the wild flowers to flourish. Most important of all, each species was

TOP: *Flower meadows near Muker, Swaledale*

ABOVE: *Mastiles Lane — one of the 'green lanes' along which Cistercian monks drove their sheep*

RIGHT: *In Swaledale there are sixty stone field barns within a kilometre of Muker*

allowed to flower – the wood cranesbill, meadow buttercup, salad burnet, globe flower, and many others. The colours and scents changed with the seasons, the seeds fell, insects teemed, birds and butterflies all prospered before the mower made its appearance in the meadow to cut the hay. Then came fertilisers, reseeded meadows and silage – grass cut two or three times during the summer, too frequently and too soon for flowers to bloom or birds to feed. The combined effect is to produce more crops of grass or fodder for hard-up farmers but, gradually, a more limited range of grasses begin to predominate. Spray some pesticides, add fertilisers, sow cultivated strands of rye grass – and the wild flowers of hay meadows become endangered species.

As farming evolved, new and larger cattle sheds were erected closer to the farmhouse. The old field barns were redundant and many fell into decay. The traditional landscape survives best in Swaledale, with no fewer than sixty field barns within a kilometre of Muker; and there are more than twenty nationally important meadows in the Yorkshire dales as a whole. But Richard Harvey, national park officer for the Yorkshire Dales, says that the problems of dereliction are increasing and likely to get worse. Only a massive injection of funds can avert the threat to what he calls 'one of the finest and most distinctive cultural landscapes in Europe'.

The agricultural threat to the Yorkshire Dales, like that to the North York Moors, strikes at the heart of the dilemma facing those who run our national parks: responsibility without control. Even direct areas of responsibility, such as the duty to promote public enjoyment of the parks, are not without difficulties. Paths over what are known as the Three Peaks of the Yorkshire Dales – Ingleborough, Penyghent and Whernside – have been so heavily used that on average they are 37.4 feet wide, twice the width of a B-class road. In places, the scar is 150 *metres* wide! An estimated 120,000 walkers a year climb Ingleborough and some even go up the mountains on bikes. The fragile vegetation of these moors has been completely trampled away, so that in wet weather, which is not exactly uncommon, the slopes become a morass of peaty mud. Not unnaturally, walkers seek to bypass the worst of the mud – no doubt mindful of the report in a Ramblers' Association journal of a walker sinking up to his waist in the peat – thereby making the erosion even wider. So severely damaged were most of the paths in 1985 that the Countryside Commission endorsed the park authority's £770,000 rescue scheme for the Peaks. This will involve more sophisticated methods than the boards or rubber matting tried elsewhere, not least because the boggy peat surface makes materials unsuitable as long-term solutions. Finding a durable surface which neither scars the landscape nor stifles the vegetation will not be easy. The trials will be monitored closely in the North Yorks Moors, where the popularity of the Lyke Wake Walk across the Cleveland Hills is causing similar problems.

Car-borne visitors can also be destructive. The popularity of James Herriot's books about the life of a country vet has rebounded on the narrow lanes of North Yorkshire. One-fifth of all visitors to the North York Moors never leave their cars

ABOVE: Penyghent, one of the Three Peaks of the Yorkshire Dales, where footpaths have suffered severe erosion.

FAR LEFT: The Three Peaks Race, Ingleborough

LEFT: The Lyke Wake Walk

and, for a time, the picturesque stream-bisected green at Hutton-le-Hole had more cars parking than sheep grazing. Here, the national park was able to act; a new car park and kerbstones to deter parking on the green have restored something of Hutton-le-Hole's original charm. A one-way system operates in Farndale during the short but spectacular daffodil season. More generally new footpaths, car parks, picnic areas, visitor centres and other information services have fulfilled the national parks' mandate of promoting public enjoyment in these supremely beautiful parts of Britain. Despite this statutory responsibility for recreation, however, national parks cannot impose their will. New traffic or parking schemes at Malham and Robin Hood's Bay, for example, were hotly contested by sections of the local populations and, to some extent, rebuffed.

The frustration faced by park authorities are described by Richard Harvey of the Yorkshire Dales national park: 'Changing patterns of agriculture and forestry, pressure for economic development and increasing numbers of visitors threaten to erode the traditional character of the national parks. The Yorkshire Dales national park committee is expected to balance conservation, recreation and social and economic development, and safeguard the special qualities of the national park. Whilst the committee has a special responsibility, as the local trustee of a national asset, its powers and resources are, in fact, quite limited. Many of the major challenges which it faces stem from external forces over which it can exercise little influence. Political and economic decisions taken at regional, national and international levels exert profound influence by providing or removing incentives for action. In effect, the national park committee is able only to treat the symptoms, not the cause, and what it can do in this respect is restricted by the powers and resources at its disposal.'

This analysis, which has a relevance way beyond Yorkshire, should not blind us to the successes of the parks in the first thirty-five or so years of their lives. Sometimes these are tangible and positive, such as better recreation facilities or management schemes for woods, meadows and moorland. Sometimes the success takes the form of damage limitation: the effect on landscape would have been irredeemably worse had parks not existed. The growth of the limestone quarry at Coolscar in Wharfedale, for instance, has undoubtedly been restricted by the fact that it is in the Yorkshire Dales national park. It is nonetheless a grotesque eyesore and long planning battles have been fought to prevent or restrain further expansion. Similar campaigns have been waged against potash mining near Whitby on the North York Moors. The arguments hinge upon a pledge given in 1949 by Lewis Silkin, the minister piloting the national park bill through Parliament. Mineral extraction should only proceed in national parks, said Mr Silkin, if the mineral was required in the national interest and there was no reasonable alternative source of supply. How this twofold test should be proved (or disproved) has occupied public inquiries concerning the parks ever since. A more fundamental difficulty has been that many quarries were already in existence before the creation of the parks. Quarries can also be reopened after years of closure on the basis of earlier planning permission, as was touted at Ribblehead. Limestone had been quarried in Ribblesdale and Wharfedale for centuries, just as iron ore and alum had long been mined on the North York Moors. Quarrying, like farming, is an element of the working countryside which is characteristic of Britain's national parks.

Unlike national parks in countries such as the United States and France, those in Britain are neither wildernesses nor wildlife reserves. They were grafted onto existing social, economic and political structures in the 1950s. Today nearly a quarter of a million people live in the national parks (excluding the Norfolk Broads, which has been promised a status comparable to that of a national park in 1988) and on average three-quarters of the land is privately owned. Even where land is publicly owned, it is far more likely to have been acquired for military training, forestry or reservoirs than for conservation or recreation. 'Who owns the land is not nearly so important for conservation as how they manage it,' says Adrian Phillips, director of the Countryside Commission. Perhaps so, but Mr Phillips sounded a less reassuring note in the Commission's annual report for 1985–86. The national parks, he said, were in triple jeopardy: 'under-resourced, under-protected and poorly understood'.

The national parks designated under the 1949 National Parks and Access to the Countryside Act together cover roughly 9 per cent of the land area of England and Wales, a far higher proportion than in countries where the 'wilderness' concept determines the creation of a national park. Wordsworth is often cited as the father of the park movement. The lakes, he wrote, were 'a sort of national property, in which every man has a right and interest who has an eye to perceive and a heart to enjoy'. But it was in the United States that the first national park was created – Yellowstone in 1872. As the American pioneers did not worry unduly about Indian property rights, it was relatively easy to establish federal sanctuaries free from commercial development. Apart from catering for visitors, American national parks remain virtually uninhabited and undeveloped today.

In Britain, it was to be almost 150 years before Wordsworth's vision was realised. Although the Open Spaces Society and the National Trust were formed in the nineteenth century, it was not until the inter-war years of the twentieth century that a campaign for national parks crystallised. By then the advocates of parks were no longer restricted to the poets, artists and others who drew aesthetic pleasure from beautiful countryside. The physical challenge of walking and climbing had increasingly lured people from the cities to the moors and mountains of northern England. But the public was barred from many of the wilder moorlands. The Peak District, in particular, became a battleground for greater public access (see chapter 3, pages 92–4). Conservation interests also grew impatient, especially after government proposals

For a time the stream-bisected green at Hutton-le-Hole had more cars parking than sheep grazing

in 1931 for a national parks authority had been dropped. In 1936, under the aegis of the Councils for the Protection of Rural England and Wales, the access and conservation movements joined forces to form a Standing Committee on National Parks. Now known as the Council for National Parks, it was this body which successfully campaigned for the parks we have today.

The government white paper issued in the same month as VE Day seemed to herald a new dawn. Surely those potent images of rural England which had helped to sustain the war effort could now be made reality? Four years later, the legislation to enact the white paper's principles disappointed many of the early pioneers; forty years on, national parks are still living with the consequences of their birth-pangs. There was no great controversy over the parks to be designated, although the deletion of two lowland areas (the South Downs and Norfolk Broads) was regretted; it also left these two areas particularly vulnerable to an agricultural revolution whose future impact was unforeseen. The aims of the national parks, enshrined in the 1945 white paper, remained intact and have changed little: to preserve and enhance natural beauty and to promote public enjoyment. The difficulties arose in deciding how best to fulful this mandate.

71

Kilnsey, Yorkshire Dales, threatened by the expansion of Coolscar quarry

Despite their 'national' status, the parks are administered locally. But geography does not always respect local authority boundaries and several national parks cover more than one county. Most county councils had opposed the creation of new administrative units which would weaken their traditional powers. As a result of their campaign, only two of the parks — the Peak District and the Lake District — were

given the independent planning boards originally proposed for them all. The rest were to be run by committees associated with one (or more) county council(s). And, although national government nominated one-third of committee members and provided three-quarters of the cash, local government therefore provided two-thirds of the board or committee members who decided how the money should be spent. Not that the funding was generous. Until the 1970s no park outside the Peak District had its own staff. Since then, park administration has been centralised, finances increased and staff employed to produce and implement plans for running each park. Welcome though the improvements have been, some inherent weaknesses remain.

Governments have charged national park authorities with conserving the landscape, yet decreed that agriculture and forestry should be largely excluded from planning control. National policies for agricultural support, buttressed by EEC schemes for less favoured areas (see chapter 1, pages 25–6), are the strongest influence on the farmed landscapes of

Guisborough, Cleveland – a prosperous commuter base for nearby conurbations

national parks. Sometimes these encourage overstocking which leads to overgrazing; always, until now, production rather than conservation has been the decisive factor. Industrially, too, there are development areas and schemes run nationally by organisations such as the Council for Small Industries in Rural Areas. On development, however, the national parks are able to act as planning authorities. Major cases, such as the Whitby potash mine in the North York Moors, may go to public inquiries and ultimately to a minister's desk, but the parks determine the majority of cases.

Park authorities are required by law to be conscious of 'the social and economic needs' of local people, but local authority representatives have not always found it easy to balance national and local interests. Their electors may not be numerous in national terms – nationally 0.5 per cent of the population in 9 per cent of the total land area of England and Wales – but they need jobs as much as anyone. Local views about the fate of mining applications, holiday complexes or new roads may not therefore be in harmony with the best interests of conservation. Most parks have suffered from falling populations, with an increasing proportion of second or retirement homes; one house in seven in Wensleydale is a holiday home and the percentage is growing. With agriculture shedding labour, there can all too easily be a decline in rural services which short-lived tourist seasons cannot offset. Conversely, on the fringes of the parks, villages such as Guisborough in Cleveland have become prosperous commuter bases for nearby conurbations.

National parks are inhibited in their ability to tackle the diverse problems partly by constitutional weakness and partly by paucity of funds. Even after a 13 per cent increase in funds promised for 1987–88, the total central government grant for all ten national parks was £9.8 million, compared to the £13.4 million received solely by the Royal Opera House in Covent Garden. No wonder the Countryside Commission has felt it necessary to launch a public campaign to make our national parks better known and better supported. Ninety-six million day visits were paid to the parks in 1985, yet a survey the previous year showed that barely half the people questioned could name a single national park without prompting.

Many such paradoxes attend Britain's national parks: designated as national assets, yet largely locally controlled and privately owned; chosen for their 'wildness', yet home to 250,000 people; shaped mostly by agriculture, though farmers are largely exempt from control; proclaimed for public enjoyment, though recreation may occasionally endanger the landscapes which are supposed to be conserved; overseen by the Countryside Commission, whose advisory role lacks the executive powers enjoyed nationally by the Nature Conservancy Council. Given these difficulties, there is one overriding paradox: hamstrung and underfunded since birth, the national parks have been successful against the odds.

Despite serious losses, it is in national parks where afforestation, intensive farming, quarrying and motorways have

73

been most effectively resisted. Access has been improved. Four-fifths of the country's (admittedly, very few) access agreements negotiated with landowners are found in national parks. Although all national park authorities recognise that further work is required to develop the rights-of-way network, new waymarked walks have tempted increasing numbers of visitors to abandon their cars. Other recreation facilities range from riverside picnic sites to restored barns for overnight accommodation. Though the funds available to national parks are paltry, they have enabled the park authorities to pioneer conservation schemes for uplands and woodlands which have been taken up elsewhere. These schemes even include two restrictions on farmers' freedom from local control.

First, limited controls over farm (and forestry) buildings and roads have been extended from parts of the Peak District, Lake District and Snowdonia to all ten national parks; but sanctions are confined to the design and location of buildings, not their existence. The second form of control is more substantial, but also potentially flawed. Under the 1981 Wildlife and Countryside Act, farmers in national parks are obliged to notify the park authority in advance of any activity for which they intend to seek a Ministry of Agriculture grant. If the park authority objects, a decision on the grant application goes to the Ministry of Agriculture. If the ministry upholds the objection, the park authority must offer a management agreement which compensates farmers for the profits 'lost' by being unable to improve his farming operation as, perhaps, his counterparts outside national parks could have done.

In practice, most park authorities bypass the formal need to involve the minister and begin to negotiate a compensation-based management agreement with the farmer as soon as they object to a proposal. The cost of such an agreement sometimes deters park authorities from making any objection at all. If an agreement is concluded, whether voluntarily or as a result of a ministerial decision, it means that one impoverished public body will pay a farmer money for his inability to achieve public grants from another body in order to pursue a project deemed to be against the public interest! There is some evidence that the guidelines have stimulated proposals for farm improvements which would not otherwise have been contemplated. Farmers can ignore the park authorities altogether, if they are willing to forgo Ministry of Agriculture grants. Some farmers on the North York Moors have done so, confident that agricultural improvement would yield sufficient profit even without the aid of grants. Sometimes, too, grant applications (and the theoretical 'prior notification' to park authorities) are made retrospectively – too late then if the work is environmentally damaging, even if the grant is subsequently refused.

In the first five years of the Act, eighty-three 'compensation' agreements were negotiated by national parks. Some management agreements involved no money at all, simply advice and manpower to look after stone walls or to improve public access. Every acre of meadow, moorland or

74

ABOVE: North York moors, near Fadmoor

RIGHT: Dalby Forest, North Yorkshire

ancient copse saved from the plough must be welcomed and the Yorkshire Dales national park authority says that most disputes with farmers have been settled amicably, with the farmers agreeing to modify their original proposals. The North York Moors national park authority has also developed a farm conservation scheme, through which a project officer can help farmers devise comprehensive farm plans which combine conservation and agricultural improvement. There is undoubtedly a more fruitful dialogue between park authorities and farmers today than when the Wildlife and Countryside Act became law in 1981. But the Act offers no sanctions against farmers (or foresters) who proceed unaided by government grants or against activities for which no grants are available.

A potential third weapon in the national park armoury is the landscape conservation order. Some such power of last resort has been advocated by the Council for the Protection of Rural England (CPRE) since 1971. Government proposals issued for consultation in December 1986 would confine landscape conservation orders to the wildest and most unspoiled parts of national parks and SSSIs; such orders would be too weak and too limited, in the view of conservationists, even to stop moorland from being ploughed. National park authorities would welcome landscape conservation orders where voluntary agreements fail; management agreements cannot provide general protection for the 5625 square miles of national parks in England and Wales. Even if national park authorities overcome a reluctance to pay farmers for doing nothing, they simply do not have enough money to fund widescale compensation. In the mid-1980s the two Yorkshire national parks each had around £150,000 a year for conservation, roughly the same as the cost of a new car park at Helmsley. Both parks therefore saw the more broadly conceived environmentally sensitive areas (ESAs) as a better answer to the problems afflicting their moorland or meadows. For the first time, the parks could say to farmers generally that there is money in conservation. (The background to ESAs is explained in chapter 5, pages 177–80.)

Nationally, the £6 million a year allotted to ESAs in 1987–88 is trifling set against the £2.5 billion spent on agriculture and food policy as a whole. Locally, it will be quite significant. The budget for each of the areas was expected to be around £1 million a year, roughly that given to each of the Yorkshire national parks for their entire expenditure. However, national parks fared poorly in the initial selection of ESAs. The Ministry of Agriculture argued that national parks already received some funds which it could use for conserving landscapes. The one exception in the first ten ESAs designated in England covered what was called the Pennine Dales. This area extends beyond the northern boundaries of the Yorkshire Dales national park into Teesdale and Weardale in County Durham. In all, nine dales are covered by the scheme, which will seek to encourage farmers to maintain hay meadows, dry-stone walls and field barns. It is hoped that many farmers badly hit by the slump in farm incomes, will welcome the

75

additional cash offered to maintain the traditional landscape which they, as much as visitors, enjoy.

Yet the whole of the national park — indeed, any national park — could fairly be classified as an environmentally sensitive area. Why else did so many people campaign for so long for their protection? Until something like the ESA concept and landscape conservation orders are extended to the entire area of all national parks, the parks will remain vulnerable to agricultural change. The heather moors can still be ploughed, valley woodlands decline for lack of management, stone walls and hedges be allowed to decay.

Because the national parks cover the best of the moorland and dale scenery of Yorkshire, they attract the fiercest controversy if perceived to be under threat. But there are fine stretches of countryside in these Pennine shires outside the two national parks (technically, one should say three national parks, since small areas of Greater Manchester, West Yorkshire and South Yorkshire squeeze into the Peak District national park). Between the two Pennine parks, the moors of West Yorkshire and Lancashire are rarely far from cities or towns. Not that you feel oppressed by industry high on the moors above Haworth. Here, little seems to have changed since Emily Brontë wrote *Wuthering Heights*, the supreme novel of moorland life.

These moors also have their softer side; fast-flowing streams which race down twisting, wooded valleys such as that cut by Hebden Water west of Halifax. Many of the earliest textile mills were sited in valleys such as this in order to harness the power of the rivers. For more than a century the freedom of the fells provided a ready escape from the industrial towns of Lancashire, Yorkshire and Durham. The spread of car ownership has enabled more people to go further afield, so that the Yorkshire Dales receive 7.5 million day visits a year — 80 per cent at weekends — and the North York Moors 11 million. Yet there is still great demand for the countryside on the doorstep: each year over a million people now visit the West Pennine Moors between Blackburn and Bolton. Almost half of this moorland is owned by the North West Water Authority for reservoirs and a catchment ground for water supply.

In the Pennine shires generally, reservoirs have been among the more dramatic changes to the countryside wrought by man. Remote valleys were flooded to provide secure water supplies for the factories and homes of industrial Yorkshire and Lancashire. In the past, reservoirs not only transformed the landscape but also barred the public from large tracts of moorland. Fears of pollution were used to justify widespread restrictions on public access. Improved purification methods have allowed restrictions to be eased in some areas, including the West Pennine Moors. Elsewhere on the Pennines, old battles for public access are far from resolved. The Brontë moors have been singled out for special attention by the Ramblers' Association in its 'Forbidden Britain' campaign. So, too, has the Forest of Bowland in Lancashire. When the ramblers' campaign was launched in

The Forest of Bowland — access has been improved but the AONB remains a prime attraction for foresters

1986, access to 62 square miles of Bowland was limited to a strip 7.5 miles long and 40 feet wide. Here the landowner was worried by the supposed threat to his grouse moors. Some members of the public, it is true, deposit litter as liberally as cows leave dung. Evidence from moors where public access has been improved is not conclusive, but ramblers' leaders claim that landowners' fears are overstated, particularly in an area as relatively wild as the Forest of Bowland.

Tucked away beneath the Lake District and beside the Yorkshire Dales, Bowland is somewhat under-appreciated, even in Lancashire. Yet its 310 square miles of moorland, crags, rivers and wooded valleys known as 'cloughs' constitute one of the largest areas of outstanding natural beauty (AONBs) in England. The official designation includes Pendle Hill, south of the Ribble Valley, but otherwise it covers one large chunk of mostly open country north of the Ribble. Almost half the region is moorland, crossed by few roads and infrequently penetrated by tourists. For a 'forest' it may appear to have remarkably few trees, but its name reflects its medieval role as an area for deer rather than the modern conception of woodland. As deer hunting declined, the moors became used for sheep grazing or grouse rearing, further whittling away the trees which were indeed once there. Nevertheless Bowland remains far more wooded than the neighbouring dales, with oak, ash and hornbeam in the valleys and skirting the foothills.

Lancashire has little deciduous woodland, so these woods have particular importance. But many are poorly managed and an increasing proportion of Bowland's woodland is coniferous. The rectangular lines of plantations such as those near Dunsop Bridge jolt the harmony of bare fells, green fields and wooded cloughs. As farming profits decline, areas outside national parks will become prime candidates for further afforestation. According to the Lancashire branch of the CPRE, Bowland faces a twofold challenge: the afforestation of bare land and the replanting of existing broadleaved woodland to produce a conifer crop. Without controls over forestry or farming, designation as an AONB can do little to repel such attacks.

How the land is farmed and managed is crucial to the survival of all rural landscapes, not just those enjoying varying degrees of official recognition. Beyond the Howardian Hills (designated an AONB in 1987) and Vale of York are the Yorkshire Wolds, the most northerly range of chalk hills in Britain, their name mercifully unchanged as a result of local government transfer from the East Riding of Yorkshire to Humberside. The medieval sheep runs on the wolds have long been devoted to arable production, but since the 1970s the steep slopes of the downland valleys have also come under attack. These slopes, for so long unploughed, had remained a northern outpost of a distinctive chalk flora. Agricultural grants made it economic to 'improve' the rough grassland, ploughing, reseeding and spraying the delicate plants of chalk downland out of existence.

Humberside has its share of 'barley barons', as befits a county which borders Lincolnshire. The trend from pasture to arable land also penetrated into North Yorkshire, with the characteristic destruction of hedgerows, particularly in the Vale of York. A quarter of the hedgerows in Yorkshire and Humberside disappeared between 1947 and 1982, according to the Countryside Commission. Only in East Anglia and the East Midlands was the loss greater. Humberside has also lost a third of its ancient woodland in the last fifty years, according to the NCC, with other surveys putting tree losses in Yorkshire at between a quarter and a third. Straw-burning and the loss of wildlife have been other consequences of more intensive agriculture in these counties.

Humberside has an additional problem: the smell and waste produced by 650,000 pigs. One in ten of the nation's pigs live their brief lives in Humberside, mostly in Holderness, and the disposal of their waste worried the Royal Commission on Environmental Pollution in 1979. The waste is made into liquid slurry, an unappealing mixture of excreta, urine and water. The National Farmers' Union has criticised what it calls the small minority of its members who have allowed

slurry tanks to overflow or spread slurry in wet weather so that it pollutes rivers and water-courses. A small minority, maybe, but prosecutions for pollution are increasing yearly. A report from the all-party House of Commons Select Committee on the Environment in May 1987 called for new powers to combat agricultural pollution of water supply. Planning controls can now ensure that new intensive livestock units are sited at least 400 yards from any houses.

Farming in the Pennine shires takes many forms, from tiny one-man hill farms for sheep to arable lowlands, from mixed livestock farming in the river valleys to vegetable crops on the Lancashire plain. The latter is the most fertile region in these counties, a swathe of grade-one agricultural land north of Merseyside devoted to the intensive production of salad crops and vegetables. Elsewhere in these northern counties four areas were among the forty-six originally identified by the Countryside Commission and Nature Conservancy Council (NCC) as candidates for selection as ESAs: the two national parks, the lower Derwent Valley and the AONB straddling the Lancashire–Cumbria border, Arnside and Silverdale. Only the Pennine Dales were among the ESAs initially chosen by the Ministry of Agriculture, but all the areas have some protection. The National Trust owns several tracts of Arnside and Silverdale, two woody hilltops overlooking Morecambe Bay, while the NCC has emerged as the Derwent's benefactor.

The lower Derwent Valley is an area of wetland between York and Goole, known also as the Derwent Ings. The river regularly spills over its banks as water pours off the uplands each winter. The grassy water meadows, enriched by silt deposited during the annual floods, are mown for hay in midsummer and then grazed by cattle and sheep. It is a

ABOVE LEFT: The Yorkshire Wolds near Stamford Bridge

ABOVE RIGHT: The River Derwent near Bubwith, Humberside

pattern of pastoral management which has made the Derwent Ings one of the best regions for wildlife in northern England – it sustains sixty-one species of water plants as well as meadow flora, thirty-five species of fish and the increasingly rare otter, and a rich array of birds either breed there in summer or arrive for winter. There is no technical reason why the Ings should not be drained and converted into fertile arable land, just as happened in the fens or has been threatened in the Somerset Levels. Drainage schemes have been proposed, but they struck few chords among local farmers. 'It's not right to destroy something that can never be replaced,' said one. Since the NCC declared the whole of the Ings an SSSI, the threats have receded.

Under the 1981 Wildlife and Countryside Act, the NCC can compulsorily purchase SSSIs under threat – assuming that it has the money. Since over 3.5 million acres of Britain – roughly 8 per cent of the land – are covered by SSSI designation, compulsory purchase clearly has to be a last resort and confined to the most important sites. The cost of buying 6000 acres of marshland in the Ribble estuary of the Lancashire coast in 1979 was £1.75 million, almost a quarter of the NCC's annual budget at that time. At stake was one of a shrinking number of coastal marshes around Britain. The Ribble estuary was particularly important for wading birds which would have lost their habitat if plans to drain the marshes and convert them to arable crops had not been averted.

There is far more variety to the north-west coast of England than most of the 6 million visitors a year to Blackpool might ever suspect. The shallow silted Dee estuary south of the Wirral attracts huge flocks of birds to its sand and saltmarsh; the Ainsdale sand dunes near Formby, some of which are big enough to be known as hills, sustain pines inland and rare natterjack toads in the wet slacks between the dunes; and Morecambe Bay, where nearly 50 square miles of sand and mudflats are exposed at low tide, lures the greatest concentration of wintering shore-birds to be found anywhere in the country. Change the tide pattern, of course, and you change the habitats. Yet this is what could happen at Morecambe Bay, the Ribble and Dee, where power-generating tidal barrages have been proposed. The Mersey and, a little to the north, the Alt estuary are also threatened by development proposals, despite the Alt's recognition as a Ramsar site of international importance for wildlife.

Morecambe Bay is overlooked by Arnside Knott, a limestone hill in the Arnside and Silverdale AONB – a splendid natural grandstand, with the broad sweep of the bay in the foreground and the Lakeland fells beyond. Arnside once had a port, with its own boat-building yard, but the ever-shifting sands of the bay changed all that. Bypassed by most tourists, the area's varied charms of rocky shore, marsh, limestone pavements and wooded hills are a perfect antidote to bustling Blackpool or crowded Coniston. Certainly, the CPRE thinks so; it bitterly contested plans for fifty holiday chalets which it felt were inappropriate for so tranquil a spot.

ABOVE: A tidal barrage is proposed at Morecambe Bay, haven for wintering shore-birds

BELOW: *Chalk cliffs at Flamborough Head*

The eastern coast of the Pennine shires is altogether more rugged, with 400-foot chalk cliffs at Flamborough Head and the coastal rocks of the North York Moors national park. South of Flamborough Head lies the most rapidly eroding coastline in Europe. The shoreline of Holderness lies a quarter of a mile back from where it was 200 years ago. Sixteen villages between Bridlington and Spurn Head have been swallowed by the sea since the Domesday Book recorded their existence in 1086. Spurn Head is an elongated spit of sand and shingle that juts out into the Humber estuary, 3 miles long yet in places barely 50 yards wide. Or, at least, that's what it is was in 1987. It has changed shape several times over the centuries, on occasions being washed away altogether by winter storms or breaking into a series of small islets. The fragility of the Holderness coast stems from its geological origins. After the last Ice Age, layers of boulder clay were deposited at the foot of the old line of chalk sea cliffs which now form the wolds. This soft clay is no match for the power of the sea which, in theory, could eventually crash once more against these former cliffs, now many miles inland. Man is marshalling his defences with groynes and sea walls designed to slow down, if not repel, the relentless advance of the sea. At Spurn Head, few experts foresee long-term success: a single storm was sufficient to breach the road to the spit-head in 1978. Until Spurn falls victim once more to the sea, it is a haunting place to watch seabirds. Even more spectacular are the precipitous Bempton Cliffs, north of Flamborough Head. In a reserve now run by the Royal Society for the Protection of Birds are the only gannetry and the largest seabird colony on the British mainland. These cliffs form part of a heritage coast, a distinction shared with 34 miles of shoreline further north, where the North York Moors national park reaches the sea.

This coastline of rocky cliffs has avoided the holiday camps, bungalows and caravan sites found further south in Holderness and around Filey; at 666 feet Boulby Cliff, north of Staithes, is the highest point on England's eastern coast. Tiny Robin Hood's Bay is the only settlement which breaches the shore between Scarborough and Whitby, two resorts enhanced by their ruined castle and abbey respectively. Part of the long-distance Cleveland Way now follows this shore, tempting sufficient numbers from their cars for wooden boards to be laid along heavily used stretches of the path. Other paths are so lightly used that national park staff regularly clear away undergrowth. More often, though, problems are caused by too many visitors in too few places.

Half the cars parked in the entire Yorkshire Dales national park have been shown by surveys to use eight sites. The park authority also worries about the number of caravan sites, particularly as the largely treeless dales have little natural screening. And there can be conflict between competing recreation interests: for example, birdwatchers are opposing schemes to make more of the lower Derwent navigable to larger pleasure boats. Despite severe local problems and sometimes fierce controversies, recreation pressures in these

Pennine shires are generally less intense than those for housing and industrial development. Nowhere is the urge for development felt more strongly than around the urban fringe of the old nineteenth-century conurbations, and it poses as difficult a dilemma as conservationists can face: how do you balance protection of unspoiled countryside against a region's desperate need for jobs?

Many local authorities woo firms with promises of 'green-field' sites and encourage the creation of 'science parks'. If an opencast coal mine is proposed, people who believe it will take them off the dole can be forgiven for putting their livelihood before the landscape. But science parks and open-cast mines have done little so far for overall unemployment levels and nothing for the decay of the great industrial cities for which the counties are famous. It is also arguable (as explained in chapter 1) that development of opencast sites (found in Lancashire, West Yorkshire and South Yorkshire) hastens the closure of deep-mine pits which employ more people.

It is sometimes claimed that new roads contribute to the revitalisation of run-down areas, even though the motorways and ring roads which already criss-cross West Yorkshire and Lancashire appear to have had little success so far. Future plans are therefore viewed with some scepticism by local branches of the CPRE.

Nationally, the CPRE rarely opposes new motorways or roads in principle. True, it tends to be more enthusiastic about schemes such as the 'Dales Rail' venture, through which the Yorkshire Dales national park hopes to boost traffic on the magnificent, but threatened, Settle to Carlisle railway line. And moves to encourage freight traffic on the railways are certain of a warm response from conservationists, not least because carrying more freight by rail would lessen the damage inflicted on ancient market towns. CPRE groups generally also welcome bypasses, although there may (as at Burscough in Lancashire) be arguments about alternative routes. Conservationists often argue than an existing road should be examined for possible improvements – perhaps made into a dual carriageway? – before a motorway and associated link-roads are allowed to carve into unspoiled countryside. This, for instance, was the response to the proposal for a new M65 to link Burnley, Nelson and Colne with the M6 and M61 south of Preston.

The M65 could easily develop into the second trans-Pennine motorway, linking up with a route down Airedale in Yorkshire. The Department of Transport no doubt hopes that it will seem perverse to end the motorway high on the Pennines, as at present planned, little more than 15 miles from Bingley. Business interests have long hankered for an alternative to the M62 between Leeds and Manchester; it is pointed out that an extended M65 would not go through a national park. The British Road Federation still favours a motorway through Longdendale between Manchester and Sheffield. This route across the northern tip of the Peak District national park (also known as the Woodhead Pass)

was scuppered by strong opposition in the 1970s. However, link roads remain in position as a long-term threat to this dramatic Pennine valley.

Conservationists have learned to be wary of the Department of Transport's intentions. Motorways can be built by stealth; an improvement here, a bypass there and – well, why not link the two new stretches after all? Even though many of the new roads have been welcomed by private motorists as much as by haulage firms, there is an additional reason for scepticism. Motorways in Yorkshire and Lancashire provide links to the ports which exporters undoubtedly need. Yet importers gain equal benefit and new roads can also siphon commercial development away from the cities. Five separate proposals for shopping and leisure complexes around the city of Sheffield were before the planners in 1986, mostly strategically located near motorways or ring roads. Leeds faces similar pressure. Across the Pennines development has spilled out from the old textile valleys into what is effectively a new town, as Preston, Leyland and Chorley coalesce near where motorways merge in central Lancashire. Further south, commercial developers and house-builders have cast avar-

83

ABOVE LEFT: The elongated spit of Spurn Head has changed shape several times over the centuries

LEFT: Boulby Cliff – the highest point on England's eastern coast

ABOVE RIGHT: Whitby Abbey

icious eyes on the green fields of Cheshire, now barely half an hour by motorways to Manchester or Liverpool.

Most of the northern cities have their green belts, but they are all under pressure from developers. In Cheshire, the county council in the mid-1980s wanted to relax its restrictions on development, to the dismay of not only local conservationists but neighbouring councils. These councils saw

prospective employers settling happily for congenial Chester rather than rehabilitating derelict sites in the cities. The government agreed that such a danger existed, and the Cheshire green belt remained intact, although in places barely so; less than 2 miles of open space now separates the north of Chester from the south of Ellesmere Port. These fields are crossed by motorways and powerlines, with an oil refinery on the marshy banks of the Mersey. Nevertheless cows graze here and people can walk across fields and along a canal towpath. Crucially, without this pocket of greenery, the urban sprawl would extend from Chester through Ellesmere Port and Birkenhead to Liverpool.

The briefest of glances at any map reveals the vulnerability of the northern shires to this kind of in-filling. The Manchester conurbation already stretches from Oldham to Altrincham and from Bolton to Stockport with scarcely a break, a distance of 20 miles in each direction. Much the same can be seen in West Yorkshire around Leeds and Bradford. The pockets of land which separate other northern towns are often small, but vital. Although the West Pennine Moors between Blackburn and Bolton has been designated a country park, there has been strong pressure for new 'executive' housing in the green belt around Darwen.

Graham Sandham, director of Lancashire CPRE, says that such development is unnecessary and short-sighted: 'There is more than enough derelict land already available to meet the housing needs of the next few years, as anticipated in the county's structure plan.' Nor is the battle to uphold green belts motivated solely by a selfish middle-class desire to preserve a local rural environment. Labour cities such as Sheffield are among the strongest champions of a green-belt

policy, as Merseyside County Council explained in a 1985 report a year before its demise:

There is no evidence that development has been driven away as a result of a tight Green Belt policy. Indeed, there is some evidence that it has had the positive influence intended of encouraging investment in the urban area. Evidence ... shows a dramatic change in the pattern of urban growth, with a much greater proportion of development between 1976–1982 taking place on reclaimed or vacant land within the existing urban areas rather than on farmland, which was typical of the 1960s and 1970s.

The great cities of the north, the backbone of the industrial revolution as much as the Pennines are the geological spine of England, fear that a weaker green-belt policy would under-mine their attempts to tackle the dereliction of the past. Determined efforts have been made to improve the environment, not only in the inner cities with schemes such as the renovation of Liverpool's Albert Dock, but also around the urban fringes. Metropolitan counties led the way, until their abolition in 1986.

Despite their name, metropolitan counties covered a sur-prisingly large amount of countryside – 70 per cent of South Yorkshire, 60 per cent of West Yorkshire and 57 per cent each of Greater Manchester and Merseyside was classified as countryside. This countryside is heavily used. A survey conducted for the Countryside Commission in 1984 showed that half of all visits to the countryside are within 10 miles of people's homes. Several of the metropolitan counties developed excellent countryside units, which cleared streams, improved and waymarked footpaths, built stiles, planted trees and published leaflets to help people discover (and respect) the countryside on their doorstep. Sometimes this work had

85

ABOVE LEFT: Dentdale, on the Settle to Carlisle railway line

ABOVE CENTRE: The M62 between Leeds and Manchester

ABOVE RIGHT: The Mersey Flats – part of the fragile green belt near Chester

the bonus of clearing up the blight cast by an industrial past. Rother Valley country park in South Yorkshire and Moses Gate country park near Bolton were created largely from derelict industrial land, while river valleys east of Manchester, such as the Medlock, have been reclaimed after years of pollution and decay. Abolition of the metropolitan counties was a blow to the countryside for, between them, they had developed twenty-five major country parks and twenty-four countryside management schemes.

The Countryside Commission sought to help district councils fill the gap left by the metropolitan counties. In Merseyside and Greater Manchester joint units were set up; however not all the Merseyside districts joined their unit, and neither unit had the resources of its predecessor. The picture in Yorkshire is similarly mixed. The four districts in South Yorkshire established their own countryside units, but one year after abolition of the metropolitan counties only two of the five West Yorkshire districts had any clear policy for the countryside. Although an attempt to create a joint unit for the former West Yorkshire metropolitan area failed, the Countryside Commission still favours a coordinated approach to countryside planning. Meanwhile the Commission is giving grants for specific projects, such as the completion of the Rother Valley country park, the restoration of the Rochdale Canal between Sowerby Bridge in West Yorkshire and Manchester, the creation of a 9-mile Brontë Way footpath across the Pennines and a coastal management project around the Formby sand dunes. North-west England was also the birthplace of the Groundwork Trusts, experimental partnerships between councils, schools, business and voluntary groups designed to improve local environments. Six trusts in Lancashire and northern Cheshire have cleared rubbish, laid hedgerows, hired wardens for nature reserves, restored towpaths, planted trees and generally improved recreation.

The Groundwork schemes reflect a positive approach to countryside management and, with their emphasis on partnership and voluntary action, they have shown what can be done to rehabilitate an often neglected countryside. The Countryside Commission is helping Groundwork to expand, to south Leeds among other places. But it does not see such local action as the complete answer to the problems of the urban fringe, where so many of the pressures on the countryside are in conflict. For the farmers, the land is vulnerable to damage from the public, yet ripe for sale to developers. For the public, the land is readily accessible, yet often scarred by decay. For the planners, the land is a cockpit of competing interests, often involving battles between different recreation groups as well as with landowners. In its 1986 annual report the Commission said:

The countryside around our towns and cities carries the scars of past development and faces the uncertainty created by its potential for future development. Strong policies are required from central and local government to deal with these problems together with

The green belt around Darwen has suffered from a demand for new 'executive' housing

positive measures to remove the uncertainty and dereliction and realise the potential of the urban fringe.

The contrasting worlds of urban fringe and national parks come as close in Yorkshire and Lancashire as anywhere in England. Most visitors to the two national parks come from the northern cities, their appetites whetted by the proximity of the local moors. Safeguarding the national parks and improving the urban fringe are high priorities for the Countryside Commission, and rightly so. The two concerns are complementary, each enhancing the other and bedevilled by lack of money and institutional weakness, yet each responsive to constructive management and adding immeasurably to the character of these Pennine shires.

3

THE MIDLANDS

One hour's drive from Birmingham and you could be amid the wooded valleys of the Welsh borders, the gritstone moors of the Peak District, the limestone villages of the Cotswolds or the arable plains of Bedfordshire.

The name 'the Midlands' does not evoke alluring rural scenes; 'Heart of England' is preferred by a tourist industry which leans as heavily on literature (Shakespeare's Stratford) and legend (Robin Hood's Sherwood) as on landscapes. Yet the bleak image of the Black Country belies the diversity of the English Midlands. In few other regions is natural beauty more easily accessible or countryside so varied.

Proximity to urban centres has helped to shape the rural history of the Midlands, with towns providing markets for farms and quarries and countryside easily reached for recreation. Seventeen million people live within 50 miles of the Peak District, the oldest of Britain's national parks and the only one in the English Midlands. No national park is under greater pressure than the Peak District, with an estimated 20 million visits made to the park each year. Nor do these visitors all sit idly in or beside their cars. Walking has become a mass pastime, to a degree which would have astonished the pioneers of the 1930s who were arrested in trespasses on Kinder Scout to promote the 'right to roam' the moors (see page 92). Half a century later, plastic matting was temporarily laid on Kinder Scout where the boggy surface had been eroded by the popularity of the long-distance footpath, the Pennine Way.

In the 1930s, the campaign for a Peak District national park was fuelled by demands for greater access and concern about quarrying. Both issues remain unresolved, despite the creation of a national park with not only independent planning powers but also greater financial resources than any of

Chester

CHESHIR

S

Shrewsbury

SHROPSHIRE

HEREFORD AND WORCESTER

Hereford

The Peak District, where the lowlands meet the uplands

its counterparts. Outside the national park, the rest of the Midlands landscape is even more susceptible to development pressure. Areas of the greatest beauty may warrant the most stringent protection, but the charms of rural England derive as much from the ubiquity of pleasant countryside as from showpiece sites: simpler fare complementing the headier attractions of national parks or areas of outstanding natural beauty (AONBs), yet crucial for everyday pleasures.

Countryside Commission surveys show that most trips to the country are made locally – 60 per cent to areas within 2 miles of a town. This 'wider' countryside, as it is known to organisations such as the Countryside Commission – it should never be called 'ordinary' – represents four-fifths of England and Wales. It is country which, perhaps, we take too much for granted: the common land on top of the hill, the leafy lane for autumn blackberrying, the river meandering through grazing meadows. Or it could now be an altogether less appetising prospect: the common staked by fences, the lane laid bare by the uprooting of hedgerows, the canalised river bissecting fields of – that new phenomenon of early summer – oil-seed rape.

Agricultural change is the greatest single influence on the English landscape quite simply because 80 per cent of the surface is farmed. That is why a crisis for farming is a crisis for the countryside. In the Midlands, intensity and forms of farming vary greatly – from treeless arable prairies in counties bordering East Anglia to sheep rearing in the uplands and dairying on the Cheshire plain. Only the upland farmers will be cushioned from the impact of the falling prices and cuts in production expected as European governments strive to reduce costly food mountains. The Midlands countryside is acutely vulnerable because its accessibility enhances the commercial viability of housing, industry or recreation developments proposed for redundant farmland. Within a decade, an area equivalent to Devon and Derbyshire may no longer be needed nationally for full agricultural production.

Agriculture's difficulties offer opportunities as well as dangers, though. New recreation facilities could be created, wildlife encouraged by less intensive production, access extended by agreements on the future of common and unenclosed land. Steps have been taken in all these directions as, after years of conflict, many conservationists and farmers find themselves in unaccustomed unity over the threat to rural landscapes. 'What a really golden opportunity there is now at hand to forge links of real purpose between farming and conservation objectives,' says Sir Derek Barber, chairman of the Countryside Commission. This burgeoning harmony faces its greatest challenge in the wider countryside, where constraints against development are weakest. Even in national parks, the pressures are unrelenting.

In the Peak District, wedged between cities and motorways, the lowlands meet the uplands. Around Edale, the limestone dales and stone-walled fields of the White Peak

91

Rock formations at Kinder Scout

give way to the gritstone moors and crags or 'edges' of the Dark Peak and south Pennines. The Peak District hills are not particularly high, some just reaching 2000 feet. But Kinder Scout and Bleaklow, the highest points, feel like mountains nonetheless: sombre peat moorlands broken only by bogs and rocky outcrops of millstone grit. For many walkers today Kinder is the first challenge of the Pennine Way, which starts in Edale and ends 250 miles away near the Scottish border. As you clump up the hill, the bustle of Sheffield and Manchester a dozen miles or so across the moors seems another world.

The extensive open country so close to great cities spurred enthusiasm for 'the great outdoors' in the years after the First World War. Hiking and cycling clubs boomed. Yet access to the highest and wildest parts of the Peak District was severely restricted. According to *Trespassers Will Be Prosecuted*, a pioneer rambling book published in 1932, only 1212 acres out of 150,000 acres between Manchester and Sheffield were open for the public to wander over at will, with only twelve public footpaths more than 2 miles long in an area of over 230 square miles. Gamekeepers, zealously guarding some of the country's finest grouse moors, dealt roughly with walkers, prompting a mass trespass in 1932 on Kinder Scout. Five men were imprisoned, but the publicity helped to place the Peak District — and access generally — at the forefront of the campaign for national parks.

Fleetingly, it appeared as though the Kinder pioneers would be victorious. A government-appointed committee, whose 1947 report foreshadowed the creation of national parks, included a recommendation for a formal right of access to all open land — but it was never built into the legislation which introduced the parks. Park authorities were left to conclude local agreements in which landowners were paid to grant access. As part of the agreement a warden service has to be established and restrictions on the public during the shooting season may also apply. In the Peak District, agreements were negotiated giving access to 76 square miles of Kinder, Bleaklow and the 'eastern edges'. Access payments consume a quarter of the park's recreation budget, which may be one reason why such agreements have not caught on elsewhere; those in the Peak District represent two thirds of all access agreements in England and Wales. Farmers generally are opposed to access agreements, bridling at the thought of being mere 'park keepers'. Although a further 20 square miles of Peak moorland are open to public access, thanks to the National Trust and Sheffield Corporation, half the main moors still lack any formal right of public access. The Peak Park Joint Planning Board, as the national park authority is known, hopes that more access agreements can be secured. Despite the worries of landowners, experience has shown that public access to moors does not affect grouse numbers.

Away from the hills, the impact of visitors is not always neutral and by no means confined to walkers. Joining ramblers in the Peak District these days are climbers, hang-gliders, yachtsmen (and women), cyclists, anglers, canoeists, pony trekkers, pot-holers, picnickers and touring motorists. Pro-

ABOVE: Goodrich Castle, Hereford and Worcester

RIGHT: Flash, Staffordshire. Once almost entirely wooded, the Peak District we know today has been shaped by agriculture

moting public enjoyment is a primary aim of all national parks, reflecting those early battles for access. However, recreation interests are frequently in conflict with the Peak park's overriding duty to conserve the natural beauty of the landscape.

Dovedale, a winding valley in the south of the park, is probably the park's biggest single attraction. Families have long ambled along the riverside path, frequently with push-chairs, before picnicking on grassy banks while older children splash in the stream or jump across stepping stones. By the mid-1970s this potentially idyllic area was under intense threat. Up to a million people a year were converging upon the valley, as many as visit the entire Northumberland national park. Riverside paths were being churned into bogs, meadow flowers trampled to extinction; cars (and litter) over-flowed from inadequate car parks.

Dovedale was saved by the existence of a national park with the money and mandate to intervene. Car parks were moved from exposed hillsides to the wooded valley floor. The main path was rebuilt, with streams running in culverts underneath the new surface. Footpath erosion on the peaty, boggier moors of the Dark Peak is less easily solved, but recreation policies are not confined to defensive measures.

New paths for walkers and cyclists have been created along the routes of disused railways to lure people away from heavily used routes. Sometimes a policy of benign neglect is pursued, by omitting to provide new facilities which might swamp essentially quiet areas. In Manifold Valley, car-parking space remains limited as a means to control numbers. In two other valleys – Goyt and Upper Derwent – cars are banned at weekends. Despite the successes, the park authority faces a daunting task in maintaining, let alone enhancing, even existing public rights of way. A survey of 4000 miles of

footpaths in 1985 revealed 2200 signposts missing, 1300 obstructions and 90 bridges needing repair or replacement.

The Peak's location in the heart of England influenced its natural and economic development long before its accessibility fostered the demand for outdoor recreation. The coalescence of upland and lowland landscapes is responsible for its visual appeal and ensures that wildlife is varied; many upland species are found here at their most southerly location in England. Woodland was once similarly rich, with upland and lowland species flourishing in close proximity: lime and ash were dominant on limestone, oak and birch on gritstone. Virtually the entire Peak District, apart from the highest peat bogs, was once wooded, but barely 2 per cent of the national park is now covered by broad-leaved trees. These are mostly survivors of eighteenth-century plantations, with a few relics of ancient ash woodland in the White Peak and oak (such as at Padley Wood on the Longshaw estate) in the Dark Peak. This century has added conifer plantations, but again it is farming which has shaped the Peak District we know today. Sheep rearing on the moors is the main agricultural activity in the Dark Peak, dairy cattle in the White Peak.

With lower rainfall and higher temperatures, the Peak District is more conducive to agriculture than the northern Pennines. The limestone of the White Peak is particularly fertile, so cultivation has prospered as high as 1000 feet. Man therefore settled early in the Peak District, inhabiting caves in areas such as Manifold Valley and then leaving Neolithic, Bronze Age and Iron Age sites which are among the best in the country. When the Romans arrived, they discovered that the land could yield more than food or fodder. Lead was mined and building stone quarried, beginning a mining tradition which helps to make the Peak District the most indus-

94

ABOVE LEFT: Kinder Scout – one of the highest points in the Peak District and the first challenge of the Pennine Way

ABOVE: The Pennine Way path from Edale

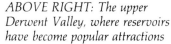
ABOVE RIGHT: The upper Derwent Valley, where reservoirs have become popular attractions

trial and populated of all our national parks. Development pressures are intensified by the demands of the encircling towns. With reservoirs flooding northern valleys and house-builders nibbling at the fringes, the national park has been under siege.

The Peak District is one of only two (the other is the Lake District) national parks run by an independent board able to precept for funds on its local authorities, although all share its planning powers. It has to approve development proposals for 'the carrying out of building, engineering, mining or other operations in, on, over or under land, or the making of any material change in the use of any buildings or other land'. Some activities were excluded from planning control, notably farming and forestry. But even if the park authority has been able to resist new developments, how could it deal with 'building, engineering or mining' operations which were already in existence before its formation?

Five reservoirs in Longdendale date back to the nineteenth century and, in all, there are over fifty reservoirs in the park — water authorities are collectively the largest landowner in the Peak District, with 15 per cent of all land. Some reservoirs have become popular attractions, notably those in the upper Derwent Valley, but access to the water is often restricted. In the mid-1980s sailing was permitted on only five reservoirs and angling on eleven. Four new reservoirs have been created since the national park was designated, with Manifold Valley, Hassop and Longdendale also threatened at various times. The scheme for Longdendale (or the Woodhead Pass) could deprive the national park of its coveted Council of Europe Nature Conservation Diploma. Existing reservoirs in the valley would be incorporated into a pumped storage scheme, with a new high-level reservoir, for electricity generation. In

1983 the scheme was withdrawn – but only for this decade. It remains in reserve as a significant threat for the 1990s.

Luckless Longdendale is also threatened by road building (as described in chapter 2, page 82). The park authority is not necessarily against new roads. It supports an improved route through Pindale as an alternative to Winnats Pass west of Castleton; the spectacular, rocky gorge of the Winnats has resounded to the rumble of traffic since subsidence closed the main road across the aptly named 'Shivering Mountain' of Mam Tor. Local traffic problems remain, around Bakewell and Castleton for example, but the park authority has broadly held the line against damaging new roads as well as against reservoirs. More recently, it has also achieved some success in a third area of conflict – mineral extraction.

Most national parks inherited some tradition of quarrying and mining when they were formed in the 1950s. For new applications, the government of 1949 laid down two prime conditions for approval: the mineral was essential in the national interest and there was no reasonable alternative source of supply. Sites were also to be restored after use. In theory, these conditions (known as the 'Silkin Test') seemed reasonable enough. But they have not prevented further expansion of the mineral industry within the Peak District. Limestone is the main target of the quarrymen, but fluorspar, lead, dolerite, barytes, gritstones and sandstones are also extracted. Nearly 10 per cent of the park's 40,000 population earn their living directly or indirectly from mineral extraction.

Mindful of local employment and the Silkin Test, the Peak park authority accepts that some mining is inevitable. Because the Peak District is the country's biggest reserve of fluorspar, in 1985 the park authority sanctioned a new mine at Great Hucklow, subject to conditions about disposing of waste. No such accord exists in respect of limestone, of which the Peak District is again one of the country's largest sources. Much comes from an enclave around Buxton, which was excluded from the park in 1951. But a dozen quarries exist within the park itself. So is their output in the national interest? Yes, say the operators, because the high quality makes it suitable for the chemical industry. No, say the conservationists, because more than half the limestone from the Peak District national park area is used as aggregate for road-building and the construction industry. As other regions could supply the lower-grade stone for roads, at least some limestone extraction fails to pass the Silkin Test. And, according to this test, such extraction cannot be justified in a national park *even if the environmental impact is not great.*

In fact, it's hard to imagine uglier blots on the landscape than some of these limestone quarries. Eldon Hill quarry has gouged a massive hole in the hills west of Castleton, spewing forth dust and scarring the view for miles around. Tunstead quarry, straddling the park boundary near Buxton, is even larger, with a face nearly 2 miles long, the largest in Europe. Both quarries existed before the park was created, and both are among those which have sought extensions. In all cases, the park authority has resisted extensions, so the decisions

ABOVE: The 'Shivering Mountain' of Mam Tor

went, after public inquiries, to the government. In 1953 Eldon Hill was allowed to expand – until 1997. Tunstead also succeeded, taking 250 acres of Old Moor in 1978. But then, in 1986, Topley Pike, also near Buxton, failed to win an extension. A year later a further proposal to extend Eldon Hill beyond 1997 was also quashed, with the inspector finding 'no off-setting justification of a particular need for the mineral' to be set against damage to the environment, rural character and natural beauty.

It was the first time that the park authority had defeated any mineral proposal in the Peak District, let alone having done so twice within twelve months. But other proposed extensions are pending and there are already signs that the mineral industry will not take its defeats lightly. For the Topley Pike and Eldon Hill verdicts also effectively dismissed the Silkin Test as having only historical significance. The inspectors thought the park's overall mineral policy had more relevance – and this had been altered by the government to allow the area 'to contribute more effectively to the national demand for minerals'. Subsequently, the government sought to clarify its policy towards quarrying: developments in national parks, it said, should be demonstrated to be in the public interest, taking into account national need for the mineral, alternative supplies and local employment, as well as effects on the landscape.

In the disputes over Topley Pike and Eldon Hill, the park authority was supported by objectors from many voluntary bodies, including the Council for the Protection of Rural England (CPRE). Together they won an epic battle – essentially the victory means that the quarries will close at the end of the century. However, the war is far from over and Gerald Haythornthwaite, of the Sheffield and Peak District branch of the CPRE, still regards mineral extraction as 'one of the most potent dangers to the Peak District'.

For more than sixty years this branch of the CPRE has been a thorn in the flesh of would-be developers, proving as adept at raising money as at generating publicity. Large tracts of land have been presented to the National Trust and the Sheffield green belt was successfully advocated by a branch whose officials played key roles in the park movement nationally. Gerald Haythornthwaite believes that vigilance is as necessary today as ever. Overcrowding, minerals, water and roads are his main worries, but another issue is looming larger in CPRE's fears – agriculture. Controls over the design and siting of farm buildings have avoided too many eyesores, but they do not quell deeper anxieties about what is happening to the land itself.

A moorland survey published by the park authority in 1981 found that 8 per cent of the moors – about 16 square miles – were bare or becoming bare of vegetation. Elsewhere heather and cotton grass had declined, acid grassland and bracken increased. Overgrazing of up to three times the ideal density, atmospheric pollution, accidental fires and recreation pressure were blamed for the changes. On lower land in the Dark Peak, wet meadows have been drained. In the White

BELOW: Limestone quarry near Buxton

Peak, agriculture emerges more clearly as the mainspring of change. Hay meadows have been ploughed and reseeded to produce greater yields of silage, stone walls and field barns neglected. Only twenty-seven hay meadows with a good range of flowers were found in a survey commissioned by the park authority in 1984. Ken Parker, head of the park's landscape and recreation section, says, 'The character of the Peak District landscape depends upon certain key features such as dry-stone walls (and not post and wire fences), the spring splash of colour from the flowers in the fields, the song of birds such as skylarks, the hilltop clumps of broad-leaved trees or the wild open spaces of the moorland dominated by the purple heather in late summer. All these have declined since the park was designated and we need to find ways to halt, and if possible reverse, these trends.'

As explained more fully in chapter 2, national park authorities have few powers to curb the actions of farmers. One in four notifications to the Peak park joint planning board in 1984–85 from farmers claiming Ministry of Agriculture grants were received *after* the work had been carried out. In such cases farmers were less likely to receive a grant, but the damage to the landscape might already be irreparable. Retrospective applications made a mockery of the requirement for so-called 'prior notification' and stirred doubts about the willingness of farmers to work voluntarily with conservation agencies. Since then, the number of such applications has declined: the proportion was one in eight during 1985–86, while under a new grant scheme, retrospective applications are only considered if the work is deemed environmentally beneficial, such as planting hedgerows. Even so, the incompatibility between two sets of public grants – one favouring production, the other conservation – remains. If anything, it has been intensified by the government's acceptance that increased production is no longer required.

Such difficulties increase the case for landscape conservation orders as a power of last resort where the voluntary approach has failed. The problems posed by agriculture within national parks also underline the scale of the challenge faced elsewhere. In national parks, there is prior notification, however flawed; there are controls over location and siting of farm buildings; there is money available for conservation work, such as schemes for woodland management and moorland restoration; special projects, such as the Peak District's 'integrated rural development' experiment, may be undertaken; and, we are promised, there will be landscape conservation orders for at least some parts of the parks. Yet, despite the extra protection and funds available to national parks, Ken Parker says, 'The landscapes which were the reasons for the Peak District's designation as a national park are in decline.' How much more vulnerable therefore is the wider countryside – areas of diverse farmland throughout the Midlands – which lack any veneer of protection? It is here that landscapes have been changed most dramatically by an agricultural revolution, born of a wartime emergency and

98

nurtured by peacetime subsidies, whose consequences were as largely unforeseen as they are unloved.

The Second World War destroyed Britain's reliance on cheap food from abroad. For a century Britain had traded manufactured goods for the foodstuffs of the world. Domestic agriculture languished, unable to compete with countries where wages were lower and the climate more favourable for mass production. Overall output showed little increase in value between the 1860s and the 1930s, with growth in dairying and horticulture masking a steady decline in cereal production. The 1930s were years of depression for farming as well as industry. Land prices tumbled, bankruptcies soared. At the outbreak of war, barely a third of the nation's food was produced at home. The U-boat blockade transformed British farming. Increasing production became a patriotic

LEFT: Eldon Hill quarry will be allowed to expand until 1997

BELOW: Napton-on-the-Hill, Warwickshire

duty — 'digging for victory' — and the result was a triumph. Twice as much food was produced at home in 1945 as in 1939.

The national consensus about the need to produce more food survived the end of coalition government. Memories of the 1930s' slump reinforced the political desire to buttress British farmers against poor harvests and cheap competition. The 1947 Agriculture Act established the framework in which guaranteed prices and capital grants were offered to farmers as incentives to increase production. The principle was little affected by Britain's membership of the EEC. For all its complexities, the essence of the common agricultural policy is the same: price support and capital grants to give stability to farmers and security to European food supplies. Nobody envisaged that domestic production, within either Britain or Europe, would one day produce more food than was needed.

Because food production seemed so paramount and environmental side-effects so unlikely, farming was largely excluded from the system of planning control established in 1947. This provoked little criticism at the time. The wartime Scott Report concluded:

Farmers and foresters are unconsciously the nation's landscape gardeners and there is no antagonism between use and beauty.

A minority report dissented from this view, but it aroused little support; there seemed to be other priorities. Pressure groups such as the CPRE welcomed the 1947 Town and Country Planning Act as a means to control the suburban sprawl and ribbon development which plagued the 1930s. Although downland was ploughed for wheat and barley during the war, previously farmers had made few radical changes to the landscape for the best part of a century. All this altered after the war. Not only did farmers have guaranteed prices but, from 1957, all farmers could apply for capital grants to modernise their farms. Lest they did not know how to proceed, the government set up the Agricultural Development and Advisory Service (ADAS) to provide free technical and financial advice. ADAS also established its own research laboratories, which, along with those of the chemical companies, fostered further technical advances. Farming was becoming an industry, increasingly intensive and increasingly specialist, and the countryside was its factory floor. By subsidising output, the policy favoured farmers on the most fertile soils, such as those in East Anglia. But new machines (there were still 300,000 working horses on farms in 1950), higher-yielding strains of crops, pesticides and fertilisers enabled more marginal land to increase production, too.

Small farms had helped to shape the character of the countryside and sustained the rural economy. Many were now swallowed up by their larger neighbours; the 454,000 farms which existed in England and Wales in 1953 had dwindled to 242,300 by 1981, and a quarter of these were too small to be classified as full-time. By the mid-1980s 12 per cent of all farms were producing more than half the total output. The number of full-time farmworkers fell by two-

100

Golden Valley, Hereford and Worcester. Despite the crisis in agriculture, productivity is still increasing

thirds from a total of around half a million in 1951. This posed problems for the social fabric of rural life, as jobs declined and farmworkers' cottages were snapped up by weekenders — 'two nations in one village', as sociologist Howard Newby called it. But the greater productivity of farming more than fulfilled the government's initial objectives. Since 1947 milk production has doubled, wheat is up five times, barley sixfold. Productivity is still increasing. According to the Ministry of Agriculture's annual review of agriculture in 1987, the average wheat yield per acre was then just under 3 tonnes, compared to a little over 2 tonnes a decade earlier; milk yields averaged 4950 litres per cow, compared with 4250 litres at the start of the same ten-year period. Overall, home-produced foodstuffs satisfy about 80 per cent of domestic needs, compared with 63 per cent in 1977. The higher output of cereals stems partly from a more intensive use of land and partly from the fact that a greater area of land has been devoted to arable crops. Both trends have significantly affected the countryside.

The consequences of intensification in the Peak District have already been mentioned: overgrazing of moorland, conversion of hay meadows into silage, reseeding of grasslands and uprooting of woodlands. Farm amalgamations also mean more redundant buildings and fewer workers to maintain the

101

30,000 miles of stone walls which dissect the White Peak. For the Midlands generally, the most fundamental change involves the proportion of land cultivated for arable crops. According to a national landscape survey published by the Countryside Commission in 1986, cropped land increased from 37 per cent of all farmland in England and Wales in 1947 to 48 per cent in 1980. The percentage growth was greater in the Midlands than anywhere else, although the pace and extent of change has varied greatly. In Bedfordshire, for instance, land under grass fell by 42 per cent between 1953 and 1973, compared with 3 per cent in Derbyshire. Three fifths of the East Midlands is now arable land, leaving only East Anglia with a higher proportion. Moreover, the effects are magnified by the intensive methods employed on farmland which mostly lacks the natural fertility of the fens. Heavier soils needed heftier doses of fertilisers to increase output – nationally, the use of nitrogen fertilisers has grown by eight times since the war, as farmers sought to exploit every scrap of land. This led also to the most lamented feature of modern arable farming: the loss of hedgerows.

Some hedgerows have existed for centuries, possibly millennia in places, often along parish boundaries; counties in the West Midlands, notably Shropshire and northern Worcestershire, are among those rich in ancient, winding hedgerows. Other hedgerows were created more recently, when the open fields of areas such as the East Midlands were enclosed by straighter hedgerows of hawthorn in the eighteenth and nineteenth centuries. Whatever their form – and they often vary even within parishes – hedgerows have given lowland England its traditional mosaic of fields, woods and sunken lanes. It is hedgerows and hedgerow trees which fill the horizon and harbour much of the wildlife of farmed countryside. Or they used to. Since 1947, according to the Countryside Commission landscape survey, 22 per cent of the hedgerows – roughly 190,000 miles – in England and Wales have gone. The rate of loss has been greater in the East Midlands than anywhere except East Anglia.

The loss of hedgerows (explored more fully in chapter 5) transforms landscapes, particularly in flat terrain. One of seven areas studied in a regional survey published by the Countryside Commission in 1984 was in Warwickshire. In 1972 hedges with hedgerow trees formed 38 per cent of all horizon views in this region; by 1983, they formed only 4 per cent. Instead, there were distant views of more than a mile as arable farmers removed hedge after hedge to create large fields on the East Anglian pattern. The loss of elms, virtually wiped out by Dutch elm disease, exaggerated the change in Warwickshire, but farmland trees generally are endangered. Along hedgerows many have been cut down (lest they cast shade over the crops) and few saplings – the trees of tomorrow – survive the flails of mechanised hedge-cutting. The Countryside Commission studies found that, although considerable tree-planting had been undertaken along driveways or around farm buildings, few saplings were growing in hedgerows. Oak saplings were particularly rare.

ABOVE: Shropshire is among the counties richest in ancient winding hedgerows

ABOVE RIGHT: Long Mynd, Shropshire, where five times as many sheep graze as would be ideal to maintain the heather moorland

The survey concluded: 'In most study areas, the hedgerow tree is gradually disappearing and is not being replaced.'

Warwickshire occupies the middle ground in Midlands farming. It has swung towards arable production, although less so than counties further east such as Bedfordshire and Northamptonshire. It has retained some mixed farming, but less so than in the border counties of Herefordshire and Shropshire. In these border counties, much of the countryside appears to have escaped unscathed by the agricultural revolution in the east. 'You'll find no prairies here,' chorus farmers and conservation groups alike. Part of Herefordshire included in the Countryside Commission regional survey was found to have changed little between 1972 and 1983. Few hedgerows had gone and many trees had been planted. The attitude of the farmers, suggested the survey, was 'likely to keep the traditional enclosure landscape'. Despite greater use of fencing in 'paddock grazing', dairy farmers here, and further north in Cheshire, still need hedgerows for their stock. And, when the work is done, hedgerows and copses provide cover for game shooting.

The CPRE has encountered some flak from its border branches for what they perceived as 'shrill' attacks on farmers. 'We don't bash the farmers, we cooperate with them,' says Peter Winstanley, a former secretary of the Herefordshire branch. Generalisations about a countryside so diverse as England's or an industry with 240,000 entrepreneurs are indeed hazardous. But complacency is unwise. In Shropshire 63 per cent of semi-natural ancient woodland has been cleared or converted to plantations in the last fifty years. Five times as many sheep graze on Long Mynd as would be ideal for maintaining the heather moorland. In Cheshire, the sixth most wooded area recorded in the Domesday Book, county council

103

104

reports have voiced alarm about the 'irreversible' deterioration in the county's trees (of 630,000 oaks, only 56,000 are young), the drainage of water meadows and the ploughing of fields according to the medieval ridge and furrow system. Similar concern has been expressed in Staffordshire, while in Hereford and Worcestershire, ravaged by Dutch elm disease, new tree planting will not fully replace existing mature woodland and sometimes involves replacing broad-leaves with conifers.

Any lingering doubt about the threat should have been dispelled by the Countryside Commission's national survey of landscape change, published in 1986. This showed, first, that broad-leaved woodland in the West Midlands fell by a third between 1947 and 1982, more than in any other region of the country. Second, proportionately more hedgerows have been lost here than in any other region except East Anglia and the East Midlands. Nationally, hedgerow losses had accelerated from 2600 miles a year between 1947 and 1979 to 4000 miles a year in the 1980s, just when the worst of the destruction was thought to be over. Farmers' leaders certainly believed this to be the case, for they had been publicising a Ministry of Agriculture survey published a year earlier showing hedgerow loss at no more than 1000 miles a year. Furthermore, according to the ministry survey, more than half this amount had been replaced by new hedgerows. With nearly 6 million trees planted and 4500 new ponds dug on average during the previous five years, the National Farmers' Union (NFU) said, this survey presented a picture of 'a conservation-conscious farming industry, devoting resources and effort to maintaining, replacing and enhancing the attractions of the countryside'. However, the ministry survey was more limited than that conducted by the Countryside Commission and relied heavily on a postal questionnaire filled in by farmers rather than independent photographic and other evidence. 'Farmers care, too,' trumpeted the NFU publicity. Maybe, but it is the Commission's statistics which are the most comprehensive and least susceptible to sampling error.

It was not until the 1970s that the full impact of the

ABOVE LEFT: Farm buildings at Priors Marston, Warwickshire

ABOVE: Agricultural policies have changed the face of the countryside

postwar agricultural revolution on the landscape as a whole began to be appreciated. There had previously been worries about the effect of pesticides on wildlife and the ethics of factory farming. Ugly farm buildings had also provoked criticism; citizens who had trouble adding a porch or garage to their house could not always understand why aluminium silos or factory-style cattle sheds could be erected so freely by farmers. (Some controls were introduced in 1986, depending on the type and proposed location of farm buildings.) Initial concern about individual features eventually culminated in a more comprehensive indictment by the Nature Conservancy Council (NCC), which identified the following national changes as examples of 'the overwhelmingly adverse impact of modern agriculture on wildlife and its habitat since 1940':

- flower-rich hay meadows – 95 per cent lacking significant wildlife interest and only 3 per cent undamaged by agricultural intensification (such as reseeding and conversion to silage);

- chalk and limestone grasslands – 80 per cent lost or damaged, largely by conversion to arable production or improved grazing, but some reverting to scrub through lack of grazing;

- lowland heaths – 40 per cent lost, again largely as a result of conversion to arable or improved grassland, but also some afforestation, building and reversion to scrubland;

- ancient, semi-natural woodland – between 30 and 50 per cent destroyed either by grubbing out to provide more farmland or conversion to conifer plantations;

- lowland fens, valley and basin mires – 50 per cent lost or damaged through drainage operations, agricultural reclamation and chemical pollution of drainage water;

- upland grasslands, heaths and blanket bogs – 30 per cent lost or significantly damaged as a result of afforestation, agricultural improvement or reclamation and overgrazing.

The NCC is motivated by its concern for wildlife. Its 1984 report, *Nature Conservation in Great Britain*, said that twenty-four of Britain's fifty-five resident breeding butterflies had declined or become endangered since 1950, largely because agricultural change had destroyed their habitat. Fifteen species of dragonflies, thirty-six species of birds, four reptiles and the otter have suffered a similar decline. Nearly 150 plants have declined by at least a fifth since 1930, nearly half of them in wetlands.

While urging agricultural policies which would support rather than thwart conservation, the Countryside Commission hoped that voluntary cooperation between farmers and conservationists would reconcile their conflicting interests. 'Demonstration farms' showed how trees, ponds and hedges could be developed; countryside management schemes, with project officers, pursued similar objectives in

105

wider areas. The Farming and Wildlife Advisory Group (FWAG) – an amalgam of farming and conservation bodies established in 1969 – also espoused cooperation, and its growth was indicative of how sensitive some farmers had become to criticism. By the mid-1980s many landowners and farmers were admitting that the agricultural revolution had in some places gone too far. FWAG leaflets spoke of 'the treeless, hedgeless prairie view from the farmhouse window'; and, if the Country Landowners' Association was more circumspect, it nonetheless acknowledged in 1984 that existing policies were 'no longer tenable on economic, social, environmental and political grounds'. One reason why the NFU supports the FWAG is the fear that, if voluntary conservation fails, farmers might lose their freedom from planning control.

Small inroads into this freedom have occurred in the national parks and on sites of special scientific interest (SSSIs), but these cover only 9 and 5 per cent respectively of England and Wales. Elsewhere farmers have been unconstrained. Neither voluntary conservation nor countryside management have defused environmental concern. So long as agricultural policy was wedded to the grail of higher production, the CPRE has argued, conservation would be confined to field-corner copses or ponds.

Of course, any interest in conservation was as welcome as it was significant. As long ago as 1969 the RSPB (Royal Society for the Protection of Birds) had helped to establish the Farming and Wildlife Advisory Group. The CPRE was then beginning a long campaign for conservation to be a duty of the Ministry of Agriculture. By the early 1980s some of the more destructive grants, such as those for draining wetlands or removing hedgerows, were withdrawn or reduced. Conservation grants for works such as restoring ponds or managing trees were introduced in 1984 and subsequently expanded and increased. The NFU endorsed codes on straw-burning and footpath ploughing which demonstrated a more sympathetic attitude towards conservation issues. Interviewed in 1987, Simon Gourlay, the NFU president, said, 'There's nothing immoral about maximising profit, but sometimes farmers pushed their quest for maximising output further than was good for the countryside. Since the excesses of the 1950s and 1960s farmers have become increasingly aware of conservation and are now taking the environmental aspects very seriously. On the other hand conservationists have come to recognise that farmers are under pressure to make a living.'

In 1986 the Ministry of Agriculture officially acknowledged conservation as one of its objectives. To outsiders, it seemed a nervous, even reluctant, embrace, largely forced upon the ministry to appease the external conservation lobby and to rebuff pressure within Whitehall from the Department of the Environment. To Michael Jopling, then Agriculture Minister and a farmer himself, it was no shotgun marriage. 'Farmers are the biggest group of conservationists in the country,' he said when interviewed in 1987. 'The beauty of the British landscape owes more to farmers than anyone else.

The Leen 'conservation' farm near Pembridge

The landscape has always been changing, but farmers and conservation can live together very well. The problems come because you have a small minority who have acted in a non-conservation way.'

As a result of the ministry's formal obligation to promote conservation, ADAS produced a plethora of leaflets advocating and explaining conservation measures, many of which have been highlighted on demonstration farms. One such farm is The Leen, a 410-acre mixed farm with dairying, beef cattle, potatoes and cereals near Pembridge, in Herefordshire. Farmer Tony Norman had begun to develop wildlife sanctuaries by re-establishing ponds and planting trees long before the ADAS underwent its Pauline conversion to con-

servation. Then, helped by ADAS and FWAG advisers, he learned how to manage hedgerows and existing trees in ways which enhance their value for wildlife. Small details can make big differences, such as the shape of hedgerows and the frequency of their trimming, the gradient of pond edges, the species of trees planted and the distance between newly planted trees. Conservation also means a degree of untidiness, allowing areas to grow wild or dead trees to remain as habitats for insects and birds. Tony Norman was motivated by his interest in wildlife, but despite his evident enthusiasm for conservation, he stresses that, first and foremost, he is a profit-seeking farmer; he has removed hedgerows to achieve better shapes and larger field sizes and uses fertilisers to increase yields. 'But the farm is not as intensive as it could be,' he says. 'Some hedgerows have been planted because thought has always been given to maintaining wildlife corridors. I am pleased by the quality of wildlife that has already come back, but I farm the best land for all that it's worth and develop conservation on marginal land and in odd corners.'

Tony Norman allocates roughly a tenth of his farm to conservation and his achievements show what can be done; one corner which was arable in 1980 now has alders, willows, a pond and nearly sixty species of plants. If he can do this, why can't others? Farmers like Tony Norman are not unusual. They live on the land and are as likely to appreciate its beauty, wildlife and history as anyone, arguably more so. But they have to make a living, and for forty years they have been encouraged by price supports and grants to do so by increasing production. Conservation has different goals; it requires some land to be left ungrazed or uncultivated, some features to be maintained. This inevitably prompts certain

LEFT: Wildlife sanctuaries have been developed at The Leen by re-establishing ponds and planting trees

BELOW: Part of the ancient herd of Herefords at The Leen

farmers to say that conservation is a luxury which they cannot afford, particularly in times when farm incomes are falling.

By the mid-1980s the conservation lobby was politically strong and vehemently expressing its dissatisfaction with the protection offered to the countryside. Efforts of conservation advisers were admired, but modest. Although the FWAG was growing rapidly, a solitary FWAG or local authority adviser could visit only about 80–100 farms a year in counties which might have 3000 or more farmholdings. Even then, only one in three of these visits resulted in a conservation plan being prepared, according to the Countryside Commission's annual report for 1985–86. ADAS added conservation to its advisory services, but there was some scepticism about whether people who had long advocated intensification could carry much conviction when it came to conservation. Conservation grants helped, but those from the Countryside Commission in 1986 amounted to a trifling £1.6 million against around £2.5 *billion* spent on agriculture and food support. The 1981 Wildlife and Countryside Act had promised some protection for national parks and SSSIs. But the principle outlined in the Act of conservation bodies having

to compensate farmers for 'lost profits' (if applications for agricultural grants were rejected) stirred opposition. Increasingly there were demands for measures to protect the countryside as a whole rather than specific sites or habitats. The CPRE demanded planning controls on agriculture, with tree preservation orders, for instance, extended to hedgerows. Many critics sought the introduction of landscape conservation orders. Above all, there was pressure to recast the system of financial support so that increased production would no longer be the sole or primary goal of agricultural policy; environmental objectives should be part of any policy for the future of farming.

Such an aim would once have been dismissed as heresy or fantasy, but by the mid-1980s the economics of agricultural policy were pointing in the direction of reduced emphasis on production. From being a net importer of many foods, Britain and Europe had become exporters – if they could find markets at all. More often than not, unwanted produce piled up in 'intervention stores', bought by EEC taxpayers to guarantee prices to farmers, yet surplus to consumer demand. It cost Britain nearly £1 million a week in 1985 just to store surplus butter and skimmed milk. In the same year, despite poor weather and a modest harvest, Europe produced 160 million tonnes of cereals – 17 million more than were required. Yields are increasing by 2.5 per cent annually and biotechnological improvements in plant breeding predicate a cereal surplus of 80 million tonnes by 1991. In the EEC as a whole, the output of virtually all the main agricultural commodities exceeds demand.

The combination of environmental and economic pressure has plunged agriculture into its biggest crisis since the war. EEC-imposed quotas on dairy production in 1984 were the first response, sending a shockwave through an industry unaccustomed to constraints. Nor were the repercussions confined to dairying. Beef farmers feared that dairy farmers would slaughter their cattle, thus depressing prices; hill farmers worried that valley grasslands would be switched to grazing for sheep, thereby eroding their livelihood; cereal farmers sometimes intensified production still further, so that they could maintain profits despite price or production curbs. European governments have not been short of ideas about how to tackle the crisis. Early retirement for farmers, incentives for diversification into recreation or forestry, price cuts and further quotas have all been canvassed and, in varying degrees, implemented. Underlying all such proposals is an acceptance that production needs to be curtailed, and it is this which puts the countryside at risk: what will happen to the land which some say is no longer needed for farming?

How much land might become 'redundant' is a matter of complex debate, depending upon assumptions about future increases in yields as a result of plant and animal breeding. The implications of less intensive farming also affect the calculations. But forecasts for Britain range from 2.5 million acres by 1991 to 10 million acres by the end of the century, if land continues to be worked as intensively as now. Everyone

One of the few surviving oaks in Sherwood Forest

agrees, however, that one of the areas of England likely to be hit hardest is the Midlands. More remote, hillier regions will be cushioned by the extra help available to less favoured areas (see chapter 2), while more fertile East Anglia, for example, will be better able to make profits on reduced outputs. The proximity of the Midlands countryside to towns also increases the viability of alternative land uses.

One option favoured by the British government is an increase in forestry. And where more obvious than in Sherwood Forest? At the moment myth is more attractive than reality. More accurate, too, since Sherwood used to be a heath interspersed with oak woodland rather than what we understand today by a forest. The historic area of Sherwood, technically a forest in the sense of having been a royal hunting preserve, is now a mix of farmland, collieries and mostly coniferous woodland. A few magnificent oaks survive, and Nottinghamshire County Council has established a visitor centre near Edwinstowe which exploits the Robin Hood legend for more than it is probably worth. Still, it could be the nucleus for the new royal forest proposed by the Countryside Commission as our legacy for the twenty-first century.

The Commission's idea of a new forest is one designed for recreation as much as timber and largely comprising native broad-leaved woodland, trees that may take eighty years or more to mature. Farmers, accustomed to cash crops, tend to look more favourably upon faster-growing conifers. Government grants for farm forestry have been stepped up and advice proffered about how to exploit existing woodland. Even so, with the extra funding announced in 1987 confined to 30,000 acres of farm woodlands a year for the entire country, few experts expect commercial forestry to play a major role in the Midlands; profit margins are too low and land uses other than forestry too financially tempting in a region which is rarely far from towns and transport links. One of the most lucrative such uses is development. For farmland on the urban fringe, the problem is not so much seeking alternative uses as resisting them. Much of the Midlands is already under intense pressure.

Development can mean the exploitation of what lies beneath the land. Staffordshire, north Warwickshire, Derbyshire and Shropshire are already afflicted by opencast coal mining and limestone extraction. Among the sites favoured by quarrymen is the limestone ridge of Wenlock Edge, part of the Shropshire Hills AONB. Sand and gravel workings are also widespread in most Midlands counties. Falling land prices will stimulate the economic viability of all mineral workings. Deep-coal mines are also spreading from traditional mining counties to unfamiliar territory such as the Vale of Belvoir in Leicestershire and, if British Coal gets its way, to a site known as Hawkhurst Moor, east of Solihull in the West Midlands. Nationally, conservation groups such as the CPRE are less troubled by deep-coal mines than opencast workings because the former consume far less land. The people of Solihull, a smart haven for Birmingham's middle-classes, take a less sanguine view; if the scheme goes ahead, the half-timbered

ABOVE LEFT: Sherwood Forest visitor centre, which exploits the Robin Hood legend

ABOVE: Wenlock Edge, part of the Shropshire Hills AONB – a site for limestone quarrying

village of Berkswell, with its Norman church, would be barely half a mile from the pit-head. Opposition has been heightened by the fact that the proposed mine would be located in the 'Meriden Gap' separating Birmingham from Coventry. At its narrowest, this band of open countryside is now less than 6 miles wide. If any farmland does go out of production here, few areas will have more suitors.

Although there is pressure for new housing around much of Birmingham – north towards Cannock Chase in Stafford-shire and south-west towards Wythall in Worcestershire – the most sustained assault has been upon the Meriden Gap, in the south-east towards Coventry. Part of this area was once promoted as 'Birmingham's beautiful countryside' in much the same way as the concept of 'Metroland' espoused the rural attractions of London's north-western suburbs. Towns grew around stations at Solihull, Olton and Dorridge

along the old Great Western Railway line between Padding-
ton, Oxford and Birmingham's Snow Hill. Widespread car
ownership later caused the initial settlements to sprawl, as
commuters no longer needed to be within walking distance
of the stations. A green belt eventually protected a swathe
of countryside between Birmingham and Coventry; however,
its sanctity is now threatened as never before.

The National Exhibition Centre (NEC) – built substantially

on green-belt land – and motorways have been prime catalysts for development. The NEC plans to double in size, with a new exhibition arena displacing woodland previously covered by tree preservation orders. The M42 through green belt around the south and east of Birmingham could effectively become the city's eastern boundary. An estate of 5000 houses is being built in a wedge between the M42, A34 and the Birmingham–Oxford railway. Along the M42, there are plans for a 'high-tech' site near the exhibition centre, hypermarkets and a service area. Villages east of the motorway such as Knowle and Dorridge would then have few, if any, green fields between them and Birmingham. The scale of housing developments need not be numbered in thousands to transform existing communities: an extra 700 houses planned for a site west of Dorridge represents a 30 per cent increase in local population.

The convergence of motorways on Birmingham exemplifies how new roads profoundly change patterns of life in the countryside as well as the landscape. Sometimes this is for the better, with bypasses taking traffic away from the narrow streets of historic market towns such as Ludlow in Shropshire. Here, as at Sudbury in Derbyshire, the bypass is well designed, fitting into the contours of the land rather than obtruding into the landscape. Elsewhere, existing roads could perhaps be improved as an alternative to allowing new routes to carve through open countryside, as the A1–M1 link will through Naseby battlefield in Northamptonshire. Bypasses and motorways invariably have secondary effects upon patterns of settlement. Towns and villages along motorways suddenly fall within the commuter zone of conurbations such as Birmingham, Sheffield or Manchester. The extension of the M40 from Oxford to Birmingham is already hoisting house prices along the Warmington Valley; the M1 and electrified rail services have turned Northamptonshire and Bedfordshire into commuter territory for London.

Towns also tend to expand towards a new road. Worcester is pushing out towards the M5 with a large housing development at Warndon; Northampton and Chester, in edging towards their bypasses, threaten to engulf villages which once were separate communities. Hardingstone near Northampton and Christleton near Chester are examples of such suburbanised countryside. Most local authorities are vigilant in the defence of the green belt, but high unemployment can undermine their resistance. As described in chapter 2, the government vetoed a move by Cheshire County Council to remove the presumption against most forms of development on their green-belt land. However, as the agricultural crisis has deepened, the government floated ideas for alternative uses of surplus farmland not entirely dissimilar from the original Cheshire proposal.

Coming hard on the heels of moves to scrap the previous presumption against development on all farmland and to remove structure planning powers from county councils, the proposals fanned fears of a builders' bonanza in the countryside. The implications of what the CPRE described as

115

Opencast coal mining threatens the village of Berkswell

'potentially the biggest change in land use since the war' are explored more fully in chapter 6.

Farming near major cities has never been easy. Worcestershire's county planner once dubbed the urban fringe south-west of Birmingham as 'the bedstead belt' because of the unwanted household goods dumped on the edge of towns. But the closer to the cities the greater is the potential value of land for alternative uses. Sometimes dereliction is cited as a reason for approving development. 'It will tidy up what's now an eyesore,' say developers, eager to circumvent irritating details such as green belts or planning constraints against building. One form of development may be encouraged. Already areas such as the Meriden Gap are dotted with sports fields, golf ranges and riding schools. Under government proposals to cope with overproduction, recreation is seen as a prime candidate for redundant farmland, particularly when the land is within easy travelling distance of urban settlements. Yet sports grounds inexorably produce club houses with car parks and lights, effectively becoming late-night social clubs, to the detriment of the countryside and the annoyance of their neighbours.

Leisure is certainly a growth industry. Shorter working hours, longer holidays and car ownership, which tripled between 1960 and 1980, have triggered a transformation in our use of the countryside. According to Countryside Commission surveys, roughly 25 per cent of the population visit the countryside frequently (at least once a week), 30 per cent regularly (at least once a month), 20 per cent occasionally (between one and six months) and 25 per cent, largely less well-off people, go rarely, if at all. On a peak summer Sunday, 18 million people visit the countryside. That's two fifths of the

116

BELOW LEFT: The Meriden
Gap – green-belt land under
sustained pressure from developers

BELOW CENTRE: The M42,
through green belt, could effectively
become Birmingham's eastern
boundary

BELOW RIGHT: The National
Exhibition Centre plans to double
its size

entire population of England and Wales, and three-quarters of them go by car.

Some places, like Dovedale, have almost become victims of their own popularity; in the same category are Symond's Yat in the Wye Valley, Creswell Crags on the Derbyshire–Nottinghamshire border, Alderley Edge in Cheshire and Cannock Chase in Staffordshire. The Countryside Commission sponsored an effective management project at Cannock Chase to combat damage caused by the sheer number of visitors; interpretative facilities were also improved so that people were encouraged to explore less visited areas. Similar schemes to disperse visitors have been launched in the Peak District.

The Countryside Commission has also promoted recreation closer to conurbations. Between 1968 and 1986 the Commission helped to create 206 country parks, 239 picnic sites and 200 recreation paths in England and Wales. The National Trust, Forestry Commission, water authorities and local authorities have all developed recreation facilities. Northamptonshire, for instance, has pioneered the novel concept of 'pocket parks' for informal use of small open spaces. More than half of the attractions listed in the English Tourist Board's annual summaries of visitor numbers have opened since 1970. Many of the new developments have had the incidental advantage of clearing up the dereliction of abandoned industrial sites. Canal towpaths have been restored (as at Macclesfield in Cheshire), disused rail lines converted into cycleways (as in the Peak District), and flooded gravel pits turned into venues for water sports or refuges for wildlife (as at Chasewater and Consall parks in Staffordshire).

Participation in sport has boomed, sometimes causing con-

117

flicts with other leisure interests. Plans to open the upper Severn for navigation pitted boatmen against anglers and birdwatchers, while motorcycle scrambling over the Malvern Hills infuriates almost everyone (at present the law permits a limited number of motor-scrambling events to take place in any one area each year without planning permission). Many visitors are content simply to go for a drive, admiring the views and perhaps stopping for a picnic or a drink at a country pub. But between one-fifth and a third — according to different surveys — go walking, the most popular of all activities in the countryside.

Again, sterling work has been undertaken by the Countryside Commission and others to improve facilities for walkers. Circular trails complement long-distance paths, and manuals are available describing how to design routes and waymarked signs. The new routes are intended to highlight parts of the 120,000 miles of rights of way which exist in England and Wales. Yet, according to a 1986 survey conducted for the Countryside Commission, as many people walk on country roads as on rights of way. Only one walker in eight ventures on a right of way which is neither signposted nor waymarked. Alan Mattingly, director of the Ramblers' Association, fears that some local authorities invest too much time and effort

LEFT: A bypass has taken traffic away from the narrow streets of Ludlow

BELOW: Warmington, Warwickshire, where the extension of the M40 from Oxford to Birmingham has hoisted house prices

RIGHT: Symond's Yat in the Wye Valley – a victim of its own popularity

in showpiece schemes at the expense of their legal obligation to maintain all rights of way. Roy Hickey, of the Countryside Commission's recreation and access branch, adds, 'We have this huge resource of rights of way for which local authorities are responsible but which they find difficult to maintain. A lot of our effort is directed towards getting the idea accepted that it is legitimate to spend money on countryside access.'

Agricultural change has not helped. Footpaths which once followed hedgerows may lead across a field of corn once the hedge has disappeared. Although farmers are legally obliged to reconstitute paths after ploughing, a national survey published in 1985 showed that 59 per cent of rights of way in arable areas were affected by ploughing. Nor is the problem confined to arable counties such as those in the East Midlands. A survey conducted by the Ramblers' Association in Herefordshire found 96 per cent of all paths ploughed into oblivion or seriously obstructed by barbed wire or missing bridges. Stung by such findings and calls for legal action against farmers, the Countryside Commission and the Ministry of Agriculture jointly published a ploughing code in 1986. Ramblers are sceptical that it will have much effect. Bulls can also be a deterrent to enjoying a public right of way, yet legally − if they are beef bulls and accompanied by cows or heifers − the farmer is entitled to keep them in fields crossed by footpaths. The point of the distinction may not be appreciated by the average walker.

Such hazards could be one reason why so many people choose to walk on roads. This nervousness is also reflected in the popularity of familiar and local countryside for walking. The image of the long-distance rambler, with heavy boots and bulging rucksack, is misleading. Two-thirds of country walks are less than 3 miles in length and half of these occur on a familiar route within an hour's drive of home. So, once again, it is the wider countryside which is the most heavily used − not national parks or areas 'managed' for recreation. And it is this countryside which is most threatened by development pressures.

Some recreations may pose problems in themselves. If golf courses, riding schools and sports fields occupy redundant farmland, informal access will be restricted and the countryside transformed into little more than an urban park. Larger projects such as the holiday centres proposed at Sherwood, Rutland Water and Symond's Yat could overwhelm narrow country lanes, as the residents near Alton Towers theme park in Staffordshire know all too well. Yet farm shops and pick-your-own facilities should help some farmers to weather hard times in areas where the bed-and-breakfast trade is limited. These are examples of what agricultural economists call diversification; others are the pursuit of new crops, the production of organically produced foodstuffs and the development of rural craft workshops or recreation facilities.

Another piece of jargon has recently assumed even greater importance: 'extensification'. It is used to describe less intensive farming of land to produce lower yields. Environmentally sensitive areas (ESAs − see chapter 5, pages 177−80) are, in

Damage to Cannock Chase has been checked by a scheme to disperse the huge numbers of visitors

effect if not intention, a form of extensification, with their emphasis on low-input farming. In March 1987, European agriculture ministers agreed a package of 'socio-structural' measures which included an extensification scheme. Under this, farmers could be offered aid to reduce production of cereals, beef and wine by at least 20 per cent for a minimum of five years. How the objective will be achieved is left to individual countries. In Britain, there is no shortage of ideas, but also no consensus.

Fertilisers may be applied in lower dosages than previously, incidentally easing fears about nitrate pollution of water supplies — a government report in 1986 admitted that 1 million people were living in areas where nitrate levels exceeded European limits; these included parts of Stafford-shire, Worcestershire, Warwickshire and Nottinghamshire. Another route to extensification would be to leave larger field 'headlands' – the areas near field boundaries where machines turn round – unploughed and unsprayed. Experiments by the Game Conservancy have shown that this greatly benefits wildlife. For these reasons, extensification appeals to conservationists more than other options for dealing with the agricultural crisis. 'There is not too much land,' says CPRE, 'but too much food.' It is unlikely to be a complete answer.

Enforcing codes or laws about lower fertiliser use would be difficult, while reducing production (also difficult to monitor for commodities used as animal feedstuffs) could push more farmers into bankruptcy. In the halcyon days of ever-increasing production, many farmers entered into costly bank loans for new equipment or farm buildings. In 1987 farm loans were a fraction under £6000 million, twice the 1980 total. If interest rates and other costs stay high, lower output and falling prices could destroy farmers' profitability. On this capital-intensive treadmill, the temptation will be to intensify production still further. Farmers on marginal land such as much of the Midlands would be at a disadvantage compared to those whose land is better suited to both arable or livestock.

The NFU is therefore among those supporting an extreme form of extensification – known in the inevitable jargon as 'set aside'. Essentially, this means that part of a farmer's land would lie fallow in order to reduce production. To the NFU, this would be a temporary – and compulsory – expedient while ministers prepare a long-term integrated policy to replace the abandoned vision of ever-increasing output. Farmers would be compensated for the land they take out of production and this would be easier to monitor than reductions in intensity. John MacGregor, who succeeded Michael Jopling as Agriculture Minister in June 1987, sees 'set aside' as the means to achieve the desired 20 per cent cut in cereals. But the NFU is not alone in questioning whether this can be done voluntarily. American experience also suggests that land set aside would be marginal land which is least profitable for farming anyway, while the remaining land is worked more intensively than ever. Conservation gains – if any – will depend upon the frequency of rotation and degree of pesticide control, and marginal land simply abandoned would soon become derelict.

Many of these options for farming's fragile future will chill the heart of those who love the countryside. The potential gains from increased recreation and small-scale extensification, such as larger uncultivated headlands, are modest set against the risks of afforestation and commercial development. However, the crisis for agriculture should be looked upon as an opportunity for enhancing the countryside by promoting environmentally benign farming.

Conservation grants have already been increased, some harmful grants (such as those for removing hedgerows) removed, advice services expanded (and, in the case of ADAS, exempted from charges) and the principle of ESAs extended. Five Midlands areas were among forty-six ESAs in England

BELOW: Restored gravel pits in Cheshire

BELOW RIGHT: The Malvern Hills

OVERLEAF: *The Clun Valley –
one of the ESAs chosen to begin
operation in 1988*

and Wales proposed by the Countryside Commission – the Shropshire Hills, Clun Valley, Nene Washes and Valley, Peak District and Wyre Forest. Although all forty-six areas were regarded by the Countryside Commission as being threatened by agricultural improvement, only two, Clun Valley and the North Peak, were among the ESAs chosen to begin operation in 1988. In the Border landscape of Shropshire's Clun Valley, the rough grasslands of the gentle hills are being improved, the twisting hedgerows are deteriorating and the oak woodlands damaged by grazing.

Many conservation groups would like to see the ESA principle of funding farmers who maintain traditional landscapes available throughout England, certainly in national parks and AONBs. The Ministry of Agriculture says the need for European cooperation makes this impossible. Difficulties of obtaining agreement between twelve countries with remarkably diverse agricultural industries also inhibit action on curbing the use of fertilisers. Action by Britain alone would put our farmers at a critical disadvantage. Farmers at a FWAG conference in 1986 – and therefore, by definition, sympathetic to conservation – thought that uncertainty was increasing intensification. A discussion panel on arable farming concluded, 'It was felt that until the EEC as a whole began to deal with the problem of surpluses, UK farmers should continue to produce as much of their high-quality products as they can in order not to be at a disadvantage to other producers.'

At the very time when the NFU sought to make common cause with groups such as the CPRE, and were more anxious than ever to promote farmers as 'stewards of the countryside', practical conservation was becoming a casualty of farming's economic difficulties. 'We have to recognise that the more

123

hard pressed farmers become, the less able they will be voluntarily to forgo income in favour of conservation,' NFU president Simon Gourlay told a London seminar in 1987. Outside the ESAs, there was simply not enough money to make conservation worthwhile.

One way forward was suggested in an experiment in the Peak District called 'integrated rural development'. Backed by the European Commission and six British government departments or agencies, this explored a comprehensive approach to rural life involving social, economic and environmental policies. Grants for maintaining herb-rich hay meadows, restoring redundant buildings for community use, maintaining stone walls, starting new businesses and educational projects, plus a wide variety of other schemes, were all funnelled through one organisation. The first phase of the experiment, focusing on the villages of Longnor and Monyash, was an undoubted success; over thirty-five jobs were created, the landscape improved and community spirit fostered after years of rural decline. The second phase – in a third moorland parish – encountered more resistance since some local farmers feared the project would jeopardise the livestock allowances which are the lifeblood for most hill farmers. With agriculture nationally in turmoil, some farmers were reluctant to try a new approach. In the end, however, half the farmers in the third parish decided to participate.

Ken Parker of the Peak District national park authority says, 'We have shown that integrated rural development is not just an interesting theory. It is a practical possibility. In total, fifty new jobs have been created in these three different parishes in a wide variety of activities, showing that economic decline can be stopped. At the same time, the environment has been improved and community self-confidence bolstered because virtually every scheme was implemented by local people. All this has been achieved in just four years since the scheme started, reversing decades of decline in population, job opportunities and environmental qualities at very modest cost.'

The scheme has influenced government thinking about ESAs and the work of the Development Commission in attracting small firms to the countryside. More fundamentally, it has suggested that elements of the countryside should not be looked at in isolation. By encouraging activities such as a tourist information centre in the village shop or the maintenance of stone walls, integrated rural development implicitly acknowledges that the countryside needs people if it is to be maintained in the form we love. And, indeed, why not subsidise the shepherd as well as the sheep, the shop as well as the silo? People need the countryside to refresh and invigorate their lives. You cannot say that a source of pleasure enjoyed by 18 million people on a single Sunday is undervalued, but it is certainly underfunded and underprotected. Conservation and public access should form part of a comprehensive package for the new age of agriculture about to dawn, not least in our underestimated Midlands.

125

4

THE WEST COUNTRY

No part of England is further than 100 miles from tidal water. As an island nation the sea has moulded our history, and nowhere is this more evident than in south-west England.

The maritime tradition lies deeper than the legends of smugglers' coves and shipwrecks evoked by Daphne du Maurier's novels. From great ports such as Plymouth and Bristol, navies have sailed to battles on high seas and pilgrims departed to settle new lands. In parts of the West Country, more people lived off the sea than off the land. Many still do, indirectly. Tourism has become a major industry, luring more visitors to the region than anywhere in England except London. For all the delights of the West Country's moors and hills, nobody doubts that the area's prime attraction is its sinuous shoreline.

A third of the heritage coast designated in England by the Countryside Commission is to be found here. Four areas of outstanding natural beauty (AONBs) and one national park cover other stretches of unspoiled coastline. Between them, these designations cover the best of the contrasting shores to be found in south-west England: from cliffs of granite pounded by Atlantic waves on the north coast to sleepy, wooded estuaries in the south, from sandy beaches to rocky creeks. Nowhere else in England has as rich or diverse a coastline, so it is little wonder that it has attracted such unparalleled official honour. Yet this very beauty brings dangers – of crass commercialisation, insensitive development or simply too many people in too small a place.

Agriculture may also transform the margins where land and sea meet, with thrift-speckled grassy clifftops coming increasingly under the plough. Although the impact of intensive agriculture has generally been less dramatic in the West Country than in eastern England, farmers have nonetheless

GLOUCESTERSHIRE

● Gloucester

● Stroud

AVON

● Bristol

● Bath

WILTSHIRE

Ilfracombe ●

SOMERSET

● Salisbury

● Taunton

DEVON

DORSET

Okehampton ●

Exeter ●

● Dorchester

● Bournemouth

Plymouth ●

● Weymouth

ABOVE: Cliffs near Botallack, Cornwall

OVERLEAF: Gunard's Head, Cornwall

wrought controversial changes on the landscapes and wildlife of moors such as Exmoor and Bodmin, the downs of Dorset and Wiltshire and the wetlands of Somerset. The coast may be the West Country's most distinctive feature, but its inland areas do not lack attributes. It is here that you find southern England's only national parks. There are also ten AONBs, whose sites range from the tip of Cornwall to the Cotswolds.

None of these areas is immune from the nationwide problems posed by recreation, agricultural change and development, although the intensity of pressure varies within the region. Around Bristol and Swindon, it is house-builders and industrialists who are gobbling up green fields, while on Dartmoor the aggressor has been the Ministry of Defence. Even within single counties there is the paradox of some villages dying because schools and shops close while others are invaded by new housing estates. Prosperity and poverty are neighbours throughout much of the West Country, particularly since the imposition of EEC milk quotas curtailed the income of the region's dairy farmers. Not that the 15 million visitors each year can yet observe much evidence of decay in their rush to the sea. Through the car window, it mostly looks a verdant landscape with trees and banked hedgerows. The shoreline appears largely untrammelled by development. But can this rural idyll survive mounting economic threats?

The Royal Society for the Protection of Birds (RSPB) has identified nine West Country estuaries or harbours where development proposals menace sites important for waterfowl. From Barnstaple in north Devon through the Camel, Hayle, Fal, Plym, Dart, Teign and Exe estuaries to Poole harbour in Dorset, birdlife and landscapes are at risk. 'All these places are sites of special scientific interest [SSSIs],' says Kevin Standring, planning officer for the RSPB. 'Developers always say, "There are plenty of other places the birds can move to." But that is no longer true. Recent studies have shown that all the best feeding sites are now full. There is nowhere for the displaced birds to go. The birds come from as far away as Siberia, Canada and Scandinavia, and they come because of our relatively warm climate and deeply indented coastline. Britain is bound by EEC directives and, in some cases, by other international agreements, to take care of these places.'

The threat to the birds is reason enough for an army of people to feel concern – the RSPB grew from a mere 8100 members in 1959 to 509,000 by 1987. Even people able to do little more than distinguish a gull from a puffin would find their walks along clifftops or estuaries impoverished without the wail of seabirds; the sounds of the countryside, for all its apparent tranquillity, can rarely be divorced from its sights. If wildlife loses a habitat, man's enjoyment of the countryside invariably suffers too. An example of such loss is the more sterile world of a coniferous forest against the teeming vitality of oak woods. Or here, along the coast of south-west England, the intrusion of barrages, docks, yacht marinas and oil terminals into estuaries and harbours loved by human visitors as well as birds.

Several of the development proposals threaten river estuaries along the southern shores of Cornwall and Devon. This is a softer, more sheltered coast than that to the north, deeply indented when sea levels rose after the last Ice Age to turn what were once river valleys into tidal estuaries. These natural harbours have long been exploited by man, with ports at Falmouth, Fowey and Dartmouth, as well as the great naval base at Plymouth. Nowadays many of the smaller harbours have more yachts than fishing boats or commercial craft, but the life of their communities still centres on the water. By and large, development has not yet marred the physical beauty of the estuaries. Fowey's china-clay trade, for instance, takes place away from the narrow streets of the old town. Putting barrages across estuaries, as proposed for four sites along this coast, would be much more intrusive, with secondary effects far upstream. Without the scouring effect of tides, some creeks would swiftly silt up, despite the artificially high water levels maintained by the barrages. If this makes the waterfront simply less attractive (although thereby more vulnerable to later development), some of the other proposals highlighted by the RSPB are more immediately threatening — notably the proposal for a new deep-water port near Dartmouth and the pursuit of oil in Poole Harbour.

The controversy over a new port with its associated warehouses and other industrial development on the east bank of the Dart exemplifies a wider debate about the merits of providing jobs as against conserving the landscape. Here, on one side, was the district council arguing that development would create at least 500 jobs in an area of high unemployment. On the other side were the conservationists, backed by rival south-west ports who feared a further loss to their already declining coastal trade. The entire 22-acre Dart site lies within the South Devon AONB and adjoins some fine oak woodland owned by the National Trust. 'It's an area of the highest landscape quality,' says Richard Lloyd, regional officer for the Countryside Commission. 'Given the configuration of the landscape, even a relatively small development would become a significant element in the scene. The Dart port would be a major intrusion, particularly when viewed from the river. It would also set a precedent for further development in the future.'

Although the conservationists were united in opposing this plan, they recognise the dilemma of jobs versus the environment. People who live in AONBs need work. The Countryside Commission believes that new industrial units should be sited on the edge of towns or villages rather than in unspoiled countryside 'unless there is a national need and no alternative locations are available'. These were precisely the arguments used by the oil industry to support the establishment of a terminal on Furzey Island in Poole Harbour. BP began by drilling for oil at its Wytch Farm site in nearby Purbeck, which grew into the largest onshore oilfield in north-west Europe; but BP said that, to exploit its full potential, drilling needed to be extended to Furzey — in the middle of a harbour guarded zealously by an army of well-heeled

129

yachtsmen and naturalists. Heritage coast, AONB, SSSI, listed
as a proposed protection area under the EEC Birds Directive:
BP could scarcely have chosen an area more garlanded with
bureaucratic acclaim. It is also, quite simply, very beautiful.

Initially, BP was able to screen its wells and 'gathering
station' amid trees, but later stages of the development lack
similar cover. A 56-mile-long pipeline from Wytch Farm
across the New Forest to BP's refinery on Southampton
Water also troubled conservationists, but was approved by
the government in 1987. Few people dispute that any oil
well in Poole Harbour itself must be environmentally damaging. The consequences of spillages in these weak tidal waters
would certainly be catastrophic for the redshank, shell-duck,
Brent geese and other birds for whom this is home. Conservationists acknowledge that BP has sought to minimise
the worst effects of its activities, yet worries remain. Dorset
has become Britain's largest onshore oilfield without the
arguments ever being vented at a public inquiry, other than
one into the pipeline. A precedent has thus been set — and
other companies may lack the resources and environmental
concern shown by BP in Dorset.

Of all the threats to the coasts of south-west England, the
one that was greatest before the Second World War has
somewhat receded. Tighter planning controls have mostly

*River Truro near Malpas, which
would be affected by a Fal estuary
barrage*

Herons on the River Dart

put a stop to the sprawl of caravan sites or retirement bungalows which began in the 1930s. Enough eyesores remain from that period of the first motor-car boom. Walking along the coastal footpath east of Exmouth, you come upon dramatic stacks of red sandstones jutting from the sea at horseshoe-shaped Ladram Bay. Equally hard to miss are fields of caravans unscreened by a single tree. Beer Head further east is just as bad. Most counties have similar horrors, desecrating the very countryside and coast whose beauty has drawn holiday-makers to this corner of England for more than a century.

'A very strange stranger it must be, who does not see charms in the immediate environs of Lyme,' wrote Jane Austen of Dorset's dark cliffs, romantic rocks and sweet bays in *Persuasion.* Despite an early nineteenth-century fashion for sea bathing, it was the Great Western Railway later that century which first opened up the south-west coast to mass tourism. The line between Dawlish and Teignmouth is still as exciting as any in England, thundering along the shore above beaches and through rocky tunnels. But most branch lines which once turned remote harbours into resorts have long since succumbed to market forces. For thirty years most visitors have arrived by car. It does not take many cars, let alone coaches or caravans, to clog the narrow, high-hedged lanes of Devon and Cornwall, so traffic jams have become part of West Country folklore. For years, newspapers stationed reporters on the Exeter bypass each summer bank holiday to interview weary motorists and harassed AA men. Completion of the M5 motorway has shifted the jams from Exeter, but blackspots remain.

The proposed solutions have often angered conservationists, with a succession of rows over the north Devon link road between Tiverton and Barnstaple. Even more controversial was the argument over the route for an Okehampton bypass. Nobody disputed that a bypass was needed. Traffic pouring off the M5 and dual-carriageway A30 had crawled through Okehampton for years. But should it go south of Okehampton through Dartmoor national park or north across medium-grade farmland? A public inquiry favoured the southern route and this was subsequently supported by the government. However, under the Acquisition of Land Act, a government department cannot purchase open space without offering suitable land in exchange or subjecting its proposals to what is known as a special parliamentary procedure. In this case, the land offered in exchange was agreed by the government to be inadequate, so a joint parliamentary committee of MPs and peers examined the proposals again. They concluded that there was insufficient justification for any incursion into the national park and urged the government to accept the northern route. To the dismay of conservationists, including the Countryside Commission, the government used its parliamentary majority to overturn the committee's verdict and insist that the southern route go ahead. What will be lost in Devon is part of a national park, the wooded slopes of Okehampton Park and the medieval deer park of Okehampton Castle. What has been lost nationally, for spurious reasons of alleged speed of construction, is the principle that national parks should be spared development if alternative sites exist.

For some West Country communities, bans rather than bypasses are the only solution to traffic chaos. Tiny harbours such as Clovelly and Polperro at times overflow with visitors, netting far more tourists than fish. Their cobbled streets are too narrow or too steep for cars, so clifftop car parks have been provided and the villages have become pedestrian zones. This has saved villages from exhaust fumes, although not from commercialisation. Yet the glory of the south-west coast is that it has so many faces: from sophisticated Torbay to sedate Sidmouth, from the surfing beaches of north Cornwall to the gently lapping waters of south-coast creeks, from the wooded cliffs of Exmoor to the sand dunes and heath of Studland Bay, from picturesque fishing villages to bustling naval ports.

One factor in the continuing survival of so much magnificent coastline has been the National Trust. The Trust was formed as much to look after open spaces as the great houses with which it has become popularly associated. During the 1930s the Council for the Preservation of Rural England (as the CPRE was then known) produced the first report

Dartmouth marina

highlighting examples of development despoiling the coastline: bathing huts, refreshment kiosks, car parks, insanitary picnic sites, sprawling bungalows, as well as caravans sited or designated with no thought for their impact on the landscape. Despite the greater powers granted to local authorities under postwar planning acts, the coastline was granted no special protection. In the 1950s the Cornish region of the National Trust therefore began to buy up large tracts of the county's coastline. Its initiative helped to inspire Operation Neptune, launched by the Trust nationally in 1965 to acquire 900 miles of coastline. In its annual report for 1962–63, the Trust estimated that the rest of the 2750 miles of the English and Welsh coast were already 'beyond redemption'.

Operation Neptune more than doubled the length of shoreline owned by the National Trust, so that by 1981 it possessed 400 miles. In north Somerset, south Devon and Dorset as well as Cornwall, the Trust snapped up coastal land which came onto the market. Although such ownership deters inappropriate development, it is rarely the end of the story. At Kynance Cove on the Lizard peninsula and at Studland Bay

in Dorset, for instance, the Trust faced problems caused by the pressure of visitors. Heathland flowers were being trampled to death, grass worn totally away. Elsewhere new farming methods were transforming the appearance of clifftop fields. Neither the benevolent ownership of the National Trust nor the official designations of the Countryside Commission left the coast unscathed. Something positive was required, concluded the Countryside Commission in the 1970s. Something more than the negative planning constraints theoretically extended to AONBs. Its solution was the idea, devised in 1972, of heritage coasts.

Heritage coasts are shores of outstanding beauty or possessing important wildlife (in practice the two attributes are often connected) where the Countryside Commission and local authorities seek to protect the landscape. Roughly a third of the coastline of England and Wales now rejoices in this label, much of it in the West Country. The intention was to promote positive management in conjunction with local authorities. Dorset had one of the earliest heritage coasts and here, along the Purbeck coastline of Lulworth Cove and Durdle Door, progress has been made. Footpaths have been repaired and waymarked, car parks screened by trees or resited, eyesores cleared, access agreements negotiated with landowners, farmers advised about how to conserve the landscape. Unhappily, an internal report prepared for the Countryside Commission in 1983 concluded that such success was untypical.

Ten years after the first heritage coasts were identified only twelve of the thirty-five areas then designated had any management at all. 'While development has in general been controlled,' said the report, 'on most heritage coasts it would not be possible to know that you are on one.' Things have improved a little since then, but Countryside Commission pleas for project officers and wardens to be appointed have coincided with a national squeeze on local authority spending. In Cornwall, whose 140 miles of heritage coast constitute a fifth of all such shoreline in the country, a project officer was initially appointed jointly with the National Trust, although the scheme now also involves Cornwall County Council. Kynance Cove has become something of a showpiece of restoration, with the principles of traffic management applied to footpath routes. Spurred by such success, the Commission remains wedded to the principle of heritage coasts, and rightly so; at their best, they help to conserve the landscape and to enhance public appreciation of what the Commission calls 'a vital component of our landscape heritage'.

Predictably, nature has proved the most effective guardian of the landscape, as along Exmoor's majestic coast, where the steep cliffs and paucity of inlets keep farmers, developers and even tourists at bay. Here there is also a public body dedicated to promoting precisely the balance between conservation and recreation desired for heritage coasts. Exmoor's national park authority is no more awash with funds than the other national

135

A new deep-water port is proposed on the River Dart near Dartmouth

parks, but at least within its small budget its objectives are clear. A national park authority should certainly be better able to finance the waymarking of footpaths and visitor centres than many hard-pressed councils. There are also controls on development in conservation areas at Porlock Weir, Lynmouth and Dunster with their distinctive cottages of thatch, cob and stone. Between them, the Exmoor national park authority itself and the National Trust own more than half of the 30 miles of coast within the national park. This helps to ensure that the 'hog's back' cliffs, where stretches of sessile oak woodland alternate with gorse and heather, are managed sensitively. Elsewhere on Exmoor, life has not been so equable.

A fifth of the moorland of Exmoor which existed in 1947 had disappeared thirty years later. Coniferous forests took some of the land, but the main culprit was agriculture. With the crucial help of government subsidies, moorland was either resown with rye grass and fenced to provide better grazing or, nearer the fringes, drained and ploughed for crops; pesticides and fertilisers were widely used. Both forms of agricultural improvement destroy the heather and moorland grasses which were the prime reason for Exmoor's designation as a national park. Only a quarter of the national park now remains as unimproved moorland. Even the largest tract at Brendon Common north of Simonsbath extends for barely 4 miles from north to south. Six moorland plants have become extinct since 1930, according to the Nature Conservancy Council (NCC). And the smaller or more fragmented the central moorland becomes the more endangered is the surviving wildlife.

Still less moorland would exist today had it not been for a public outcry, led by the Exmoor Society and the CPRE in the 1970s, which proved to be a catalyst for conservation nationally. The Society said:

Unless a halt is called *now* to the reclamation and enclosure of wild and open moorland (both grass and heather) there will be so little left that Exmoor's continued existence as a national park will be an expensive farce.

In 1977 an inquiry by Lord Porchester recommended that the national park authority designate those areas of moorland which it wanted to conserve 'for all time' and that it should make moorland conservation orders over vulnerable land. Farmers who owned land covered by such orders would be compensated for their inability to improve the land and increase their output. This compensation, said Porchester, should be on a once-and-for-all basis, but farmers fought what they saw as excessive constraints. The election of the Conservative government in 1979 scuppered the chances of any overall implementation of the Porchester recommendations. Park authorities were obliged to prepare maps of moorland they wished to conserve, but were not given the powers to impose conservation orders. Management agreements offered to farmers also differed significantly from those proposed in the Porchester report.

Under a voluntary deal struck between the national park

authority and farmers, management agreements would compensate farmers *annually* for a loss of income incurred by not improving the moorland. The government, keener on voluntary agreements than statutory regulation, agreed to provide 90 per cent of the cost of these management agreements. Farmers promised prior notification to the national park of anything which might affect the moorland, although the park authority still lacked ultimate powers to prevent damaging or destructive action. The principle of compensating people for notional lost profits was as controversial as it was costly, but it enabled the moorland losses to be stemmed and foreshadowed significant changes in the 1980s. The National Farmers' Union, aware that its public image was taking a battering, urged restraint and cooperation amongst its members. When the government brought in the 1981 Wildlife and Countryside Act, the Exmoor example, with significant changes, was treated as a model for the national scheme of compensation and prior notification for national parks and SSSIs.

Nationally, there was nothing like enough money for widespread compensation and, to some extent, the Exmoor precedent has been overtaken by schemes such as that covering environmentally sensitive areas (ESAs – see chapter 5, pages 177–80). Nevertheless the climate of cooperation fostered within Exmoor has avoided too many clashes, although a maverick farmer might still seek compensation for not growing wheat on ludicrously unsuitable moorland. Other agricultural changes continue to threaten not only Exmoor but Dartmoor too.

The South West's two national parks are frequently bracketed together in the public mind. Although geologically dissimilar, both have heartlands of wild open moor roamed by wild ponies, with buzzards and ravens soaring overhead.

ABOVE LEFT: Poole Harbour –
menaced by oil exploration

ABOVE RIGHT : Red sandstone
and caravans at Ladram Bay

Purple heather and golden gorse blend with subtle moor grasses to create an illusion of wilderness. With virtually no trees and with streams hidden in combes, it seems as though you can see for ever. The greater size of Dartmoor conveys a feeling of raw nature unique in southern England. Towards the fringes of the moors, the parks present a softer face, with sheltered villages, mixed farmland and rivers tumbling through wooded valleys to the sea. Wild moors and farmland, granite tors and thatched cottages, peat bogs and clapper bridges provide the contrasting faces of Dartmoor. An esti-mated 8 million visits are made to Dartmoor each year; in isolated places, visitors may pose a threat to the landscape they have come to enjoy. However, such pressures are pin-pricks set against the fate of the two national parks them-selves.

ABOVE: It does not take much traffic to clog the narrow high-hedged lanes of Devon and Cornwall

FAR RIGHT: Okehampton Castle

RIGHT: The Okehampton bypass will bisect Dartmoor

At almost any point along the fringes of Exmoor you can see examples of what is happening. Fields of bright-green, well-drained grass give the moor a manicured appearance totally out of character with its untamed nature. Wire fences also inject an alien element into a landscape renowned for openness. As if this were not enough, reseeding the grassland destroys most of the varied moorland vegetation which gives the moor its seasonal subtleties and its appeal for wildlife. It was the intensity of modern farming, not the farming itself, which posed the first postwar threat to the moors. Today there is a second threat: that bracken will engulf the heather if hard-up farmers abandon grazing on the moors altogether. 'Ungrazed it would be difficult to see over, let alone walk on,' says the Dartmoor national park authority.

The moors which we have inherited are no more 'natural' than any other landscape below 2500 feet in this country. Dartmoor and Exmoor were inhabited in the Bronze Age, when prehistoric man began to clear the cover of trees. Dartmoor was then in its heyday as a place for human settlement. Extensive remains of field boundaries, stone circles and villages are evidence of primitive agriculture. As man learned how to cultivate the more fertile lowlands, the moorland settlements were abandoned. In the Middle Ages both

moors became royal forests for hunting deer. For centuries deer shared the moors with cattle and sheep, feeding on the heather and cotton grass, sheltering in the valley woodlands. Red deer still roam freely on Exmoor today.

Some farmers had continued to graze their livestock on the moors long after most early settlers decamped to the valleys. In 1815, following word of an agricultural revolution in the east of the country, an Enclosure Act ended the legal protection afforded to Exmoor as a royal forest. The land was divided among private owners, who were free to do as they liked. Early attempts to improve the moorland were unsuccessful, although the nineteenth-century pioneers bequeathed a legacy of fine beech hedges. Twentieth-century technology proved better able to tackle the problems posed by 70 inches of rainfall a year and sodden soils. The moors were soon ringed by farmland and the stage set for the conservation battles of recent years. Surviving unimproved moorland in the heartland of the old royal forest includes, poignantly, some abandoned farmsteads around Simonsbath dating from the first doomed agricultural improvements.

Dartmoor's greater size – 30 per cent larger than its northern neighbour – makes it less vulnerable to substantial nibbling away round the edges. The thinner soils and blanket bogs over its granite plateau also render it less hospitable to intensive agriculture. But neither of these factors fully explains why more than half of Dartmoor survives as moorland. In *The History of the Countryside*, Oliver Rackham has no doubt about the prime reason for the difference between the two national parks:

Dartmoor, in contrast [to Exmoor], has never had an Enclosure Act and remains mostly intact. Such are the consequences of tampering with the legal status of wild vegetation.

Some fields were established, bordered as often by walls as by hedges, but Dartmoor was never fully enclosed because a large proportion of it had been 'common land' since at least the thirteenth century. Almost 100,000 acres of Dartmoor are subject to a variety of common rights, covering not only sheep and cattle grazing but peat digging and fuel collection. Dartmoor national park authority pioneered new ways to manage common land. In 1985 the Dartmoor Commons Act created the first commoners' council in the country with statutory powers to control matters such as how the land is grazed. Limits on numbers of animals can be imposed if areas suffer from overgrazing. The 1985 Dartmoor Commons Act also gives the public – for the first time – a legal right of access to all common land, so long as they don't abuse that right by causing damage. Dartmoor's attempt to promote better management and access helped to point the way to proposals agreed in 1986 between landowners and conservationists for all common land in England and Wales.

If the agreements forged locally in Exmoor and Dartmoor work, they should lessen the agricultural pressures on these national parks. But they will not remove them. The parks were nominated by the Countryside Commission as potential ESAs, which would have given the farmers positive inducements to manage their land in ways which maintain and enhance traditional landscapes. Hill farming is a hard, financially unrewarding business and the farmers may need additional help if the grazing essential to keep moors free from bracken is to continue. They may also need help to maintain hedges or walls. Traditionally, this was a job done by farm workers in winter, but many farms have shed labour. The number of farming jobs on Dartmoor and Exmoor fell by two thirds between 1952 and 1972. ESA status would give moorland farmers extra cash which could be used to employ hedgers, but neither park has so far been chosen. The future remains uncertain, not only on the moors but in the more fertile fringes, where the traditional pattern of mixed farming is also jeopardised by curbs on output and prices.

TOP: *Polperro*

ABOVE RIGHT: *North Cornwall, near Bude*

RIGHT: *Lulworth Cove*

FAR RIGHT: *Pentewan caravan site, Mevagissey*

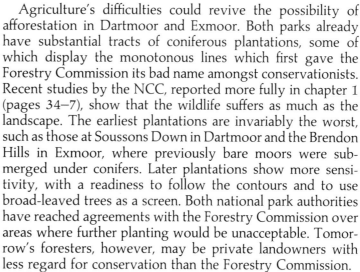

Agriculture's difficulties could revive the possibility of afforestation in Dartmoor and Exmoor. Both parks already have substantial tracts of coniferous plantations, some of which display the monotonous lines which first gave the Forestry Commission its bad name amongst conservationists. Recent studies by the NCC, reported more fully in chapter 1 (pages 34–7), show that the wildlife suffers as much as the landscape. The earliest plantations are invariably the worst, such as those at Soussons Down in Dartmoor and the Brendon Hills in Exmoor, where previously bare moors were submerged under conifers. Later plantations show more sensitivity, with a readiness to follow the contours and to use broad-leaved trees as a screen. Both national park authorities have reached agreements with the Forestry Commission over areas where further planting would be unacceptable. Tomorrow's foresters, however, may be private landowners with less regard for conservation than the Forestry Commission.

The parks are already concerned about woodlands in private ownership, particularly the relatively small areas of native deciduous woodland which remain. About 5 per cent of each park is broad-leaved woodland, yet most, perhaps all, of the moors were once covered by trees. Wistman's Wood,

141

an eerie oak copse huddling along a bank of the West Dart River 1400 feet above sea level, is possibly a remnant of Dartmoor's original tree cover. It is certainly among England's highest surviving oak woods. More substantial oak and birch woodlands are found in the river valleys and along the moorland fringes. These were traditionally managed for timber and fuel, but as these needs declined many woods fell into a tangle of neglect. Tree preservation orders have been applied to many woods, yet these cannot ensure their future regeneration. Too many trees are old and dying. Four-fifths of Dartmoor's woodland is estimated to be unmanaged and in decline. The typical small farmer lacks the skills and resources to manage woodlands, particularly as these are likely to be in a poor condition.

So precarious is the future of broad-leaved woodlands, yet so valuable are they as an element in the landscape and for

142

wildlife, that some woods have acquired special protection. Yarner Wood in south-west Dartmoor is now run by the NCC. Horner Wood, south of Porlock in Exmoor, is managed by the National Trust and provides a vibrant contrast to the open spaces of Dunkery Beacon a few miles away. Elsewhere in Exmoor, the national park authority has bought more than 1000 acres of woodland and developed a plan to manage others in ways to ensure their survival. Mostly, though, the authority can do little more than exhort or protest. Some landowners have understood the message that their old woodlands are dying, only to replace them with fast-growing and more profitable conifers. If such people are willing to forego all public forestry grants, there is nothing that can be done to stop them.

Planning controls in the national parks are flimsy. Both south-western parks have seen valleys drowned to form reservoirs, while new firing ranges at Willsworthy on Dartmoor were sanctioned by the government despite the park authority's opposition. The Ministry of Defence owns or has rights to use just under a sixth of Dartmoor, more than any national park except Northumberland. (Curiously, Exmoor is the only national park without any military presence, beyond low-flying aircraft shattering the contemplative solitude.) Few people dispute the intrinsic incompatibility between promoting an area for its natural beauty and allowing it to be used as a military training ground.

Dartmoor has become the most bitter battleground between the conservationists and military because the army has commandeered so much of the highest, wildest and best moorland of this small and highly pressured national park. Dartmoor also has eight times as many visitors as North-

umberland. Half of its central moorland is used by the Ministry of Defence and for much of the time, apart from weekends and the month of August, this land, theoretically dedicated to public enjoyment as a national park, remains out of bounds, with the noise and visual intrusion of military activity polluting far wider areas. Conservationists accept that it is unrealistic to expect that the army will suddenly vacate land some of which it has been using since 1870. But the Countryside Commission, which is statutorily responsible for advising governments on national parks, believes there should be a full, phased withdrawal by the military from Dartmoor. Conservationists strongly resist attempts to extend Dartmoor's military areas, as happened in 1980, when 'dry' or adventure training began at Cramber Tor, or to make existing facilities more permanent, as implied by proposals for new barracks to accompany the Willsworthy ranges.

Perversely, military training can safeguard some vegetation. 'Live' shells thudding into natural tors and ancient monuments or tanks churning up grassland are scarcely ideal conservation techniques. But they may be less damaging overall than the deep ploughing, reseeding and pesticide-spraying in the armoury of modern farming – and not just on Dartmoor. The army ranges at Lulworth in Dorset and Salisbury Plain in Wiltshire have largely preserved traditional grasslands which elsewhere were going under the plough. In recent years, the image-conscious army has enlisted naturalists to help prepare conservation plans for their sites which aim to protect the most valuable species. Archaeological sites are similarly protected, although not infallibly so. This is second-best conservation, though, since public access to such areas is invariably limited; most of us will have to accept the

ABOVE LEFT: Durdle Door

ABOVE CENTRE: Porlock Weir – a conservation area where development is controlled

ABOVE RIGHT: Only a quarter of Exmoor national park remains as unimproved moorland

expert's word that rare flowers, herbs and insects survive under the crossfire.

Humans find military occupation of attractive countryside less congenial. News that the army was seeking to extend six training grounds elsewhere in England prompted strong local protests in 1987. If these had been replacements for sites on Dartmoor, the army might have found reluctant allies among national conservation groups. Although the Ministry of Defence declined to publish documents detailing long-term plans, it appears that the extended training grounds would be additions to the army's territories. There were no plans for further reductions in the areas of Dartmoor used for training; if anything, the intensity of use there will increase. For all the army's efforts to be seen as good conservationists, bigger vehicles and increased firepower consume larger areas of land, so future training may be more damaging to the countryside. Public access will certainly be a casualty, as seen by the closure of 30 miles of public footpaths on Salisbury Plain in 1986.

Equally incompatible with the concept of a national park is large-scale industry, yet around Lee Moor in south-western Dartmoor are some of the world's largest opencast china-clay mines. One pit alone is 300 feet deep and covers 100 acres. Great tips of waste are piled up here, not unlike those near St Austell nicknamed the Cornish Alps. Tin, copper, lead, limestone, iron and silver have also been exploited; granite is still quarried. National park status may be insufficient cause to deny a nation supplies of rare minerals, if there are no comparable sources elsewhere. China clay, for instance, is confined to the south-west of England, and a tungsten mine has recently been sanctioned on the edge of Dartmoor on similar grounds of national rarity. Such sites may be the exception to a general prohibition on development, but they demand the highest standards of landscaping and subsequent restoration.

144

AONBs, the second division of official landscape protection, are even more vulnerable to arguments that the economic need for minerals outweighs the environmental case to preserve the landscape. The Mendips, Quantocks, Cotswolds and the Purbeck Downs have all been quarried for one mineral or another, usually from a time long before they were designated as AONBs. Near Charterhouse, on the plateau of the Mendips, are the remains of an amphitheatre established when the Romans mined here for lead. In time, nature can repair many of the ravages of man and, occasionally, man can find imaginative new uses for abandoned industrial sites. On Owermoigne Heath in Dorset, a former gravel pit has been sown with grass to form a tree-screened caravan site in summer and grazing ground in winter.

BELOW: Abandoned farm near Simonsbath

Many AONBs are predictably popular with visitors, notably those covering large stretches of the coast. Inland, too, recreation pressures are frequently intense. Cheddar in the Mendips, Bourton-on-the-Water in the Cotswolds, Corfe Castle in Dorset and Stonehenge in Wiltshire are all nationally known tourist attractions. Equally serious are the effects of

ABOVE: *Bright-green, manicured fields are starkly out of character with Exmoor's untamed nature*

ABOVE RIGHT: *Haytor, Dartmoor*

145

tourism on areas less able to provide facilities. The Quantocks is one of the smaller AONBs, just 38 square miles in size, and visited mostly by local people from Taunton and elsewhere in Somerset. Many visitors drive off the unfenced roads onto the thin soils of hills made more fragile by high rainfall.

Several AONBs within south-west England were identified by the Countryside Commission as potential ESAs: West Penwith (with the Cornish AONB), Bodmin, the Mendips, South Wiltshire Downs and parts of the North Wessex Downs, plus the national parks of Dartmoor and Exmoor. But only two West Country ESAs were chosen: West Penwith, between St Ives and Land's End and the Somerset Levels and Moors.

Man's perception of scenic beauty tends to dwell on hills and coasts. Only three of the first thirty-six AONBs designated in England and Wales lack these features: the Wye Valley, High Weald and Dedham Vale. Nobody paid much attention to the flat, frequently waterlogged fields of the Somerset Levels. Yet this is the largest surviving area of a type of land which once covered a quarter of the British Isles. Wetlands take several forms: marsh, fen, bog and mire. Often there is a combination of a saltmarsh fringing the sea and inland fen underlain with peat. Such was the case in East Anglia, and it was the analogy with the fens that awakened interest in the Somerset Levels. In 1971 a Ministry of Agriculture report, *Modern Farming and the Soil*, pointed out that it was only poor drainage and fragmented holdings which held back the Levels from achieving the same potential fertility as the fens. In other words, Somerset could become like the Cambridgeshire and Lincolnshire fens: an arid prairie devoted to wheat, barley or sugar beet. If this prospect whetted the appetites of any farmers, it sounded a belated warning for conservationists.

The Somerset Levels and Moors are the flood plains of five rivers which flow into the Bristol Channel near Bridgwater. Technically, the Levels are the coastal belt of clay soils and the Moors are the lower-lying inland river valleys, often with peaty clay soils and bordered on all sides by hills. Because the Levels are higher than the Moors, the slow-moving rivers find it difficult to reach the sea and winter tides regularly cause the land to flood. Farmers cannot do much with land that is submerged, so for centuries there have been attempts to drain the wetlands. Until recently these lacked the momentum of the drainage movement in the east of England. In the sixteenth century a scheme proposed by the Dutch engineer Vermuyden, and backed by King Charles I, was defeated by local commoners, who were quite content to use the land

LEFT: *Dartmoor's thinner soils and blanket bogs over a granite plateau make it less hospitable than Exmoor to intensive agriculture*

ABOVE: *A large proportion of Dartmoor has been 'common land' since at least the thirteenth century*

simply for summer grazing when the floods receded. Improved drainage was installed between 1770 and 1830 to accompany the Enclosure Acts, but it was relatively modest. In fact, the drainage would later enhance the appeal and importance of an area apparently bypassed by twentieth-century agricultural developments.

The Somerset Levels began the second half of the twentieth century much as they had ended the previous century. Drainage dykes known as 'rhynes' fed water into the rivers, but the fields still flooded most winters. The water level remained high. Wide, open views were broken only by clumps of willow or alder along the rivers, rhynes or roads. The presence of so much water caused a shimmering haze to hang over the meadows at dawn. In spring, as the cattle returned to graze, the meadows themselves were rich in flowers. The moisture from winter flooding (and a lack of pesticides) was ideal for flowers such as marsh marigold or marsh orchid. A typical field would have forty or fifty plant species: some – depending on how heavily they were grazed or cut for haymaking – would have as many as seventy different flowers and thirty different sedges and rushes. In or alongside the shallow water of the rhynes were rarer plants like marsh fern, water fern, flowering rush and bogbean. But by 1980 only 10 per cent of the Levels and Moors were estimated to retain the full range of wetland species.

Nevertheless, the experts were enthusiastic about what remained. 'The best aquatic flora and fauna of any grazing marsh in Britain,' says Brian Johnson of the NCC. 'By far the best area for wading birds in south-west England,' says the RSPB, adding that the Levels are also an important staging

148

post for migrant and wintering birds. This rich wildlife
inheritance – and the area sustains far more than mentioned
here, including butterflies such as the now uncommon
marbled white and mammals such as the even rarer otter –
is threatened by anything which disrupts the traditional management of the land. The interdependence of nature is such
that, if one link goes, all else suffers. And the key to change,
past and present, is drainage.

Pipes under fields, deeper rhynes and diesel pumps can
drastically lower water tables, making it feasible for farmers
to sow artificially cultivated strains of grass which increase
yields from diary cattle by 25 per cent. Or they may plant
cereal crops for which Europe's common agricultural policy
has in the past guaranteed high prices. If Britain (or Europe)
had a shortage of either milk or cereals, there might be some
justification for such changes. In particular, there might be
some reward for the taxpayers who subsidised anything up
to 80 per cent of the drainage and other 'improvement' costs
which enabled farmers to transform their land. Given these
incentives to intensify production, it is perhaps surprising
that more farmers did not do so.

Nationally, according to the CPRE, 175,000 acres of
wetland was subjected to field drainage between 1971 and
1980 – an area the size of the Isle of Wight every five years.
But this was by no means the limit of the drainage. Water
authorities and internal drainage boards virtually quadrupled
their spending in the decade from 1974 on 'improving' rivers
and arterial drainage channels. Drainage boards are a curious
form of public body, heavily funded by central government
grants yet with minimal public accountability. Farmers dominate the boards and so are in a position to propose drainage
schemes from which they will be the principal beneficiaries.

The undemocratic nature of the boards' constitution might matter less if the environmental consequences of drainage were not so dire.

149

Rivers are sometimes 'canalised' to help them drain away flood water more quickly. Meanders are straightened, trees lopped. Rhynes are deepened, cut by machines which uproot the waterside vegetation and dredge the bottom of the dykes. The insects which provide food for birds and fish lose their breeding places. So, too, do the warblers, kingfishers and otters which live amid the rushes and reeds of the rhynes. The water plants which flower on the surface of the rhynes cannot flourish if ditches are too deep or water flows too fast. Nor can they or the vegetation on the banks survive the regular spraying of pesticides to keep drainage channels clear or 'improved' land free from weeds. Pesticides and fertilisers not only filter into rhynes (through the field drains) but also stifle any orchids, marigolds and other wild flowers of the meadows which have survived the lower water levels. According to the NCC, half the lowland fens, valley and basin mires which existed in 1947 have been lost as a result of drainage, reclamation or chemical pollution; twenty-three of our forty rarest wetland plants are threatened with extinction.

Although the nineteenth-century rhynes increased the wildlife interest of the Levels, modern drainage jeopardises birds as much as plants. Without the willows, there are no nesting holes for owls or redstarts. Without the vegetation along the rhynes, there is no protection for the sedge warblers or whinchats. Without fish in the pesticide-polluted rhynes or rivers, there is no food for herons or kingfishers. All wading birds — and, in particular, their chicks — need moist conditions to bring worms and other invertebrate food to the surface. Ploughing the meadows for arable crops destroys

ABOVE LEFT: Wistman's Wood — possibly a remnant of Dartmoor's original tree cover

ABOVE CENTRE: Willsworthy ranges

ABOVE RIGHT: Clay tip near St Austell — one of the 'Cornish Alps'

the breeding ground of yellow wagtails. The overall effect upon birdlife of 'improving' wetlands was shown with stark clarity in a comparison of two areas in the Somerset Levels conducted by the RSPB. The area of traditional summer pasture had the ten main characteristic species of the Levels; the area which had been drained had only four – gone entirely were the echoing songs and sight of snipe, curlew, redshank, grasshopper warbler, sedge warbler and meadow pipit.

In the 1970s, modern drainage and intensive farming techniques threatened to destroy in a decade the fragile balance between man and nature which had allowed the wildlife of the wetlands to flourish. But the Levels were slowly finding some champions. Somerset County Council, declaring the Levels a 'special landscape area', established a 'demonstration

farm' and published a series of leaflets offering advice on how to pollard willows, maintain rhynes, meadows and other landscape features. The NCC, using powers under the 1981 Wildlife and Countryside Act, designated certain parts of the Levels as SSSIs. The RSPB bought chunks of unimproved West Sedgemoor.

Such attention was not always welcome locally. Some farmers burned effigies of NCC staff whom they accused of interfering with their livelihood. But many farmers wish to stay in dairying and the NCC payments for lost profits came to be accepted as a means of boosting farm income already under pressure from milk quotas. Qualification for payments under the ESA scheme depend upon more positive action to safeguard the landscape, but the omens are promising. Ten years of work by Somerset County Council and the NCC have given them considerable expertise. 'We know about

LEFT: Bourton-on-the-Water

ABOVE: Corfe Castle

how to manage rhynes in ways that will not only keep the wildlife but also fulfil their drainage function,' says the NCC's Brian Johnson. 'I believe we have achieved a credibility locally by showing that our methods are practical and can still give farmers a profit. We have also shown that converting reseeded grass to traditional sward, by changing water levels and by changing the herbicide/pesticide regime, we can help meadows begin to regain their wildlife. What we are recommending is changing a gear downwards — reducing input and output but maintaining profits.'

The second of the West Country's ESAs has been designated partially in order to save an even older landscape — that of Iron Age Britain. The rocky coast and granite headlands of West Penwith in the tip of Cornwall could scarcely be more dissimilar to the Somerset wetlands, apart from their archaeological importance. The moist soils of the Levels produced not only a thriving peat industry but also perfect conditions to preserve the world's oldest known trackways, dating from 4000 BC. The archaeological remains of West Penwith are somewhat younger, but more visible: chambered tombs, standing stones, abandoned villages and a network of tiny irregular fields dating back to the Bronze and Iron Age more than 2000 years ago. No other part of Britain, arguably

The Quantocks, near Broomfield, Somerset

The Somerset Levels is the largest surviving area of a landform which once covered a quarter of the British Isles

no part of Europe, has so many archaeological remains in so small an area. The hedgerows have not only a greater antiquity but reflect a distinctly Cornish character: built on bases of stone (no rooted hedgerow tree would survive the Atlantic gales that buffet this exposed peninsula) and covered by layers of turf, wild flowers and shrubs.

Small dairy farms traditionally posed no threat to these remains or the heathland which lies between the Celtic fields and the sheer cliffs. But fluctuating fortunes in dairying can cause difficulties. If profits are high, there is pressure to intensify; grassland or moors may be improved and traditional stone buildings demolished. If profits are low, hedges and buildings may be neglected, and there is a temptation to sow crops, which could lead to ancient monuments being ploughed. Either way, hedges may be removed – as, indeed, they were. The Cornwall Committee for Rescue Archaeology estimated that more hedges were destroyed in West Penwith between 1963 and 1976 than in the previous seventy-five years. Over 100 acres of moorland around the Iron Age village of Chysauster have been improved for pasture since 1980. Without the help promised for ESAs, a unique landscape and significant wildlife would be in grave jeopardy. But West Penwith is not the only part of the West Country where the

cold wind of farming economics now blows as gustily and unpredictably as the Atlantic gales. Away from the uplands and more remote regions, farmers lack the additional financial assistance accorded to what, in Euro-jargon, are called less favoured areas (see chapter 1, page 25).

The West Country is vulnerable in an age of agricultural retrenchment because it is heavily dependent on livestock farming. As a generalisation, the further west you go in

England, the more you see cattle in the fields with sheep on the hills and moors. The cream teas of Devonshire and Cornwall reflect the West Country's traditions as a stronghold of dairy farming. Mixed farming is also strong. This has helped keep the loss of hedgerows since the Second World War to barely half the national average for England; more hedgerows, banks and ditches survive in south-west England than in any other region. How dairy farmers will react in the long term to the effect of quotas on their milk production is as yet unclear. Mixed or dairy farming is necessary for the countryside to retain its patchwork image of hedge-bordered fields; cattle and sheep grazing is necessary to maintain the moorland blend of heather, grass and gorse. Change the nature or balance of farming and, as has been seen in Exmoor and the Somerset Levels, you change the countryside.

Some parts of the West Country have already been radically transformed within a generation. In Dorset two-thirds of the downland and heathland which existed in 1934 (themselves fragments of what existed in the nineteenth century) disappeared in the next forty years. Most of the downland was ploughed for arable crops or reseeded to produce improved grassland, grass almost totally devoid of the flowers, herbs, butterflies and birds found there previously. Anything between a third and a half of the archaeological sites along the South Dorset Ridgeway were destroyed in the process. The Dorset heathland is particularly revered by naturalists because the warmer climate (an important factor for wildlife generally in the region) attracts species not found elsewhere, apart from on the much smaller and atypical heaths of the Lizard peninsula. Yet half the heathland which existed in 1919 has disappeared under conifer plantations alone – so

ABOVE: The Somerset Levels, near Langport

ABOVE RIGHT: Zennor, Cornwall, showing a typical patchwork of hedge-bordered fields

much for the 'ancient permanence' of Thomas Hardy's 'Egdon Heath'. Agricultural reclamation has also taken its toll. Although more lowland heath remains here than in any other county other than Surrey, much of it is fragmented and the best is protected in special sites or reserves.

More generally in Dorset, the major change this century has been what a Countryside Commission survey called 'the dramatic swing from sheep and associated root crops to cattle and cereals'. Where livestock is still reared, the grazing is much more intensive than it used to be. The chalk hills of the Wiltshire downs and the limestone slopes of the Cotswolds have undergone a similar conversion from grassland to arable. Where sheep once reigned, corn is now king. Drive south from Stow-on-the-Wold to Northleach in the Cotswolds and you see arable fields on every side. Look north from Dorset's Cerne Abbas in summer and the characteristic dry valley of the chalk downlands is ablaze with golden wheat.

These random impressions are buttressed by statistics. According to the national landscape survey published by the Countryside Commission in 1986, the proportion of cultivated land in south-west England increased by almost half between 1947 and 1980. Wiltshire County Council reckons that half the chalk grassland of the Wiltshire downs was ploughed up between 1937 and 1971 – and the process

ABOVE: Studland Heath, Dorset

RIGHT: Worth Matravers, Dorset. Where livestock is still reared, grazing is much more intensive than it used to be

certainly did not stop there. Historically Wiltshire had fewer hedgerows than other south-western counties, but it has nevertheless paid a price in the cause of agriculture. At least a third of that county's rich heritage of 640 scheduled ancient monuments have been destroyed or badly damaged, with a similar story of devastation in the Cotswolds, where the distinctive stone walls have frequently fallen into decay. The NCC's survey of tree losses shows that almost half the semi-natural ancient woodland in Cornwall and Somerset (the first two western counties to be surveyed) has been destroyed or converted to plantations in the last fifty years.

The greater pace and scale of agricultural advance in eastern England has distracted attention from its impact upon the West Country. Yet ancient broad-leaved woods are dying here through lack of management and rare habitats disappearing through intensive cultivation. River pollution has increased, with farm effluent blamed by the Department of the Environment for 'alarming decreases' in salmon and trout

in rivers such as north Devon's Tamar and Torridge. In 1987 a parliamentary select committee attacked as ineffective the control of pollution exercised by Whitehall and water authorities; privatisation of water authorities could make national coordination of such controls as do exist even worse.

What is already alarming is that the uncertain economic future now threatens the areas of mixed farming so far relatively unscathed by modern methods. Squeezed by falling prices and high interest charges, some farmers may choose to identify production still further. As recently as 1985, the Devon regional newsletter of the Ministry of Agriculture was urging farmers to increase the stocking rate and the use of fertilisers for their existing livestock in order to free more land for arable crops. Farmers in tourist areas may join those

already in the bed-and-breakfast trade or seek to diversify their business in other ways. Project Silvanus, a West Country scheme to help farmers in Devon and Cornwall manage and market their woodlands, is seen by the government as an example of how farm forestry can be developed in the future. Some farmers, though, will go out of business, leaving their least fertile land to become semi-derelict scrub or to be used for unsightly rubbish dumps. Neglected or abandoned farmland may fall into the eager clutches of house-builders and other developers. Along motorways and in Avon, Gloucestershire and Wiltshire, this is already the major threat to the countryside.

All south-western counties have anxieties over development. The Cornish branch of the CPRE has opposed housing plans for the coast near Bude and out-of-town hypermarkets near Hayle and Penzance. In Dorset, there is intense pressure

on the 3 miles or so of open countryside between Yeovil and Sherborne and around the Poole–Bournemouth conurbation. In Somerset, sites between the motorway and Taunton have become prime targets for housing or supermarkets. But it is along the northern border of Somerset, where it joins Avon, that the situation begins to become acute. Bristol regards itself as Britain's fastest-growing major city. Not to be outdone in the superlatives league, Swindon in Wiltshire has been described as the fastest-growing town in Europe. Between 1961 and 1981 the population of Wiltshire grew at more than three times the national average, so that it has increased by 57 per cent in the last fifty years. Nor is there any sign that the county's growth is over. Another 38,500 houses are planned in the next decade, with 9000 houses – in effect, a

ABOVE: The Ridgeway. Where sheep once grazed, corn is now king

RIGHT: Hypermarkets near the M5

160

new town roughly the size of Salisbury – proposed for a single site north of Swindon.

One factor in this population spurt has been improved communications, notably motorways but also high-speed trains and relative proximity to airports. High-tech firms have clustered along the M4 from south Wales to Heathrow in such numbers as to invite comparison with California's 'silicon valley'. Bristol, at the fulcrum of communications on the M4 and M5, and long a centre for aerospace, is now the home for electronics companies such as Inmos and Hewlett-Packard. Motorways to the north and west of the city are effectively becoming its new boundaries. Junction 17 on the M5 was built in fields north of Filton airfield in the 1960s; twenty years on, it is a jungle of hypermarkets and brash shopping warehouses with a 'science park' a little to the north. But housing is transforming Bristol more than commerce. Between Patchway and the M4, plans have been approved for 8500 new houses. This is no minor in-filling, but developments large enough to be small towns in themselves: 8500 houses near Patchway, 4500 near Weston-super-Mare, 2000 near Clevedon, 1500 houses at Falfield.

A green belt is supposed to contain the sprawl, but already villages edge ever closer towards each other. Nailsea has spread southwards to within half a mile of Backwell, while new proposals would push it within a similar distance from Wraxall. A 2-mile gap beneath the wooded Tickenham Ridge is all that would then separate Nailsea from Clevedon. Meanwhile Kenn, which has won best-kept village prizes in its time, would become little more than a suburb of Clevedon if development proposals are approved. Much the same is happening north of the city, beyond even the line of the

ABOVE LEFT: Berkeley Castle, Avon

ABOVE: The Frome Valley could become yet another housing estate

RIGHT: Chipping Campden

M4. The Frome Valley near Winterbourne is one target for developers. At present a pleasant valley, with a riverside footpath much used by local residents, it could become yet another housing estate. Chipping Sodbury, once a self-contained village, has barely a mile of countryside between its western fringes and the Bristol conurbation.

Once covered by concrete or smothered by stone, the countryside has gone for ever. So long as land remains derelict in cities such as Bristol, there will rightly be battles over the developers' hunger for green-field building sites. In Wiltshire, it is Swindon, Chippenham and Trowbridge which are devouring the surrounding countryside; near Salisbury, there have even been plans to site a supermarket on meadows near the cathedral. In Gloucestershire, there is pressure around Cheltenham, Chipping Camden and Stroud, where the open space of Selsley Common has been threatened. In both counties, housing targets set for the 1990s were reached by the mid-1980s, often demanding extra spending on roads or schools that had long been sought by established rural communities. In Dorset, the county structure plan envisages 60,000 more houses by 1991, with two new 'towns' in the countryside north of Wimborne.

Towns such as Swindon are now pressing for buffer zones to stop their ceaseless sprawl, but problems are not confined to the mega-developments beloved of house-builders; small projects, perhaps of no more than a dozen houses, can irrevocably alter the character of rural communities. They may be villages within commuting distance of nearby towns, such as Broad Hinton and Chiseldon near Swindon, Painswick between Gloucester and Stroud or Kington Langley near Chippenham. Or they may be tourist attractions such as Lower Slaughter in the Cotswolds, where the River Windrush trickles down the centre of an immaculately spruce village street. At Puncknowle in Dorset twenty-six new houses represented a 25 per cent increase in the size of the village. In south Wiltshire, a county structure plan envisages each

parish having an average of thirty-four new houses over ten years. 'Such policies constitute a blank cheque for speedy suburbanisation,' says the Wiltshire branch of the CPRE.

More houses generate more traffic on roads which were once simple country lanes. New developments also impose great strain on public services, with additional schools, medical facilities and police services tending to lag behind the house-builders. Sometimes it is not just the number of houses but their style which offends. In the larger developments, it is the architectural monotony which sometimes repels: 'Twinned with Legoland' was one graffiti-writer's verdict on Yate, a 1960s development outside Bristol. In smaller projects, the fashion for 'executive-style dwellings' adds nothing to a village's vernacular tradition and mostly puts the new houses out of reach for local people. If too many houses go to people who don't work in the village (or who have retired) this can intensify the problems of rural life.

Nowadays the life of villages rarely revolves around the local farms. The trend towards arable farming since the war has meant that farms have lost much of their workforce. Livestock farming has also become far more dependent upon machines than men. Houses no longer required by farm

labourers have been snapped up as weekend cottages. Their owners often bring a superficial prosperity to an area, as they may be better able to repair their properties in traditional styles – Dorset, for instance, now boasts twenty-eight registered thatchers. But too many second homes or retirement homes can mean too few families to keep the village school alive. Once the school goes, families drift to the bigger settlements. The young people may be forced to leave the village in order to find work or houses they can afford. The village shop then founders, particularly if supermarket chains offer a free bus service to their 'super stores', as happens around Taunton. It may be the only bus that calls, if the village does not have enough active residents to justify regular services in these profit-conscious times. Jobs as well as houses are required if villages are to survive the new agricultural age.

ABOVE: Lower Slaughter and the River Windrush

RIGHT: Yate: 'twinned with Legoland'

LEFT: Opencast mining is planned in the Forest of Dean near Parkend

ABOVE: A new nuclear-power station at Winfrith will devastate the surrounding heathland

ABOVE RIGHT: Otterton

Conflict between the need for jobs and the demand for recreation in the countryside can be as fundamental as that between modern farming and nature conservation. Opencast mining at Oakenhill near Parkend in the Forest of Dean will do nothing for the environment, but it will provide jobs in a traditional mining area. Quarries blight Dartmoor and the Purbeck hills, among other places, but local people need the work as much as the country needs (some of) the minerals. Whether or not the country also needs new nuclear-power stations at Winfrith Heath in Dorset and Hinckley on the Somerset coast is debatable. Certainly, the four giant cooling towers proposed for Winfrith would devastate the surrounding heathland; yet there will be people living locally as anxious to secure jobs there as others are concerned about questions of cost and safety. Economic gains should be balanced against environmental losses – not least because it is the natural beauty of the countryside which has established tourism as a prime source of income for the West Country.

Sometimes bodies such as national park authorities are accused of putting their visitors' interests before those of the residents. Often the interests coincide. Removing electricity and telephone wires from a village such as Otterton in Devon makes it more attractive for tourist and local alike. Dorset and Somerset have set up countryside units which have overseen widespread tree-planting, often to replace elms. Although no substitute for managing existing woodlands, the programmes have been deservedly popular. County councils, the Countryside Commission, the National Trust and other organisations have done much to enhance the countryside of south-west England in the last fifteen years. Canals have been restored, country parks and picnic sites established, footpaths improved (including the creation of the country's

165

longest long-distance path, along the coast from Minehead in Somerset to Poole, 515 miles away in Dorset), visitor services developed to help people understand and appreciate what they see. Farm museums have helped to bridge the gulf between town and country. National agreement over common land offers hope of greater access to areas such as Bodmin Moor, where fencing and limited rights of way impede easy access to parts of the moor, including Brown Willy, at 1377 feet the highest point in Cornwall. The Blackdown Hills in Somerset have been earmarked as a future AONB – giving them greater (if incomplete) protection from future development – and the Cotswolds AONB will be extended.

These and other achievements have appealed as much to the West Country's own inhabitants as to the annual influx of tourists from further afield. Of course, there are problems. Traffic still clogs Dartmoor, despite the national park's road schemes; the stone circle of Avebury and the castle of Corfe remain desperately in need of bypasses; riversides, sand dunes and heaths are still being worn away by the tramp of feet. And more fundamental threats loom. Housing development, agricultural uncertainty and recreation pressures could transform the West Country – from the rocky shore of Land's End to the Midlands fringes of the Cotswolds, from the Forest of Dean on the Welsh border to the rolling Wessex downs. The risks are there, but so, still, is a countryside as rich and varied as any in England.

166

Stone circle at Avebury

5

EASTERN ENGLAND

Nowhere has the once familiar landscape of England been more extensively transformed than in its eastern counties. This could have been said more than 300 years ago, when Dutch engineers revived the visionary schemes of the Romans to drain the fens for agriculture.

Or 150 years ago, when John Clare, the ploughman poet of Cambridgeshire, decried the enclosure of open commons into hedge-lined fields. But today we are witnessing an era of change as dramatic as any in the past. 'Instead of small fields lined by hedgerows and trees, we now have fields of up to 500 acres,' says Paul Edwards, director of the Suffolk Preservation Society. 'One field I know contains the sites of four former farmsteads!'

This new agricultural landscape bears no similarity to that lost in the years of enclosure which so saddened John Clare. What Clare evokes in his poetry is a land of open commons, with trees and rough grassland, where flowers blossom and birds sing. What farmers have created since the Second World War, at the behest of politicians in Whitehall and Brussels, is an arable prairie where not only flowers and birds but animals and people are more rarely seen. The flatness of much of the land makes this twentieth-century agricultural revolution even more dramatic. Often as far as the eye can see, there are no trees, no hills and no buildings: just an endless 'field' of grain, with the occasional yellow blaze of oil-seed rape in summer, or the furrowed earth in winter crossed by electricity or telephone cables.

Paradoxically, it is the fertility of the soil which has encouraged the intensive arable farming which now makes so much land look bleak. 'The bread basket of Britain' is how some farmers describe the eastern counties, with Lincolnshire also cultivating substantial proportions of the country's cauliflowers, sprouts and other vegetables among a larderful of

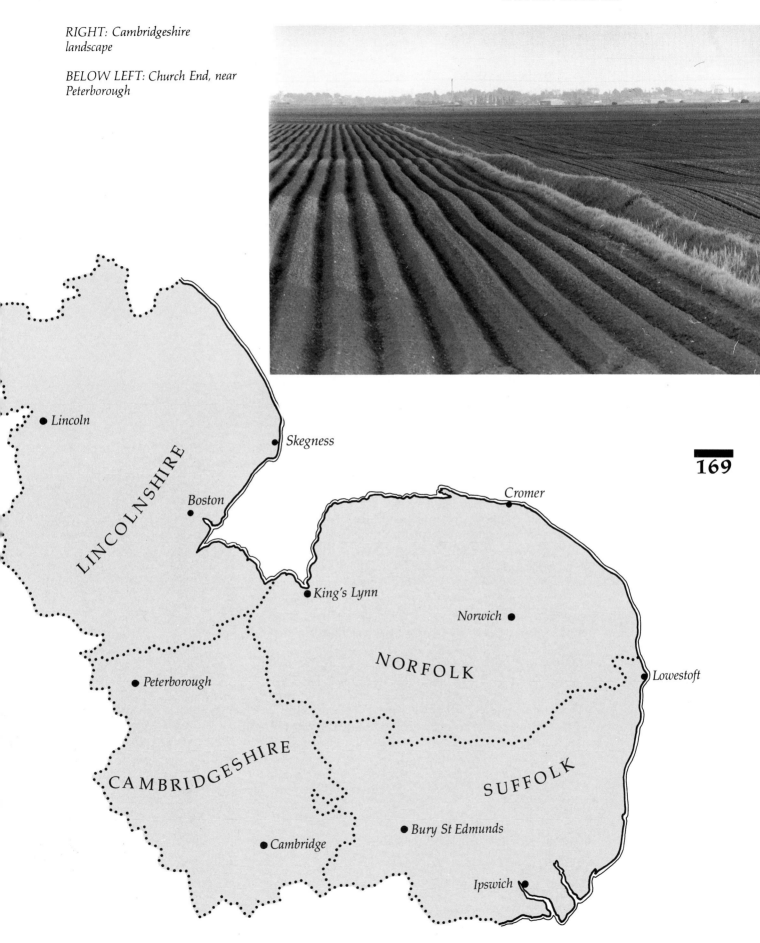

RIGHT: Cambridgeshire
landscape

BELOW LEFT: Church End, near
Peterborough

169

produce. Half the country's bulb fields can be found in Lincoln-shire, around Spalding. But the goal of ever-greater efficiency has not only levelled hedgerows and uprooted trees on land that has long been sown with crops; it is also held to justify the encroachment of arable farming upon traditional grazing pastures. Among the areas coming under the plough have been the chalk downland of the Lincolnshire Wolds, the marshes of the Norfolk Broads, the grassland of the Suffolk river valleys and the heaths of Breckland and the Suffolk coast.

LEFT: *The flatness of much of the land makes the effect of the agricultural revolution even more dramatic*

BELOW: *Bulb fields at Spalding*

BELOW RIGHT: *Flatford Mill, Dedham*

170

Sometimes the issues which excite conservationists seem too rarified or specialist to arouse comparable concern amongst the general public. Rightly or wrongly, the plight of a rare species of, say, spider endangered by loss of habitat will never have the impact of threatened or impaired landscape. Yet in the Suffolk River Valleys and the Lincoln-shire Wolds, for example, the interests of experts and day trippers often coincide. It is areas such as these which accord more with our general perception of beauty than the treeless vistas which increasingly surround them. It is such places which nourish the wild flowers, butterflies and birds which give life to the countryside, whether or not you can identify a single species. In these areas, too, people traditionally have had greater rights of access. Anything which erodes their character or diversity exemplifies the present crisis.

Apart from the huge agricultural impact on the region, previously small and rural villages around cities such as Cambridge and Norwich are becoming little more than suburbs for commuters. Alternatively, the loss of agricultural jobs, country bus services and village schools is draining the life-blood of more remote communities. Along stretches of shoreline designated as 'heritage coasts' for their unspoiled beauty, plans exist for nuclear-power stations, military instal-lations and ritzy yachting marinas. Tourist coaches crawl down narrow lanes to 'Constable country' in Dedham Vale, while boats clog the waterways in the Norfolk Broads.

The broads epitomise many of the problems facing the countryside today, as well as some of the attempts by national and local agencies to overcome them. For many people, the broads mean no more than a place for messing about in boats – each year the 130 miles of rivers and navigable lakes in Broadland accommodate up to 750,000 visitors. Some 200,000 hire boats for the week, 400,000 take trips on passenger boats, and 150,000 are estimated to use private vessels, over half of which are now motor-powered. Many of the waterways are overcrowded, with queues forming at narrow bridges such as those at Wroxham and Ludham. But sometimes, as along the River Bure between Coltishall and Horning, congestion is caused solely by volume of traffic. On land, too, Broadland villages such as Potter Heigham have been swamped by crowds. Communities which once centred upon their quay or staithe now sprawl outwards, with tatty shops along the streets and ugly chalets along the waterfront.

Not all Broadland villages have succumbed to tourist pressure. Stokesby, Ranworth and Belaugh are among those which retain a charm derived from not only their location but from the use of local building materials: clay pantiles or reed and sedge for roofs, red clay bricks for walls and flint for churches. Ranworth is also one of the few places where landlubbers can see something of a broad. Nearby is another. The footpath along the southern shore of the Bure opposite Horning leads downstream to Cockshoot Broad; here you

will find a broad very different from those used as highways for boats. It is also very different from how it appeared in the early 1980s.

Cockshoot Broad is less than half a mile long and is not navigable. In 1980 the water was in places only 6 inches deep and the broad was ecologically dead. Today wildlife is returning to Cockshoot. The renaissance of this tiny dead-end broad, described later in the chapter, assumes a significance beyond its size because its problems were typical of those which alarmed the Nature Conservancy Council (NCC) and Countryside Commission. 'Unless action is taken soon,' said the Commission in 1983, 'the Broads may be damaged beyond repair.' What the Commission and others perceived to be the threat to the broads themselves was part of a wider concern about the area. Broadland includes grazing marshes, woodland and fens as well as broads and river. And it is the confluence of these landscapes which makes Broadland attractive to wildlife. Among its nature reserves and sites of special scientific interest (SSSIs) are two of the thirteen UK reserves rated as internationally important by the 1971 Ramsar International Wetlands Convention. But the need to designate 'sites' or 'reserves' has been heightened by the changes occurring to Broadland as a whole.

That man should be the cause of the most recent changes is ironical since it was man who created the broads themselves. Until 1951 they were thought to be remnants of former river estuaries, but geological detective work proved that they originated from holes dug for a medieval peat industry. Some holes! Fritton Lake is 2 miles long, 200 yards wide and 15 feet deep. From the thirteenth century, sea levels rose, flooding the peat workings to create shallow lakes, many of which were subsequently linked to rivers by navigation

LEFT: *Potter Heigham*

ABOVE: *Cockshoot Broad*

channels. The broads have shrunk in size, perhaps by as much as two thirds, as dead vegetation and sediment silts the lakes. But, according to Oliver Rackham's *History of the Countryside*, this silting is now five times as rapid as it was in the nineteenth century with consequences far beyond those of size. He writes:

Since 1965 most of the plant and animal life has disappeared. The Broads are no longer the Paradise of my childhood: plants such as the water soldier are nearly extinct, and even frogbit and hornwort are rarities. Fish, insects and birds have similarly declined.

In places, the silting is ten times worse than a century ago. Even the visitor whose memory goes back no more than thirty years will notice the lack of waterlilies, reedbeds and other aquatic plants which were once features of Broadland. These provide food and shelter for insects and invertebrates, which in turn feed fish, birds and animals such as otters. Only four of the forty-one major broads now possess the clear water, lush vegetation and varied wildlife which existed in most of them before 1900; thirty-one broads are virtually dead.

The decline of the broads has accelerated since the Second World War. The main cause has been the pollution of the water by phosphates from sewage-treatment works and nitrates from fertilisers used on farmland. Although phosphates and nitrates are both 'natural' plant nutrients, the greater volumes draining into the water have transformed the broads. At first the extra nutrients encouraged a richer growth of vegetation, albeit of a coarser kind. But as the nutrients continued to increase, they produced conditions suitable for millions of microscopic plants called algae. These turned the water a cloudy, muddy green, not unlike pea soup, and shaded out the partially submerged aquatic plants. As the algae die, they add to the mud lying beneath the water and encourage the silting of the waterways. To make matters worse, the 'wash' from motorboats has eroded the increasingly reedless river banks by up to 3 yards in ten years, adding still more mud to the murky waters of the once crystal-clear broads.

173

Only the handful of broads which are isolated from the main waterways (thereby avoiding motorboats and sewage) have retained anything of their pre-twentieth century quality. Upton Broad is one such example. Attempts to save the rest of the broads were hindered by the lack of any overall authority responsible for the area. Broadland was not among the national parks set up in the 1940s and 1950s, despite strong claims for its inclusion. In 1978 local councils established a Broads Authority which, with Countryside Commission backing, began to assess the extent of environmental damage and what could be done about it. A decade later the authority is due, in 1988, to be granted status equivalent to that of a national park as a measure of not only its achievements but also of the scale of the threat facing the broads.

Cockshoot Broad is one of its successes. In 1982 it was dammed and separated from the phosphate-enriched River

BELOW: Upton Broad

Bure. But this in itself would have been insufficient to ensure its salvation since in summer phosphates are released from mud already in the broad. So 40,000 cubic metres of mud was pumped from the broad – with dramatic results. More than twelve species of aquatic plants are growing again, and the broad hums once more with the buzz of insects and the call of birds. In other broads, too, there have been improvements as a result of phosphate reduction at sewage-treatment works. Research has shown that certain artificial water plants can stimulate enormous numbers of microscopic animals known as zooplankton which are capable of removing the algae from a broad: harness them and you have a potent force for restoration. Experiments are also being conducted by the broads authority to combat bank erosion, ranging from artificial protection of vulnerable shores to controls on the numbers and speed of motorboats on particular broads.

Despite such encouraging developments, the outlook for many broads remains grim. In terms of overall policy, it is by no means certain that the revamped Broads Authority proposed by the government will have sufficient powers over navigation or water quality to ensure that the objective of 'conserving and enhancing the Broads for ever' can be achieved. In terms of specific action, dredging as at Cockshoot is expensive, and the cost of phosphate reduction at the sewage works is also high. Although the creation of the new broads authority should mean that extra funds are available, it is unrealistic to expect the pollution of decades to be reversed overnight – particularly as the release of nitrates washed off farmland continues unabated and uncontrolled. Some waterways, such as those of the River Yare, have such high nitrate levels that the Broads Authority believes water plants may never return – even if phosphates were reduced from all the sewage works. Nonetheless, the example of Cockshoot Broad proves that, given the cash and inclination, some life can be restored to this unique maze of winding rivers and tree-lined lakes; likewise, the restoration of Broad Fen on the River Ant shows that fenland, too, can be revived after fifty years or more of decline.

The fens are waterlogged areas where the reed, sedge and grasses were traditionally cut to provide thatch for roofs or hay for cattle. Regular harvesting kept the fenland open and provided an ideal misty habitat for birds such as the bittern, marsh harrier or bearded tit. The Broadland fens are almost the last refuge in Britain for the swallowtail butterfly, while the fen orchid is among their rare plants. But, as demand for thatch declined and marsh hay was supplanted by other animal feeds, harvesting became less frequent and the fens began to be invaded by scrub woodland. Left to itself this natural succession would transform the open fen into a wet woodland with greatly reduced wildlife and landscape interest. At Broad Fen the dykes which gave access to the fen were cleared and dredged, reed and sedge beds restored by mowing, and trees coppiced by conservation volunteers and Manpower Services Commission (MSC) teams working under Broads Authority guidance. Within four years species which

174

RIGHT: High nitrate levels in the River Yare mean that water plants may never return

BELOW: Broad Fen

had been absent for decades, such as bog pimpernel and the white-flowering grass of parnassus, were growing again at Broad Fen. Work is continuing here (now aided by a management agreement with the landowner) and at other fens to restore or retain the traditional landscape.

Waterways, fens and alder carr woodlands are three of Broadland's four faces; the fourth is that of the grazing marshes, and it is this which pushed the broads to the front line of the conservation battles of the 1980s. The small village of Halvergate, north of Reedham, has become identified with both the threat to the grazing marshes as a whole and the pioneering scheme which disarmed the danger, at least in the short term. At first sight, the marshes are perhaps the least picturesque of Broadland landscapes. Yet they possess a beguiling quality all their own. In spite of their semi-natural origins (undrained, they would be fenland) the marshes have a wildness rare in lowland England.

The marshlands were formed out of mudflats and fens. In the seventeenth century windpumps were introduced to control water levels and, although now replaced by electric pumps, many windpumps remain. These pumps, along with a few willow trees, are the only breaks in the seemingly

LEFT: *Halvergate, where the grazing marshes scheme was pioneered*

ABOVE: *Farm buildings near Thetford*

endless marsh criss-crossed by dykes beneath huge skies – apart, that is, from cattle grazing serenely in summer. But in the last twenty years approximately a third of the grazing marshes have been converted to crops. The rate of conversion increased when Britain joined the EEC. Cereals were more profitable than cattle-rearing, particularly when farmers could obtain grants to install deep drains and convert their land to crops. Indeed, farmers were encouraged by government agencies to do so.

The switch to arable farming requires electric pumps to drain the land, and these need unsightly powerlines. Some drainage dykes are filled in and others deepened. More than 100 water plants have been identified in marshland dykes, but these won't grow if the ditches are too deep or the sides too steep for sunlight to reach the bottom. The flora is further damaged when fertilisers and pesticides are applied to the fields or when slurry accidentally spills into drainage channels. Gaunt, prefabricated buildings spring up to store the crops and concrete roads laid for the new farm machinery. Visually the results are unattractive; for wildlife, they are catastrophic.

During the summer, traditional grazing marshes provide nesting grounds for a wide variety of birds. The breeding populations of the mute swan, shoveller, oystercatcher, lapwing, redshank and yellow wagtail have regional or national importance. Most of these birds build their nests on the sides of dykes or in the grass itself. Some species can nest in arable areas, but they still need the marshes for food. In winter, large numbers of waders and wildfowl feed on the marshes, among them bewick swan, mallard and golden plover. According to the Broads Authority, it is likely that any major drainage scheme would result in the loss of most of the important birdlife.

Everything that makes the Broadland marshes unique – whether for landscape or wildlife – therefore depends upon the continuance of grazing. Yet everything that was being done by the Ministry of Agriculture, the Anglian Water Authority and the local drainage boards up until the mid-1980s encouraged the conversion to arable crops. That the

environmental destruction of the marshes was heavily sub-sidised from public funds fuelled the anger of conservationists, largely led by the Council for the Protection of Rural England (CPRE). The requirement under the 1981 Wildlife and Countryside Act to make payments in excess of £100,000 in the form of management agreements to compensate farmers for lost profits if they abandoned notional arable plans – in other words, to do nothing they hadn't done previously – further heightened the controversy. Eventually, a broads grazing marsh conservation scheme was introduced in 1985, by which farmers were paid £50 a year for each acre which they managed according to strict guidelines, including the management of grazing. The scheme began with the Hal-vergate Marshes and Haddiscoe Island but was later extended to the north and south, even into Suffolk alongside the River Waveney.

Ninety per cent of the eligible land was covered by the scheme, forestalling, at least in the short term, further con-versions to arable land. Its success reflected the desire of many farmers to maintain traditional methods, if at all possible. Not every farmer wants to spend all his days on a tractor, and not every scrap of land warrants conversion to arable, especially at a time when cereal harvests are piling up in EEC grain mountains. The ethos of the grazing marsh scheme was profoundly different from that of the earlier management agreements based on the principle of lost profits. These had been essentially negative as well as costly. The broads authority found that farmers themselves were also critical of a system which gave enormous compensation to a few but nothing to those who conformed with society's wishes. The grazing marsh scheme offered positive support for livestock practices which maintained the traditional landscape and wild-life.

The Halvergate scheme was spearheaded by the Country-side Commission, which won the support of the Ministry of Agriculture. Its success, allied to vigorous parliamentary lobbying by conservation groups such as the CPRE, was a significant element in persuading the government to adopt the principle as a national policy for environmentally sensitive areas (ESAs). The concept required much argument by Michael Jopling, then Agriculture Minister, within Europe since it involved financial support for farmers in areas which were potentially fertile. But ministerial persistence prevailed: in 1985 the principle of ESAs was authorised as EEC policy under Article 19 of the Agriculture Structures Regulation, and a year later it was enshrined as a key element of the 1986 Agriculture Act.

The ESA principle was a historic departure from previous policy. For the first time the Ministry of Agriculture accepted direct financial responsibility for conservation-minded farming. Until then, conservation or compensation had been founded by environmental agencies. Also for the first time, financial support for farmers in certain areas would be linked to conservation rather than production. The objectives of the scheme were, first, to conserve and enhance the natural beauty

BELOW: *River Waveney tidal creek*

177

of the designated area; second, to conserve its flora, fauna, geological and geographical features; and, third, to protect buildings and other objects of historic interest. Conservationists welcomed it warmly, although they tended to see the scheme as a first step to something more ambitious for the country as a whole. Then the arguments began about which areas would be designated – and how many.

The ministry asked the Countryside Commission and the NCC to suggest possible areas in England and Wales. To its ill-disguised irritation, the two government-funded agencies initially identified 152 areas in England and Wales that were endangered by modern agricultural practices. These were reduced to forty-six – including Suffolk's river valleys and coastal heaths, Breckland and two Cambridgeshire valleys, the Nene and Ouse Washes – but even the final shortlist of fourteen was criticised by the Ministry of Agriculture as far too high. However, Mike Taylor, head of the Countryside Commission's conservation branch, says, 'They are all at risk in one way or another and need assistance.'

The conservation agencies see the concept of ESAs as setting an example for a new era of farming. William Wilkinson, chairman of the NCC, says, 'We hope that the development of European Community agricultural policy will move in a direction in which conservation is less dependent on the designation of special areas, but more broadly based in encouraging conservation management on all farms, wherever they be located. With this in mind, we hope that the development of the ESA concept will provide mechanisms for conservation which could, in due course, be extended to the whole of the farmed countryside.'

The Ministry of Agriculture takes a more modest approach, not least because the annual budget allocated to ESAs in their first year of operation was £6 million for nine areas – five in England, two in Scotland and one each in Wales and Northern Ireland. This sum will be doubled for the financial year 1988–89 as one of the measures announced by Michael Jopling in February 1987 to deal with the problems posed by surplus farm production. Even so, argues the ministry, European regulations restrict ESA support to specific areas. Although it agrees that the concept may offer lessons for the wider countryside, the ministry insists that ESA grants cannot be applied across the board as the NCC and organisations such as the CPRE would like.

The initial group of ESAs came into existence in 1987. Farmers were offered five-year agreements to pursue the kind of farming practices which maintain traditional landscapes. These practices were spelled out in some detail after consultations between officials of the ministry, conservation organisations and farming bodies. The scheme was voluntary, although fully endorsed by the National Farmers' Union (NFU). Payments varied around the country and in some cases there were two levels of grant, depending upon the extent of the commitment to conservation. The lower level was relatively undemanding, since the ministry made no secret of its intention to persuade as many farmers as possible

ABOVE: Ouse Washes – a rejected candidate for ESA status

RIGHT: River Stour, Dedham

to do something. 'We are hoping to get more than half the land,' said one official. 'Ministers want a good turnout!' There was no obligation on farmers to prepare comprehensive plans since the ministry felt any bureaucracy would both deter and delay participation. Conservationists regretted this, as they did the continuance of production grants; farmers could conceivably get conservation grants for one part of their holdings, while intensifying production on another. The ministry says decisions on production grants will take into account the factors which prompted ESA designation; even if a farmer in an ESA has stayed outside the scheme, further intensification is unlikely to be encouraged in the area. Nonetheless ESAs are excluded from the areas proposed for the extra protection of landscape conservation orders – unless they are in a national park or designated as a SSSI.

Three regions of eastern England were among the fourteen shortlisted as ESAs: the Norfolk Broads, the Suffolk River Valleys and Breckland, the sandy heathland along the Suffolk–Norfolk border. Inevitably, the Broadland grazing marsh scheme was adopted to become one of the first ESAs to be designated. Here, as farmers knew what was involved, ministers got their good turnout – and, nationally, farmers

owning 78 per cent of the land in the first five English ESAs applied to join the scheme in their first year – but it is unlikely that the ESA grants will entice many arable farmers to convert anything but the most marginal arable land back to grazing pasture. Even though farmers in an ESA are offered more than the £50 per acre of the grazing marsh scheme, the financial reward remains modest when cereals were yielding profits in 1987 of around £150 an acre more than livestock. Many farmers' decisions will continue to be shaped as much by the overall policy for agricultural support as by the support offered by the ESA scheme. However, ESAs are a valuable test bed for conservation-oriented farming, in addition to the more immediate protection they offer for specific areas. And the other two eastern areas in the original shortlist – the Suffolk River Valleys and Breckland – were included in the second wave of ESAs to begin operation in 1988. The valleys matter because so much of Suffolk has become the domain of arable farmers. The protection of what remains of Breckland is equally critical because so much lowland heath has already disappeared.

ABOVE: Thetford Heath

The ploughing of the old grasslands means that the Suffolk valleys are the last refuge of the landscape captured in the paintings of John Constable. The crowds who come to visit Flatford Mill and the rest of Dedham Vale expect to see the Stour Valley much as it was 150 years ago. This is unrealistic for nature is never static; trees have grown, for instance, where none existed in Constable's day. In Dedham Vale, hedgerows have been removed, trees allowed to decay and meadows converted to arable – this despite its designation as an area of outstanding natural beauty (AONB) and the Constable connection. A survey of the area in the late 1970s concluded that the traditional countryside would not survive without immediate and sustained action 'to reverse the degeneration resulting from the lack of management of existing trees and hedges and the low level of tree planting in the area'. Since then a county council project has sought to help farmers maintain the landscape and to avert a drainage scheme in what it calls 'one of the most famous pastoral areas of England'. Other river valleys have not been so lucky.

Because their slopes are more difficult to plough and their bottoms harder to drain, river valleys are not ideal for arable production. But surveys of the Waveney and Deben Valleys showed that up to a third of their grassland was lost between 1967 and 1984. As in so much of England, the beauty of the valleys stemmed from the way they were farmed: cattle and sheep grazing in meadows, beside meandering rivers and in fields bordered by hedgerows. Even if the grassland has been improved by reseeding – thereby eliminating most of its wildlife value – the valleys offer a visual diversity to Suffolk which is rendered all the more valuable for its increasing rarity. 'There is little room for compromise if the variety of the landscape is to be kept,' wrote Edwin Barritt, Suffolk's county planning officer in 1983. The county council and the Farming and Wildlife Advisory Group (FWAG) have

appointed farm conservation advisers who believe that the climate of opinion among farmers in the mid-1980s is markedly different from that which existed a decade earlier. Hedgerows and trees are being planted, ponds dug or restored. But without ESA status, there were few cash incentives for farmers to turn their allegedly greater sympathy for conservation into action.

Breckland was not the only tract of heathland in East Anglia to be nominated for protection as an ESA. Unfortunately, Suffolk's coastal heaths, known as the Sandlings, never made the final shortlist. The destruction of the Dorset heaths has been widely mourned, but the losses in Suffolk and Norfolk have been proportionately greater. Heathland is in decline throughout England, so what remains becomes all the more precious. It has a wildlife which can be sustained nowhere else – the nightjar and Dartford warbler, among the birds – and an openness which has enabled centuries of virtually unrestrained public access. In lowland England, which lacks the moors and open fells of the uplands, this freedom to wander is reason enough to regret the loss of heathland – and to save what is left.

Although heaths provide habitats for some of the same plants as are found on moors, notably ling heather, these species are growing here in drier conditions than their upland counterparts. Heathland soils tend to be acid and thin, sometimes chalky (as at Newmarket) but more often sandy, as in Breckland and the Suffolk Sandlings, the most extensive areas of heath which survive in eastern England. The thin soils enabled prehistoric man to clear the woodland cover relatively easily and many of today's heaths have become archaeologically significant zones of early cultivation and settlement. The Neolithic flint mines of Grimes Graves gave Breckland Britain's first industrialised community.

Working these thin, acid soils was never very rewarding. As more fertile land was cleared of trees, the heaths were turned over to sheep grazing. Such land became the basis of many commons upon which people acquired grazing rights. Rabbits reared for their fur and meat also grazed the heaths. This grazing, along with other customers' rights to collect firewood, helped to prevent the growth of trees and established the distinctive heathland vegetation of heather and gorse, with patches of grass, that we know today. Or as we knew yesterday. Four-fifths of the Sandlings heaths have been lost this century. In Norfolk the heaths have virtually disappeared, apart from in Breckland, where just under 79,000 acres in 1934 had dwindled to barely 11,000 acres in 1980. Some of the largest tracts which survive here do so through the unlikely agency of the Ministry of Defence: Breckland's rough, open landscape is apparently ideal for training soldiers and it is only this which has repelled the assaults of farmers and foresters. (One square kilometre of the army's Breckland training grounds has yielded 307 different species of plants, more than any other area in the country.)

Heaths have been in decline for 200 years as crop rotation improved their less fertile soils; Norfolk gave its name to one

181

BELOW: *Military training area on Thetford Heath*

such system of rotation. As sheep grazing becomes less attractive – and as heather and rabbits have long since ceased to be regarded as 'crops' – the heaths are encroached upon by bracken and eventually by trees such as birch. This natural progression has been used to provide a spurious argument for annexation by the Forestry Commission: half of the Sandlings and Breckland were submerged under alien conifer plantations. House-building, airfields, power stations and golf courses have taken their toll of heathland, so all that we have left are relics of a landscape that has no apparent modern role.

Yet we would be poorer for its loss. For the naturalist, the concern may focus upon the threat to heathland's distinctive wildlife. For walkers, it may be the loss of access to open land. For everyone, concern should spring from a recognition that the hallmark of the English countryside is its diversity. Heathland is yet another semi-natural landscape which needs to be 'managed' if it is to survive. The justification for such management should be measured more in terms of aesthetics than of economics. How, after all, do you put a price upon the survival of a rare butterfly or the right to walk freely where our ancestors have roamed for 4000 years? Suffolk County Council, backed by the Countryside Commission, has launched a project to save the Sandlings, with MSC teams deployed to cut back the bracken, cut or burn the heather and establish firebreaks. Similar work should now be possible in Breckland – now that it has won ESA status.

Breckland is more concentrated than the Sandlings and more varied. Its features include chalky grasslands, sand dunes mysteriously blown inland, nineteenth-century 'hedges' of contorted Scots pine and river valleys, as well as the conifers and heathland. ESA designation should encourage sheep grazing in order to retain the heaths, among other measures to maintain Breckland's unique character. Part of this character is now wooded: the once treeless Breckland is now the Forestry Commission's largest lowland forest. The Commission has provided trails at several locations in what it calls Thetford Forest. Rights of way are relatively few elsewhere in Breckland, particularly since so much is used for military training. Lord Melchett, a Norfolk farmer and former president of the Ramblers' Association, has attacked this lack of public access: 'Norfolk is already in the deplorable position of having only half the average length of footpath per square mile compared to the rest of the country. Now we have examples of forests being sold off by the Forestry Commission and the public being excluded.'

Eastern England generally is regarded as poor in footpaths. Long-distance walker and author John Hillaby wrote after one trek that 'though I have walked from John O'Groats to Land's End I have never found anything like the obstructions that I found in Lincolnshire'. That was in 1983, since when, the CPRE says, Lincolnshire County Council has increased its footpath staff from two to a princely five. Other eastern counties also draw fire from rambling activists, despite

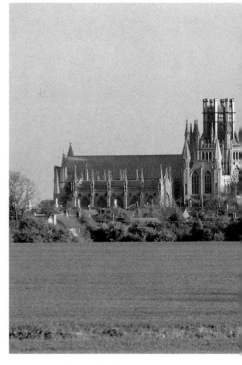

ABOVE: Ely Cathedral

schemes like Suffolk County Council's paths in the Gipping Valley, the long-distance Peddars' Way and coastal paths.

It is the ordinary rights of way, like the so-called wider countryside, which are neglected if too much attention is concentrated upon showpiece schemes, be they waymarked walks or ESAs. Yet most of England is wider countryside. There is no national park in eastern England, although, as already mentioned, the Norfolk Broads authority is promised status comparable to that of a national park in 1988. Nor did designation as AONBs prevent agricultural inroads into Dedham Vale or the Lincolnshire Wolds. The rest of the East Anglian countryside lacks even the deterrent of bad publicity which usually attends changes in AONBs, so it is here that the impact of the twentieth-century agricultural revolution has been greatest.

Eastern England first grew rich on wool. The wealth of the medieval wool trade became a matter of local pride, producing almshouses for the poor, timber-framed town houses for the merchants and great churches for the community. The spires of the churches still draw the eye across the mostly flat countryside, whether they be cathedrals as at Ely and Lincoln or unexpectedly magnificent parish churches as at Lavenham and Long Melford. But eastern England had become the arable heartland of Britain long before the Second World War prompted the government's drive to increase domestic food production. Its climate is drier than in the west – a requirement for arable crops – and the land mostly flat and fertile. Sheep-rearing retreated to the less fertile areas of the country, so that by 1947 almost 70 per cent of East Anglia was already arable land, compared to just 27 per cent of England and Wales as a whole. Since then the proportion of arable land has increased to almost three quarters of the total area, a statistically small increase which masks the significance of the changes which have occurred.

Bigger machines, better fertilisers and improved drainage enabled East Anglian farmers to capitalise upon their natural advantages of climate and soil. Wheat yields rose faster in the eastern counties than anywhere in Britain. Average farm sizes are larger, partly to make more economic use of costly new machinery; holdings of several thousand acres are common. The same expansionary ethic increased the temptation for farmers to nibble away at the more marginal land. Some such areas had long since been converted to crops – fenland, for instance, had been drained for centuries, leaving Wicken Fen in Cambridgeshire as the last extensive relic of a landscape which once covered almost 700,000 acres of East Anglia. Further north in Lincolnshire, the chalk downland of the wolds has been steadily converted to arable production since the Second World War. Previously it had been grazed by sheep and, on the lower slopes, cattle. Now in many places, as near Welton-le-Wold, the springy downland turf has all but disappeared. Where slopes remain unploughed, lack of grazing has allowed scrub to develop. Thus here, and in the river valleys and heathland of East Anglia, the apparently small growth in the proportion of land devoted

BELOW: *Wicken Fen has been restored and provided with walkways and nature trails*

183

to crops has devoured areas of great scenic beauty. Although the losses here are the most controversial, they are none-theless dramatic throughout the eastern counties of England.

A Countryside Commission survey showed that hedge-rows disappeared faster in East Anglia than any other region of England between 1969 and 1985. Roughly a third of all hedgerows have gone since 1947, although in places the loss has been even more savage. A survey by the Suffolk Preservation Society in the parish of Thorpe Morieux found that 56.5 miles of hedgerow in 1950 had shrunk to 26.8 miles by 1982. Almost half Norfolk's hedgerows went between 1946 and 1970. National and regional surveys indicate that losses have continued, even though so much of the region was already arable. A cereal-growing area of Cambridgeshire, for instance, was among seven surveyed in detail for the Countryside Commission in 1972 and again in 1983 to measure the extent of landscape change. The second survey reported that a further fifth of hedgerows had gone, mostly along roadsides, where their disappearance lacks even the justification of expanding field sizes. More farmland trees had been lost here than in any of the other study areas except one in which 'the characteristic fenland tree, the pollarded willow, [was] close to extinction'. Between 1947 and 1972 four trees in five disappeared; by 1983 the number of remain-ing trees had halved again. Eastern England has fewer trees on farmland or hedgerows than any other region of the country. Ponds go when they no longer serve any purpose to farms which have shed their livestock – or, at least, where most livestock is permanently confined to battery units of poultry or pigs. The loss of hedgerows is more serious still.

The hedgerows have been destroyed primarily because machines are large – up to 10 metres wide – and therefore need 4 or 5 metres of land in which to turn round. If the fields are too small, too much land near the field boundaries is left untilled and the costly machines are not working to optimum efficiency. So fields become larger and more rectangular. Other farmers worry about weeds spreading from hedges or the shade cast by hedges or trees. And as farmers moved from mixed farming towards increasingly intensive crop production – or were taken over by bigger, specialist enterprises – there was less need for field boundaries to be stockproof. Fences would do – and save the farmer from the chore of having to maintain his hedgerows.

A study of seven areas published by the Countryside Commission in 1984 found that, even where hedgerows do survive, their average quality has declined. To many arable farmers, said the study, 'the trimming of hedges is just an extension of mowing the "rubbish" on the banks and ditches'. Wildlife disappears along with the hedgerows. A NCC survey compared two fields, one with hedges and semi-natural grass, the other with wire fences and sown grass. The former was supporting twenty mammal species, thirty-seven bird species and seventeen butterfly species; comparative figures for the latter were five, five and zero.

The loss of hedgerows has had proportionately greater

impact upon the landscape of East Anglia than of most other regions. Much of fenland, it is true, has never had many hedges, except a few pollarded willows along the drainage dykes that form many field boundaries. But elsewhere in eastern England, with few hills and less than 5 per cent of the area devoted to broad-leaved or mixed woodland, it is hedgerows which have given much of the countryside its vitality. Birds nest there, dormice and other small animals burrow there, butterflies feed on the flowers which grow alongside the hedges. Hedgerows themselves can contain a dozen or more different shrubs and trees, whose springtime flowers and autumn fruits brighten so many country walks. The somewhat thin and straight hedgerows in parts of Cambridgeshire and around Lincoln betray their origins as the product of eighteenth- and nineteenth-century field enclosure. Many other hedgerows form ancient parish boundaries. Some experts have suggested that the number of species in a 30-yard stretch of hedge is roughly equal to its age in centuries; others feel this is too simplistic. But there is no dispute that the older hedges are generally richer in wildlife. Footpaths often follow hedgerows (particularly when the alternative is to trek across ploughed land) or use 'green lanes' between hedgerows.

All this can be grubbed out in a single afternoon by one man and his machine. Where once there was bird song, there is now only the drone of the combine harvester, often working late into the night under powerful headlights. Up to 250 plant species will decline because of the destruction of hedgerows and thirty could disappear altogether. Yet, so long as hedgerows survive, they provide corridors of life in a pesticide-ridden arable world where fewer birds or butterflies and no flowers can flourish. There are fears, too, that the loss of hedgerows will cause long-term problems of soil erosion now that some fields extend for 400 acres or more without any windbreak. Often there is nothing on the horizon, except perhaps the silhouettes of powerlines made more visible by the flatness of the land and the absence of natural features. In eastern England, with power stations on the coast, pylons and powerlines are large and commonplace as well as conspicuous. Nor are there many people or animals in the monotonous arable landscapes produced by forty years' obeisance to government calls for increased agricultural production.

Interest in hedgerows stirred public concern about stubble- or straw-burning. This practice reached a peak in the early 1980s, when thick black palls of smoke would hang over large areas of the eastern counties in late summer days. Farmers wanted to burn the stubble of one crop so they could destroy weeds and plant winter wheat while the days remained warm. Often fires raged out of control, scorching hedgerows and trees, blocking roads and keeping local fire brigades at full stretch. In most other European countries a far higher proportion of the post-harvest stubble is either used (for fuel or in the paper industry, for instance) or ploughed back into the land. A code on burning was intro-

185

ABOVE: Lincolnshire Wolds, near Louth

ABOVE LEFT: Polythene farming, Suffolk

LEFT: Where once there was birdsong, there is now only the drone of the combine harvester

duced by the NFU to try and head off calls for a statutory ban. This urges farmers to ensure a firebreak at least 15 metres wide near hedgerows, to avoid weekends and bank holidays and notify the fire brigade of proposed burning, among other recommendations. If smoke inconveniences road-users, whatever the distance of the fire from the road, farmers can be prosecuted under the Highways (Amendment) Act of 1986, but councils vary in their willingness to take action.

Local authorities in rural England tend to be torn between concern for the prosperity of their agriculture and unease about its effects on their countryside. Many councils are worried about the loss of trees and have planted saplings alongside roads. Roadsides are a frequent source of friction in arable counties. Some grass verges are churned up by tractors crossing to fields – or even progressively ploughed a little closer each year to the road. Others, lining 'green lanes' or 'droves', become cluttered with unsightly farm equipment. After a survey by the Cambridgeshire CPRE revealed widespread encroachment upon verges, the county council decided in 1986 to start prosecuting farmers who plough grass verges. Perhaps more serious, as far as ratepayers' pockets are concerned, is the cost of road repairs as heavy farm machinery and grain-collecting tankers trundle along narrow country lanes.

Many of the problems posed by modern agriculture are too daunting for any one local authority to tackle. Even bodies such as the Countryside Commission and NCC can do no more than offer advice about the effects of nitrate pollution from farm fertilisers on water supplies – a growing worry in eastern England – or agricultural subsidies which encourage intensification of farming. But constructive efforts have been made to reconcile the interests of farmers and conservationists, most notably in this region by Suffolk County Council.

Suffolk was the location for one of the Countryside Commission's first experiments in promoting conservation-minded farming. It did not concentrate all its attention on a single demonstration farm – although this was being done elsewhere in separate experiments – but sought to improve the landscape of an entire region by offering advice and practical help to all the farmers. The county council was sympathetic, partly because local initiatives such as amenity tree-planting had done little to offset the continuing loss of landscape features and wildlife habitats. And so in 1978 a project officer, Melinda Appleby, was appointed for a 10,000 acre area of mid-Suffolk north of Ipswich. Four-fifths of the land was arable, rising to 98 per cent in one of the six parishes where three quarters of the hedgerows had already been removed. Elsewhere the landscape was still a mixture of small and large fields, woods and hedges. There were some horticultural crops, a small number of cattle and a far larger number of pigs and poultry being reared in units. There was little marginal land. Melinda Appleby faced a daunting challenge.

At first, the local branch of the NFU was reluctant to

Hayley Wood, Cambridgeshire

announce that Ms Appleby would be speaking at a meeting, in the fear that nobody would turn up. Four in five farmers did eventually respond, sometimes warmly, sometimes warily, to talk about what the project might be able to offer. What the Countryside Commission could provide was basically grants and advice – about how to manage woodland or ponds or meadows. Some farmers were fascinated by wildlife and others by local history; these groups were receptive to information about their hedgerows and less likely to destroy them. Melinda Appleby told them that cutting their hedges in an A-shape allowed more light to reach the base of the hedge, which was better for wildlife. A lot of the initial effort (and very limited funds) went on tree-planting, sometimes to form shelter belts to screen farm buildings, sometimes to create copses in field corners and sometimes to produce ornamental drives. In five years over 10,000 trees were planted, doubling the original area of woodland and encouraging the setting-up of a countrywide woodland advisory service for farmers and landowners.

In all, work was done on thirty-five of the fifty-four farms in the project areas – the original area was expanded in 1981 – with full-scale conservation plans prepared for eight of these. Only six farmers failed to respond at all. One group of farmers was sufficiently interested in the possibilities to employ a full-time conservation adviser, while Melinda Appleby has since been appointed farm conservation adviser for the county as a whole. In the long run the effect on attitudes may prove as important as the impact of the project on the original area's landscape. Although meadows and hedgerows continued to be lost, it is likely that more would have gone without the project. And the planting of so many trees should ensure that at least some corners of Suffolk remain wooded into the twenty-first century.

Suffolk, like the other eastern counties, has not been a particularly wooded county for some centuries. But a high proportion of the woodland that remains is ancient, which makes the losses of broad-leaved or mixed woods all the more serious. According to the NCC, 38 per cent of Suffolk's surviving area of ancient semi-natural woodland has been either converted to plantations or destroyed in the last fifty years. The figures for other eastern counties are: Lincolnshire – 56 per cent; Norfolk – 52 per cent; Cambridgeshire – 33 per cent. Valuable though new planting of broad-leaved trees may be, it is no substitute for managing existing ancient semi-natural woodland to ensure its survival.

Harry Barnett, Suffolk's woodlands adviser, reckons that 25,000 of the 32,500 acres of woodland in the county have been neglected. To an untrained eye the woods may look impressive: sturdy oaks and ash – but too many may be of the same age, with too few to take their place. Overgrown woods become too dark for many of the wild flowers which have adapted to a coppicing regime. In many cases woods have not been managed since the beginning of this century

187

and traditional skills such as coppicing have been forgotten. With the help of Countryside Commission and Forestry Commission grants plus, for a time, MSC teams, the council's farm woodlands service won a positive response from Suffolk farmers and landowners.

Woods have been thinned, partially felled, coppiced and replanted by free labour, so long as the landowner has agreed to maintain the woods according to a management plan. At one time there were around seventy people working in the county on MSC woodland schemes. For farmers accustomed to harvesting crops (and cash) annually, managing woodlands may seem a tremendous effort for very little and very distant gain. So the service also offers advice on marketing timber or managing woodlands as 'cover' for shooting game – many woods owe their survival to shooting interests. Some farmers and landowners seek the help of the woodlands service simply because they like trees, whether for wildlife or the landscape value of, say, a copse viewed from afar.

One wood being managed under a plan agreed with the county council is Middlewood, near Offton. New rides have been opened up to let in light (and improve public access) and coppicing resumed after an absence of many years. In springtime the rides are ablaze with wood anemones, while the more knowledgeable visitor will also recognise orchids, small-leaved lime trees and innumerable butterflies. Middlewood is part of a farm whose previous owners had seen the wood simply as unproductive land which they would like to flatten and bring into arable production. Happily, the new owners are sympathetic to conservation and have also sought advice about how other features should be retained – hedgerows with a rich variety of species, for instance. None of this prevents the landowners from pursuing their primary goal of making a profit, since it affects considerably less than the 10 per cent of the farm's total land which the NCC believes that, ideally, all farms should manage in ways suitable for conservation.

Most counties now have a forestry officer who can offer advice about the various council, Forestry Commission and Countryside Commission grants available. Many counties also have advisers appointed by the FWAG or the local authorities. Conservation grants have mushroomed. The restoration of woods such as Middlewood and the retention of ponds, meadows and hedgerows as a result of conservation advice is clearly encouraging for the future – and indicative of an increasing accord between farming and conservationist bodies spurred by economic pressures and public protests. But these measures alone are unlikely to stem the tide of agricultural evolution. If agricultural policy favours the continuing intensification of crop production, conservation measures will be little more than field-corner tokenism on marginal land. Yet if governments encourage a diversification from farming, an altogether different set of problems will arise for anyone concerned with the beauty of rural England.

Eastern England's agricultural prosperity should inhibit widespread change. Although cereal prices have been cut by

ABOVE: *Middlewood*

BELOW: *Swaffham Prior*

European agricultural ministers, the high yields from these fertile soils will ensure that most areas in the region remain profitable. So it is unlikely that many conifers will be planted here, as may happen on less fertile soils. The scattered nature of the population will also limit the numbers of golf courses and riding schools. But the population of all four eastern counties is growing, as new transport links open up a region previously bereft of good communications. Not only are cities such as Ipswich, Peterborough, Norwich and Cambridge becoming increasingly popular places to live and work in themselves, but motorways and electrified rail services are enabling people to live in the East Anglian countryside and commute to London.

Commuters' cars stream to Colchester railway station from towns such as Hadleigh and villages along the Essex–Suffolk border. 'The area is under immense pressure for new housing,' says Paul Edwards of the Suffolk Preservation Society, the local branch of the CPRE. 'Every back garden that could take a house has done so. Now it's largely small clusters of new houses outside villages.' Further south, in Essex, housing pressure has become the county's prime problem (because of this, Essex is primarily covered in chapter 6 on south-east England).

Cambridge, with the M11 providing a direct link to the capital and Stansted airport, has become favoured as a centre for high-tech development, with a 'science park' north of the city to exploit the cachet and expertise of the university. With the new jobs have come demands for new houses. A miniature 'new town' for 3200 people was built at Bar Hill, 5 miles north-west of Cambridge, in the 1960s. More recently, developers proposed a much larger satellite town of 6000 houses near Waterbeach, 5 miles north-east of Cambridge, and another for 3000 homes near Wilburton, 7 miles north of Cambridge. The similarity in the distance from Cambridge is no coincidence: there is a 5-mile green belt around the City. The green belt has come under strong pressure from developers in the last ten years, with a succession of plans for hypermarkets, shops, hotels and new technology industries. Villages such as Swaffham Prior, Burwell, Bottisham and Linton are coming under pressure which could undermine their rural character.

There is similar threat to the villages around Norwich, as that delightful cathedral city becomes ever more a regional capital. Houses for another 1000 people to the east of the city at Thorpe may ease the demand, but developers would also like to build at villages such as Loddon and Saxlingham Nethergate. Elsewhere, Huntingdon, Bury St Edmunds and Ipswich are all growing in size, benefitting in part from their proximity to the A45, which links the Midlands and north to the container port of Felixstowe. Now a fast dual-carriageway, the A45, has encouraged the construction of warehouses as far from the sea as Bury St Edmunds. Their rectangular, prefabricated lines do as little for the landscape as, regrettably, they do for local jobs.

Otherwise there are few industrial or commercial scars in

189

eastern England. There are sand and gravel pits, bringing noise and dust while in production but later offering possibilities of imaginative restoration for watersports and wildlife, as at Ferry Meadows country park near Peterborough. The region is entirely without coal mines, although British Coal is investigating the feasibility of exploiting seams deep under the Witham Valley south of Lincoln. Where there has been commercial development outside the towns, it has tended to be concentrated along the coast. The qualities which give the coast much of its distinction – an unspoiled character and lack of population – makes it vulnerable to development.

The Norfolk coastline has probably suffered less than those of its neighbours. Much of the north Norfolk coast, a unique blend of sand, shingle and saltmarsh, is owned by bodies such as the National Trust or the RSPB. Such ownership helps to ensure its conservation and also signals its quality. For some 30 miles the shoreline is virtually one long nature reserve, where the boundary between land and sea is ever blurred and ever changing. It is a coast where medieval ports such as Wells-next-the-Sea and Blakeney have been stranded a mile inland by the continuing deposition of shingle off the old shoreline. The coastline – a mecca for birdwatchers in winter and summer – seems unlikely to succumb to alien development.

Lincolnshire and Suffolk have not been so fortunate. Resorts such as Skegness, Mablethorpe and Cleethorpes were popular long before the First World War. Then the motor car spawned a demand for caravans and bungalows which threatened to overrun Lincolnshire's dune-lined coast. Curbs were eventually established, although neither Mablethorpe nor Ingoldmells will win awards for beauty or town planning. The petrochemical plant at Theddlethorpe is even uglier. 'Bracing Skegness' is the prime holiday resort of the Lincolnshire coast, causing traffic problems along the way in Burgh le Marsh and Wainfleet. Further north, cars bound for Mablethorpe jam the Georgian streets of Louth. Something of the Lincolnshire coast's original quality can still be found south of Skegness, at Gibraltar Point, where a nature reserve over-

looks the Wash. The combination of dunes, marsh and sea makes the reserve internationally important, according to the NCC. If the reserve's location appeals to birds, its site near a popular holiday resort enables Gibraltar Point to demonstrate that love of nature is no obscure, minority pastime: it attracts a flock of about 60,000 visitors a year.

The Suffolk coast also has some renowned nature reserves – at Walberswick, overlooking the estuary of the River Blyth near Southwold, and Minsmere, south of Dunwich. Here you can see such rare birds as the marsh harrier, gulls and terns. The value of this coastline has been officially recognised in other ways. Like the north Norfolk coast, some 35 miles of the Suffolk shore has been designated not only an AONB but also a heritage coast.

In some places the heritage coast designation is little more than words on paper (see chapter 4, pages 135–6), but in this case Suffolk County Council has appointed a project officer to work with volunteers and MSC teams. Their tasks include the creation of a coastal footpath, the provision of discreetly sited car parks and giving advice to farmers about how to manage their land. This has undoubtedly enhanced public enjoyment of one of southern England's most undeveloped coasts. The coastal path winds across cliffs, estuaries, marshland, heath and beaches. South of Aldeburgh a 9-mile spit of shingle blocks the direct path of the River Alde to the sea. In places the spit, built up by the southward drift of beach debris along the coast, is not more than a few yards wide. And while the shoreline may be expanding here (as also in Norfolk) elsewhere along the Suffolk coast it is retreating: up to half a mile has been lost to the sea, largely destroying medieval towns such as the once busy port of Dunwich.

It is hard to think of another coast in England which has quite so much diversity within such a relatively short distance. Such towns or villages as exist are small, tranquil places with fine churches (as at Southwold or Blythburgh) or a castle (as at Orford). Little wonder, then, that in 1974 Suffolk was among the first shorelines to be defined as a heritage coast. But the unspoiled shore attracts people other than birdwatchers or walkers:

● The Central Electricity Generating Board chose a small fishing village called Sizewell as the site for a nuclear-power station in the 1960s. Then it decided to put another one there on the empty shore, prompting a four-year planning battle and a 300,000-word report by Sir Frank Layfield. Sir Frank concluded that the new power station, Sizewell B, would be a 'totally inappropriate' intrusion into the Suffolk countryside – unless local environmental losses were deemed secondary to national economic gains which, in his view, they were. In March 1987, the government gave the go-ahead.

● The Foreign Office chose Orford Ness, part of the shingle spit blocking the path of the Alde to the sea, as the site for a complex of high-powered radio aerials. In 1986 the Foreign Office sought permission to add another thirty-three aerials

RIGHT: Sizewell – a second nuclear-power station was given the go-ahead in March 1987

FAR RIGHT: Felixstowe Docks and Trimley Marshes

LEFT: Gibraltar Point nature reserve

BELOW LEFT: Dunwich, where a once busy port has been lost to the sea

BELOW RIGHT: Orford Castle

to the eleven already erected. Nine of the new ones will be 275 feet high with a 70-foot wide 'T' piece at the top of the mast.

• The Felixstowe docks company chose Trimley Marshes along the north bank of the River Orwell as the place to extend its port. Although outside the heritage coast, the marshes are part of the Suffolk Coast AONB and rated as internationally significant for migrating wading birds. In a deal with local conservationists, the company promised to provide a nature reserve on 200 acres of the site if opposition to its proposals was dropped.

• Waveney District Council and a private developer chose Southwold Harbour for a £3.5 million scheme to provide a

300-yacht marina and 300 houses. At present the harbour, along the River Blyth between Southwold and Walberswick, is an idyllic spot, perhaps somewhat run-down, with fishermen's shacks lining the banks, but that is part of its ramshackle charm. Simple wooden jetties provide berths for everything from yachts to fishing boats. A 10p ferry crosses the river in summer. It's a peaceful, beautiful place, much painted by artists and frequented by local people for walking their dogs. After strong opposition in 1986, the marina plan was dropped – or, at least, deferred, since it is accepted that the crumbling harbour walls do need restoration.

The Southwold scheme foundered not only on the strength of local opposition but also because it failed to pass two tests laid down by the government in 1982 for industrial or commercial development in AONBs. First, is the development in the national interest? Second, is there no other site? Nevertheless the threats to the Suffolk coast demonstrate the need for constant vigilance. If Southwold Harbour were to be developed, why not the other river estuaries which line the east coast? Several, say the RSPB, are threatened.

Eastern England, like Southwold Harbour, used to be something of a backwater. Skegness, Great Yarmouth and the broads drew the crowds, but mostly the resorts of the eastern counties such as Hunstanton and Cromer were devoted to genteel pleasures. Historic market towns such as Stamford or King's Lynn were bypassed or simply on roads that led nowhere. Even great cities like Lincoln and Norwich remained off the main tourist track. To a large extent this is still true; East Anglia is a destination in itself rather than a place through

which you pass. This should help to retain much of its prosperous tranquillity. But in places tourism is beginning to pose problems, as at Lavenham, where coaches now clutter the square of this pink-washed, timber-framed jewel of a Suffolk village.

The beauty of Suffolk has given it one of the richest and best-organised protection societies in England with a full-time director and office staff. The other eastern counties rely on voluntary workers, but there is no shortage of commitment, whether it be through the other local branches of the CPRE or the Royal Society for Nature Conservation. Each county has its nationally known treasures. Each also has its locally prized corners from which its people derive solace and inspiration. 'Lincolnshire is not a county noted for fine scenery,' says John Anthony, secretary of the Lincolnshire CPRE. 'But those of us who live and work here, who know all the talk of flat, boring country to be rubbish, are frequently content to let the old myths remain, so that we can continue to enjoy uncrowded roads, towns and villages. There is, in Lincolnshire, countryside as fine as any to be found in lowland England.'

The glory of rural England is that such local pride is rarely misplaced. John Anthony's paean of praise would be matched by his counterparts in Cambridgeshire, Norfolk and Suffolk. No matter that much of their time is spent fighting proposals which threaten landscapes; it is their love of the local country which inspires them to do so. Nobody who knows eastern England could doubt the validity of their concern – or the beauty of their countryside.

195

ABOVE LEFT: Southwold Harbour

ABOVE: Lavenham

ABOVE RIGHT: Lincolnshire Wolds

6

SOUTH-EAST ENGLAND

South-east England is not a place of extremes. There are no mountains or moors, no waterfalls worthy of the name, no raging torrents. Rivers meander lazily to a coast where marshes and slack tidal estuaries are more common than cliffs.

It is a cosy countryside where village greens echo each summer to the sound of cricket and polite applause. Overlooking the green will usually be the village church, still a place of architectural and spiritual homage in this more secular age. Church and inn, manor house and cottages, together they reflect a story of man's impact on the land which frequently goes back a thousand years or more. Just as today villages bear the imprint of profound demographic and commercial forces which are transforming rural life in south-east England.

Villages are an intrinsic feature of lowland England, more so than in the uplands, where settlement tends to be scattered between hamlets or isolated farmsteads. Britain as a whole is a crowded island, with eighty-nine inhabitants per square mile compared to thirty-eight in France and nine in the United States. But nowhere is more congested than this south-eastern corner of England. Romans, Saxons and Normans occupied these counties first; they established their administrative centres in the subdued south-east, with London becoming one of the world's great capitals. For centuries, London sprawled outwards, engulfing villages which today are little more than suburbs or the names of tube stations. For the last forty years, this growth has been held in check by green-belt planning policies, but these are now under acute pressure.

The greater overall prosperity of south-east England is the bait which lures developers; here is a readier market for new houses, out-of-town hypermarkets and leisure centres. Proximity to the continent intensifies the attraction, with the

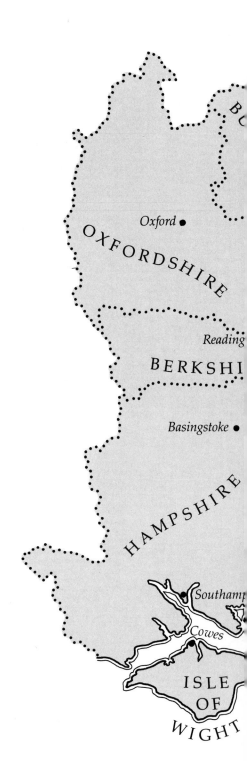

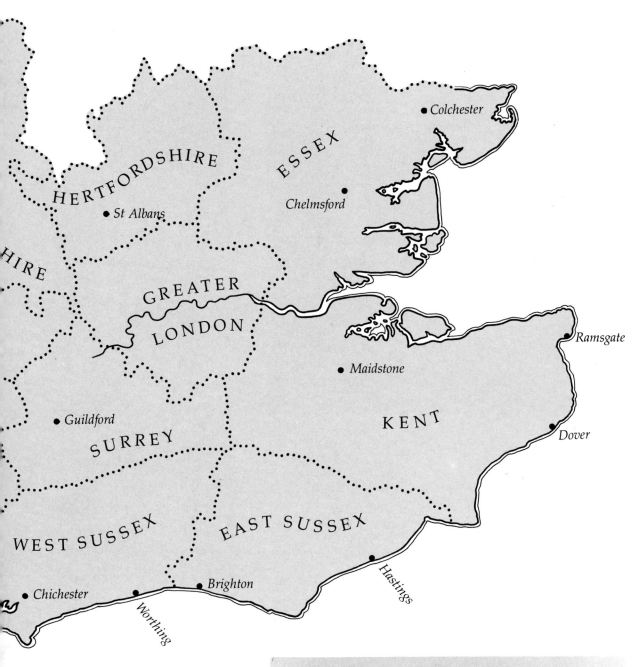

HERTFORDSHIRE

ESSEX

• Colchester

• St Albans

• Chelmsford

GREATER

LONDON

• Maidstone

KENT

• Ramsgate

• Dover

197

• Guildford

SURREY

WEST SUSSEX

EAST SUSSEX

Hastings •

• Chichester

Brighton •

Worthing •

Chichester Harbour

198

prospect of a Channel Tunnel in the 1990s. New motorways have already had potent secondary effects on large areas of south-east England: house prices go up, farmland becomes more valuable as sites for warehouses or golf courses than for agriculture, villages lose their rural character to become bases for London commuters. Development pressures are overwhelmingly the greatest threat to this countryside, particularly with the crisis in agriculture fuelling speculation about alternative uses for redundant farmland.

And 'threat' is not too emotive a word: despite the density of population, this corner of England has some of the country's most loved landscapes. Indeed, they may be so loved because they are so accessible. Just think of the countryside which can be reached within an hour of London: the North and South Downs, the Weald, the Chilterns, the Thames Valley, the salt marshes of the Essex coast, the Surrey heathland, the Berkshire Downs. A little further and there's the New Forest, a unique survival of wooded pasture from medieval England, or the coast at Chichester Harbour, West Wight or Seven Sisters. There may be no national parks in south-east England (although some have been suggested), but the region does not lack distinction. It includes landscapes as rich in archaeological sites as the villages are steeped in more recent history.

For all its lack of drama, the countryside of south-east England should be as cherished as any part of our island heritage. It has already suffered much from the impact of agriculture, and here, more than anywhere, the fear is that today's green fields will become tomorrow's housing estates

ABOVE LEFT: South Downs, near Wilmington

ABOVE: Seven Sisters

or shopping centres. One national survey in 1987 claimed plans had been published for no fewer than 1800 'superstores', totalling more than 41 million square feet. Agricultural change may despoil, but development destroys.

Settlements have always exerted an influence over the countryside, as markets for food and magnets for communications. For a century or more this influence has grown inexorably and dramatically. Four fifths of England may be farmed, but for 150 years we have been an urban society with a majority of the population living in towns. The industrial revolution spawned great cities in the Midlands and north; a single farmhouse on the banks of the Tees in 1830 became the basis of Middlesborough and a population of 50,000 just fifty years later. Conurbations were born, as towns grew into each other. By the end of the nineteenth century London had gobbled up previously separate communities such as Highgate and Wimbledon; by the 1930s the tentacles of the capital enclosed a quarter of the English population.

The inter-war years saw a boom in private house-building. Four million houses were built, many in 'ribbon developments' along new roads or railway lines which enabled people to live further away from their place of work than ever before. There were few controls over location or design. Not all developments were as infamous as the bungalows along the clifftops at Peacehaven in Sussex, but cheap building materials transported by the railways eroded regional varieties of vernacular architecture. By the Second World War, one hundred years of urban sprawl had devoured vast tracts of country and transformed much more into dormitory suburbs.

The losses did not pass unnoticed or unlamented. The Council for the Preservation of Rural England (as the CPRE was then called) was prominent among those campaigning for planning controls to curb indiscriminate building. London County Council and Surrey County Council began to buy land as open space, purportedly for recreation but partly to protect it from development. But there was no national policy until after the Second World War. Then, in 1947, the Town and Country Planning Act introduced a system which has survived, little changed in principle, for forty years. The Act was underpinned by two beliefs: that urban sprawl should be contained and that agricultural land should be protected. It foreshadowed one of the great triumphs of British planning – the creation of green belts, swathes of countryside around major cities where non-rural or non-agricultural development would not normally be allowed. The idea had already surfaced in an influential plan for Greater London, published in 1944 and prepared by Professor Sir Patrick Abercrombie, a former secretary of the CPRE. In 1955 the concept of green belts was extended beyond London to other conurbations so that by the mid-1980s 4.5 million acres of England were designated as green belt, approximately 10 per cent of the country. In southern England, Oxford and Bournemouth both have their *cordon sanitaire*, although London's, within 1.2 million acres of green belt, is by far the biggest.

'If London had not had a green belt for the past thirty years, there would have been property without a break from Henley to Southend and from Tonbridge to Luton,' says David Hall, director of the Town and Country Planning Association. 'Look at the maps in any Home Counties planning office and you will see that thousands of applications for development have been turned down because they were in the green belt. The same is true for other big urban areas.'

Green belts, supported by the broader panoply of planning

ABOVE: Bungalows along the clifftop at Peacehaven

200

BELOW: M1/M25 junction near Watford. Land prices near M25 junctions are £1m or more an acre

controls, have greatly reduced the amount of agricultural land lost nationally to urban development – from more than 60,000 acres a year in the 1930s to 37,500 acres a year in the 1970s and just 12,000 in the 1980s. Several demographic trends are now combining to intensify pressures on southern England. The postwar spurt in the birth rate has eased, but the average size of families or households has declined, thereby fuelling the demand for additional houses. There has also been a twofold migration within Britain from north to south and away from the cities, where the decline in manufacturing industry has reversed centuries of urban growth. Since 1961, rural counties have been growing while the conurbations have shrunk. London's 8.5 million population in 1966 fell to 6.7 million in the 1981 census. So, again, the demand for new housing in southern England has continued to increase, even when the national population has been relatively stable.

This demand has outstripped the supply of houses built in 'new towns' established in postwar years beyond the green belt. As a result, other towns encircling London have boomed – towns like Guildford, St Albans, Woking and Sevenoaks. Improved roads and far wider car ownership still encouraged the two-way movement of people initiated by railways: commuters leaving rural bolt-holes to work in London and townspeople descending upon the countryside for recreation. But growth in road traffic masks a greater decline in rail commuters into the capital. The new roads tempted businesses away from London, further intensifying the clamour for new houses and other developments in what was previously open country. Finally, increases in agricultural output have undermined one of the original two pillars of postwar planning: farmland no longer warrants blanket protection for agricultural production.

The stage is thus set for the biggest battle over land use since the war. Although it will be fought on many fronts, common factors are the effects of new motorways and major developments such as airports and the Channel Tunnel. The M25 has galvanised developers to draw up plans for new hypermarkets or leisure centres along its 125-mile circuit of the capital. A dozen proposals were unveiled even before the motorway was completed in 1986 – from the 'golden triangle' at the M1/M25 junction in Hertfordshire to Hewitt's Farm near Orpington, from Wraysbury in Berkshire to Claygate in Surrey. Most of the developments would be on green-belt land, with their backers arguing that the motorway has created exceptional circumstances which warrant the granting of planning approval. House-builders have also eyed the M25 eagerly, knowing that it would boost land values in towns near its route. Land prices at £1 m an acre or more near M25 junctions show what's at stake.

With the 1987 general election in the offing, ministers rallied to the defence of this beleaguered green belt. Large-scale shopping complexes were singled out for withering criticism by environment minister William Waldegrave, as 'giant speculative projects that fly full in the face of long-

201

202

established green-belt policy – a policy to which this government is fully committed'. Mr Waldegrave warned developers who pushed such schemes to the point of appeal to expect the costs of any inquiry to be awarded against them. In the short term, such ministerial views give no encouragement to the developers. But the longer-term prospects are less reassuring. Motorways elsewhere have frequently been used to overturn restraints on commercial development, including green-belt policies. Evidence presented by the CPRE to the inquiry into the M40 extension from Oxford to Birmingham listed five factors which had won developers planning approval for projects near other motorways in the past:

• the opportunity to extend existing communities towards the road, which thus forms a new urban boundary (as with the M4 at Reading);

• the possibility of exploiting easy communications and parking by siting warehousing and shopping complexes at motorway junctions;

• the need to accommodate 'essential' motorway-related developments such as service areas and hotels;

• the fashion amongst commercial developers for campus-style developments in rural (or semi-rural) locations;

• the competition between local authorities to attract high-technology industries by laying out 'science parks'.

Such developments can already be seen along the corridors created by the M4, M3 and M11. An airport is another trigger for growth, not merely in its immediate vicinity, as

ABOVE LEFT: Development land near Stansted and the M11

ABOVE CENTRE: Shakespeare Cliff, Dover. Plans to dump Channel Tunnel waste at the foot of the cliffs caused outrage

ABOVE RIGHT: The Newington area near Folkestone – under threat from the Channel Tunnel

203

at Crawley near Gatwick, but further afield. The expansion of Stansted could have similar effects upon the M11 corridor to the high-tech industries of Cambridge as Heathrow has had on the M4 and the Thames Valley. Extending the M40 towards Birmingham will increase development pressures around Oxford, Banbury, Bicester and the hitherto rural villages of north Oxfordshire. Larger than any of these developments will be the construction of a Channel Tunnel. Allied to the completion of the M25, the revitalisation of London's Docklands and the construction of new river crossings east of London, the tunnel could encourage a decisive shift of new development away from counties west of London.

Announcement of the tunnel plans focused initial attention on the proposed site west of Folkestone. There was understandable concern about the valley to be occupied by the terminal buildings, fears for the wildlife of a chalk downland along the route, scepticism about the need for an improved road link on the downs between Folkestone and Dover, outrage over plans to dump tunnel waste at the foot of Dover's white cliffs. But the repercussions of a Channel Tunnel extend far beyond the terminal site, as companies seek to build new warehouses or factories close to the M20 or M25. Ashford, earmarked as the site of a rail terminal and freight depot, claimed a 50 per cent rise in industrial rents within a year of the tunnel being announced, and there was also talk of theme parks and science parks. If jobs are created by such developments, this will foster a demand to build new houses locally for the expanding workforce. Greenbelt boundaries should be adjusted to 'different social and economic circumstances', says Kent County Council in a bullish response to the commercial opportunities offered by the scheduled opening of the tunnel in 1993.

Since the Second World War planners have attempted to strike a balance between where development should be allowed and where it should be prevented. An individual's freedom to live where he wants (even assuming he could afford to) has been subordinate to the broader interests of society as determined ultimately by elected politicians. However irksome this may be for house-builders, who talk self-interestedly about individual freedom, it has meant a presumption against non-rural development in green belts and areas of outstanding natural beauty (AONBs). This is one reason why changes in AONB boundaries, as were proposed for the Chilterns, are often fiercely resisted. With more than half of several counties (Surrey, Berkshire, East Sussex and Hertfordshire) protected by AONB status, development has been concentrated in the remaining areas of these counties. Overall increases in house building have often been remarkable enough; the number of houses in Berkshire has doubled in the last thirty years, transforming the character of the county's unprotected countryside.

Berkshire's boom partly reflects a regional policy which designated three growth areas in south-east England – Milton Keynes in Buckinghamshire, south Hampshire around the Solent, and a region straddling the Berkshire, Surrey and Hampshire borders. Milton Keynes was always seen as a new city, but what had not been envisaged was the coalescence of settlements in the other two growth areas. Look at a map and you see that 'Solent City' is becoming a reality, with little countryside left between Southampton, Eastleigh, Fareham, Gosport and Portsmouth. In Berkshire, Bracknell has edged towards Wokingham and Reading, as they have grown out towards their respective motorways. A little to the south, it is now possible to drive through Camberley, Farnborough, Aldershot and virtually into Farnham without emerging from suburban sprawl. But expansion was not confined to these growth areas. Developers leapfrogged over the green belt to expand towns such as Chelmsford, Maidstone and Basingstoke. Along the south coast there are barely 5 miles of undeveloped shore between Bognor and Brighton.

By the mid-1980s, housing targets set for the decade were already being reached. It was difficult to see how targets set for Surrey and Hertfordshire could be achieved without inroads into the green belt or in Berkshire without what the county council called 'unacceptable environmental damage'. In Berkshire, the county council therefore sought to curb the rate of house-building so that the consequences of past growth could be tackled. Traffic problems were already severe, it said, without further large-scale expansion. In any case, Berkshire was no longer a growth point; regional policy, endorsed by the government in 1986, was to encourage development in London, the older urban areas and the eastern part of the region. Nevertheless, Berkshire's attempt to scale down new house-building from 6000 houses a year to around 1000 a year within ten years sparked an angry response from house-builders. Their protests were part of a renewed assault on what they see as the rigidity of the planning system.

In the front-line of this assault are nine of Britain's biggest building companies, who joined forces as Consortium Developments to promote between ten and fifteen new 'country towns' on green-field sites in south-east England. Several sites are in green belt, all are strategically situated within easy commuting distance of London. The first site on their shopping list was Tillingham Hall, a slice of Essex green belt between Upminster and Basildon, some 5 miles from the M25. It is not particularly beautiful, but the prime purpose of green belt is to preserve openness and to prevent sprawl. If beauty were the arbiter of green belt, landowners could simply let their land fall derelict in order to secure approval for development. The Tillingham Hall site was neither beautiful nor derelict, but once it was covered by 5100 houses, precious little country would remain between London and Basildon. Similar developments were anticipated for sites in Hampshire, Essex, Hertfordshire, and elsewhere.

Tillingham Hall attracted considerable attention at a public inquiry because it was an overt challenge to the sanctity of green belts. Whoever was the victor, the outcome would have symbolic importance as a precedent. Yet this was just one of many development proposals besetting local authorities in the south-east. Some are large, like those of Consortium Developments and others near Crawley, Hook, Reading, Maidstone and Harlow; others may seem more modest — a few houses here and a conversion of some farm buildings there — but they may still transform the rural character of a village. Development pressures dominate the journals of the CPRE's south-eastern branches, emerging unmistakably as the greatest challenge to this region.

House-builders say that green-field sites are necessary to meet the demand for new housing in south-east England. Others disagree. In 1986 Prince Charles condemned developers as crazy for wanting to build over the countryside while inner cities were 'left to fester'. Conservationists led by the CPRE point to the derelict land suitable for housing already available in towns and cities. Politicans fear that increased house-building in the south-east will accelerate the flight of jobs and people from the north. What may seem little more than local disputes about housing estates therefore raise profound questions about the future of society, north and south, town and country.

Round one of the fight went to the building lobby. In 1983 it persuaded the government to propose to Parliament a weakening of the green belt: land which might be needed in the long term for development should be excluded from green belts, along with pockets of land surrounded by buildings. The joy of the developers was short-lived. The CPRE mustered the support of a hundred backbench Tory MPs and the government retreated. Round two to the conservationists. Then, round three: in 1987 the government rejected Consortium Developments' plans for Tillingham Hall. The inspector's report sided squarely with the evidence submitted by the CPRE and others during the public inquiry. He concluded that there was no shortage of housing land in the south-east;

205

ABOVE: The suburbs of Bracknell have edged towards Wokingham and Reading

LEFT: Mile Oak, near Brighton

BELOW LEFT: Tillingham Hall — green-belt land where developers proposed to build 5100 houses

no need to build on the green belt; no evidence that land prices determine house prices; and no need for new towns outside existing communities. Green belts thus remain sacrosanct. But the struggle is not over. Consortium Developments has named Foxley Wood in north-east Hampshire, outside the green belt, as its next target, with another site earmarked near Cambridge. Development pressures are intensifying, encouraged not only by the Conservative victory in the 1987 general election but by the prospect of fundamental changes to the postwar system of planning controls.

First, under government proposals floated for consultation in 1986, county councils would no longer prepare structure plans. These plans aim to reflect a balance between different interests within the individual county, identifying areas suitable for development and others worthy of protection. Berkshire's attempt to curb house-building, for instance, was part of its structure-plan review. It sought to reconcile future development with the provision of other services, not merely those of the local authorities but of water boards, the health service and other public bodies. Structure plans, because of the complexity and scale of the issues, are detailed documents and often lengthy, taking some time to wend their way through the procedures for public consultation before arriving for consideration at the Department of the Environment (DoE). Too long and too complex, said the government, announcing its preference for a single tier of development plans to be prepared by district councils. In the view of the government, structure plans had become better at stopping things happen than making them happen.

Second, as part of a package to diversify the rural economy, the government decided in 1987 that only a third of agricultural land needed to be protected as farmland. Previously, planning authorities had to consult the Ministry of Agriculture when development proposals affected 10 or more acres of any agricultural land; henceforth, such consultation is required only for plans which would involve the loss of 50 or more acres of land classified by the ministry as grades 1, 2 or 3A. These grades represent the best 35 per cent of all farmland. Ministers vigorously denied that the remaining land was being freed for development. After protests by conservationists, the planning circular was amended to stress 'the continuing need to protect the countryside for its own sake, rather than primarily for the productive value of the land'. In particular, green belts will be protected. According to a DoE report, *Rural Enterprise and Development*:

The green belts have always been the subject of special restrictions on development, not because of the agricultural value of the land they cover (which is often of variable quality) but because of the need to prevent urban sprawl, to safeguard the countryside and to assist in urban regeneration. These objectives remain as important as ever. At the same time we need to foster the diversification of the rural economy so as to open up wider and more varied employment opportunities in rural areas, and to balance that need against the protection of the environment without giving agricultural production a special priority.

ABOVE: Horsell Common

In the absence of structure plans, who will decide what needs protection? The advisory role promised for county councils is a poor substitute for the power of strategic planning, which had already been weakened by the abolition of metropolitan counties. Many district councils will find themselves not merely stretched by their enhanced responsibilities but sorely tempted to approve job-creating ventures which flout previous restraints on development. Oddly, for a government committed to deregulation, more decisions will ultimately be made in Whitehall. With 333 district councils in the country, more issues will become boundary disputes requiring intervention by the DoE. Some councils, faced with difficult decisions, will refuse permission simply to pass the buck to Whitehall when the developer appeals. The DoE has already committed itself to greater regional guidance and there will be no other body capable of vetoing piecemeal development in the countryside. With ministers trumpeting their devotion to the green belt and the environment, this should not apparently matter. However, the number of appeals granted by the government against local authority wishes has increased from 29 per cent to 40 per cent during the 1980s. This encourages developers to appeal as a matter of course, so the volume of appeals is also rising. The record does not necessarily match the rhetoric – and what will be the ground rules for reaching decisions, particularly outside green belts?

In principle, conservationists welcome the statement that countryside should be protected for its own sake rather than for its agricultural value. Poor or ordinary farmland may be valuable for landscape or wildlife, just as rural land doesn't have to be beautiful to prevent urban sprawl. Green-belt land – such as many of the commons in south-east England which have been threatened with development – does not have to be particularly large to be important. The proposals of the Common Land Forum (see chapter 1, page 29), if implemented, should save our remaining commons – not before time judging by recent threats to Horsell Common near Woking (offices), Port Meadow at Oxford (boat buildings), Boxmoor Common in Hertfordshire (road building), Walton Heath in Surrey (golf course) and Midhurst and Copthorne in Sussex (houses). But what about the rest of our countryside? One moment the government is declaring its enthusiasm for protection, the next it is canvassing alternative uses for redundant farmland. Of these, nothing is more lucrative in south-east England than development.

Within weeks of the government's announcements in early 1987 about alternative land uses for farmland, a proposal was resubmitted for a golf course in the Hughenden Valley north of High Wycombe. It was within green belt and the Chilterns AONB, in some of the open country closest to the town. Nearby, 92 acres of farmland which the National Trust was negotiating to buy was abruptly withdrawn from sale at about the same time. 'The land forms an important backcloth to Disraeli's house at Hughenden,' says Dame Jennifer Jenkins, chairman of the National Trust. 'Landowners and developers now have higher expectations of the value of property.' As

207

BELOW: Midhurst

the land is green belt, the planners have the government's clear opposition to unsuitable building. So no houses (for now) but what about the golf course? Green belts are partly designated for recreation and in some instances a well-maintained golf course or riding school may look more attractive than scruffy car dumps or abandoned gravel pits. But sports centres generate a demand for club houses, car parks and sometimes floodlights. What worries conservationists most of all is the imprecision in the new guidelines for development. Even the defences promised by the government for green belts and AONBs offer inadequate consolation, if the planning system is weakened for other areas. It is not just, say, the Chilterns which need to be protected, but the views from those hills over the Vale of Aylesbury. Who wants to reach the escarpment and gaze down on a sea of houses, car parks or the kind of garish factory now visible from Winter Hill overlooking the Thames at Marlow?

The countryside of south-east England is not without its champions. Conservation groups marshal articulate defences of their territory whenever an oil company or house-builder appears on the horizon. Admittedly, these groups can be motivated more by concern for human habitat – 'not in my back yard' or the NIMBY Syndrome, as it is known – than the natural world. Nevertheless, their interest has encouraged several local authorities to mount conservation programmes with special help for landowners to maintain endangered or rare landscapes. There are also positive policies for countryside management to cope with recreation pressures. It would be premature to hail these programmes as satisfactory solutions; economic pressures to intensify agricultural production still outweigh incentives. Nonetheless, the schemes could point the way to a future in which the country is treasured for its own sake rather than as the raw material to be exploited for commercial gain. One such programme can be found in East Sussex, where farmers are being helped to manage their woodlands – appropriately so, for south-east England is richer in ancient woodland than any other region of the country. (How tragic, then, that it was this region which was hit so savagely by the storm of October 1987.)

Trees are the natural climax vegetation for much of the British Isles. They colonised most of the country after the end of the last Ice Age, about 11,000 BC. Birch and pine were followed by hazel, alder and oak, then lime, ash, beech and the other trees which are now classified as native. By 4000 BC the 'wildwood' was at its most extensive, covering everything except the highest mountains, small areas of moorland and coastal marshes or dunes. Pollen deposited by trees and plants can now be analysed with reasonable precision to establish which species flourished where; such analysis shows that south-east England had the country's greatest variety of trees, probably because the climate was most favourable.

Lime was the dominant tree of these lowlands, with areas of hazel, oak and elm. From about 3000 BC Neolithic men began to clear the woodland to plant their crops and graze their animals. The countryside historian Oliver Rackham esti-

ABOVE: *The Weald, Kent*

RIGHT: *New Forest – rejected for ESA status*

mates that 99 per cent of the original wildwood has gone. Even the remaining 1 per cent cannot be classed as truly wild. This means neither that Britain lacks trees nor that surviving woodland is particularly recent. Thin, sandy soils were among the first to be cleared since the shallower-rooted trees were easier to remove. But these soils were infertile and so, as Bronze and Iron Age technology enabled other areas to be cleared, some sandy heathland reverted to woodland. The New Forest is thought to be such a case. Agricultural decline after the departure of the Romans also led to some reversion to woodland, although less so than was once thought.

The Domesday Book revealed a country less wooded than France is today — 15 per cent of the area surveyed compared to 20 per cent of modern France. The Weald was the most wooded part of England, with an estimated 70 per cent of the land covered by trees. The next most densely wooded region was the Chilterns. But most of England consisted of farmland with islands of wood, according to Oliver Rackham in *The History of the Countryside*:

Even the bigger wooded areas were not uninhabited wildwood; it was nowhere possible in Norman England to penetrate into woodland further than four miles from some habitation. Conversely, many villages were over four miles from any wood, and a day's journey from any substantial woodland.

The first three centuries of the Norman occupation saw further inroads into the woodland. Areas such as the New Forest which were designated as royal hunting land were

209

ABOVE LEFT: Burnham Beeches

ABOVE: Epping Forest

dwarfed by destruction elsewhere: woodland shrank by a third between 1086 and 1350. By then it had become a scarce resource which needed to be managed; it provided fuel, building materials, charcoal, and bark for tanning leather. For almost 500 years there was little change. Then, the industrial revolution undermined the economic value of managing woodland to ensure its regeneration; railways moved coal cheaply to all parts of the country, ships began to be built with steel. Forests were subjected to enclosure acts which enabled owners to abrogate commoners' rights and to convert woodland to agriculture. About a quarter of the Victorian woodland was lost to farming, so that by the late nineteenth century only 4 per cent of Britain was wooded.

Today the figure is just under 10 per cent, but this growth disguises the greatest rate of destruction of ancient woodland for a thousand years. The new woodland is overwhelmingly conifer plantations sown in the uplands, while native broad-leaved trees have dwindled by as much as half in the last fifty years. Ironically, the destruction has coincided with a greater appreciation of the ecological and historic value of ancient woodland. This means woodland occupying a site which has been continuously wooded since at least 1600. In practice, most such sites would have been wooded for considerably longer. In 1984 the Nature Conservancy Council (NCC) estimated that just over 1.4 million acres of Britain's 5 million acres of woodland is ancient. But roughly half of this sup-posedly ancient woodland has been replanted at one stage or another, mostly with non-native conifers. It is the remain-ing half – some 740,000 acres – which the NCC regards as most important.

Ancient woodland is classified as semi-natural, meaning that it is made up of native trees and shrubs which develop by either natural regeneration or regrowth from stumps left by coppicing (cutting at the base) or pollarding (cutting 8 or 10 feet up the trunk, beyond the reach of grazing animals). Woodland on a site continuously wooded for hundreds of years is always richer in wildlife than more recently wooded

sites. Plants and birds have adjusted to the traditional forms of woodland management. In fact, coppicing helps rather than hinders, since it allows the sunlight essential for plant growth to penetrate the woodland. Regular cycles of coppicing produce trees of different ages, each of which generates its own flora and fauna.

It is almost impossible to overestimate the importance of woodland for wildlife: three-fifths of our breeding landbirds, half of our butterflies and moths, and one sixth of our flowers need woodland habitats. As a generalisation, the older the woodland the greater are the number, range and rarity of species – flowers such as oxlip, lily of the valley and herb paris (which are among the indicators of ancient woodland), as well as the more familiar anemone and wood sorrel. Likewise native trees are invariably richer as a habitat for insects (and therefore birds and mammals) than alien species: the oak harbours 284 different kinds of insects compared to five in the horse chestnut and the solitary one associated with the plane tree. Once destroyed, the wildlife which teems in these woods could not be restored for centuries, if ever, while that which replaces it in plantations or farmland will be incomparably poorer.

Ancient woodland has an appeal beyond any specialist knowledge. It is a living entity, changing with the seasons and as much a part of our history as any building. Woodland also ranks high in popularity as a place for walks or picnics. The New Forest in Hampshire draws more visitors per square mile than the Peak District, the most visited of our national parks. The Chilterns, Epping Forest, Burnham Beeches and Hatfield Forest are other wooded areas long popular for their beauty. Latterly (and significantly) these areas have benefitted from protection as Crown land, National Trust holdings or common land. Epping and Burnham Beeches were among the woodlands saved from enclosure in the nineteenth century by the efforts of the country's oldest conservation group, the Commons, Open Spaces and Footpaths Preservation Society (founded in 1865, now rechristened the Open Spaces Society).

Epping is a fraction of the former Waltham Forest, which, like many medieval 'forests', was originally a place of woodland and pasture where kings owned the rights to deer and timber; they did not always own the land. The system was introduced by the Normans. Twenty-five forests were recorded in the Domesday book, among them the New Forest. Epping was proclaimed a forest in the twelfth century, while other royal forests in the south-east included Wychwood in Oxfordshire, Enfield Chase in Middlesex and Hatfield Forest in Essex. Hatfield, which is now owned by the National Trust, has survived with the fewest changes from its medieval form. For anyone accustomed to modern forests, it is a revelation: light and airy with grass pastures, scrub and marsh as well as woods – as much park as woodland. Some trees, including hornbeam and hawthorn, are pollarded, a characteristic feature of Essex woodland that has sadly been allowed to lapse at Epping. Others are coppiced and grouped into compartments bounded by banks; each compartment was

211

BELOW: Hatfield Forest – as much park as woodland

felled in a regular cycle to produce a regular supply of timber. Much of England once looked like this.

The variety of habitats in the New Forest is even more remarkable: heath, grass, bog, river valley, coast and several types of woods. Many visitors are surprised to discover that roughly two thirds of the 'forest' is not wooded at all. Where it differs from Hatfield is in the extent of plantations. More than twice as much land has been enclosed for plantation – two thirds with conifers – than sustains ancient broad-leaved woodland. But although the central core of 8350 acres of ancient oak and beech woodland constitutes less than 8 per cent of the New Forest as a whole, it is nevertheless eight times the size of the entire Hatfield Forest.

A landscape survey published by the Countryside Commission in 1986 said of the New Forest:

There is no area in Britain or indeed in north-west Europe with such an extent of old woodland, with so many old trees, or demonstrating the same lack of intervention over such a long period. Nowhere else in Britain today is it possible to find such a combination, or such an extent of mature deciduous woodland, inclosure woodland, open heathland and grass lawns, disposed together to form such a complex and attractive mosaic, with the added bonus of numerous grazing animals and a wealth of flora and fauna.

In size alone, the 141 square miles of the New Forest are a remarkable survival, reflecting a happy combination of poor soils, substantial Crown ownership and complex common rights. Since 1923 control of the Crown lands – 67,000 of the 92,000 acres overall – has been in the hands of the Forestry Commission. This is one reason why the forest has not been designated as a national park; the Commission's constitution precludes it from pursuing the primary duties of conservation and recreation incumbent upon national park authorities. However, a government instruction to the Forestry Commission in 1971 said, 'The New Forest is to be regarded as a national heritage and priority given to the conservation of its traditional character.' Since then the NCC, the Countryside Commission and local authorities have all been involved in discussions with the Forestry Commission about the forest's future. Central to these has been what to do about its increasing popularity; 7 million visits are estimated to be made to the forest annually, twice as many as twenty years ago.

The forest offers everything for a family day out: woods for walking, lawns for picnics and games, wild ponies for photographs and untrammelled access to open space on a scale rare in southern England. Management schemes have sought to limit the damage caused by the volume of visitors. Cars can no longer be driven so freely into the forest, camping sites have been restricted and where possible screened from view. Some local people have criticised 'the increasingly urban character of the recreational facilities', but the damage done by uncontrolled parking or camping was worse. There are other threats to the New Forest landscape. Oil refineries and power stations on the Fawley coast overshadow the

ABOVE: Roughly two-thirds of the New Forest is not wooded at all

RIGHT: New Forest ponies

eastern fringes of the forest, while new roads such as the proposed Lyndhurst bypass and oil pipelines could transform other areas. Grazing is in some places excessive while elsewhere insufficient to prevent scrub or Scots pine invading open glades or forest lawns. The renown of the New Forest should win extra resources to tackle such problems; other areas of ancient woodland have fared far worse, without attracting similar attention.

In 1981 the NCC launched a project to compile an inventory of ancient semi-natural woodland in each county of England and Wales. By examining maps, aerial photographs and local surveys it was also possible to estimate how much woodland had been lost. After twenty counties had been surveyed, the NCC estimated that on average between 30 and 50 per cent of ancient semi-natural woodland had been cleared for agriculture or converted to plantations since 1930, mostly since 1945. The percentages lost for counties in south-eastern England were: Buckinghamshire – 30 per cent; Essex –

LEFT: There is no area in north-west Europe with such an extent of old woodland as the New Forest

24 per cent; Hertfordshire – 43 per cent; Oxfordshire – 36 per cent; Surrey – 41 per cent. Results for other southern counties were due to be released later, but the pattern is not expected to change. Oliver Rackham believes that more ancient woodland may have been lost since 1945 than in the previous thousand years.

The biggest losses were caused by replanting semi-natural woodland. The principle was by no means novel; plantations in the New Forest 'inclosures' date back to 1698. Oak plantations have helped to establish this tree as a symbol of English woodland even though, in the wildwood, it was dominant only in the uplands. Beech was also widely planted. But since 1945 the replanting has consisted mainly of non-native conifers. Farmers, encouraged by government grants to increase production, also grubbed out woodland to make way for more productive farmland. Traditional techniques of woodland management such as coppicing had no place in the curriculum of agricultural colleges. If trees had any role, they were as new plantations – and if not conifers, then poplars to screen farm buildings or to form ornamental avenues. The surviving copses of ancient semi-natural woodland were frequently allowed to fall derelict without the special skills (and extra money) available for showpiece sites such as Hatfield or the New Forest. Only in the last ten years has there been a sustained attempt to manage existing woodlands on individual farms. It was part of a wider recognition that landscapes were being transformed. In south-east England, hedgerows have disappeared as the region reflected the national swing towards more intensive arable production; stone walls in the Oxfordshire Cotswolds have decayed; marshes have been drained and river meadows reseeded; but rivalling ancient woodland as the greatest casualty is chalk downland.

Chalk forms the main hills of south-east England: the South Downs, North Downs, Berkshire Downs, Wessex Downs and Chilterns. The Chilterns, with their extensive beech woodlands, are an exception to the pervading image of rolling green hills with soft, springy turf, plunging escarpments and dry valleys. Today the Chilterns retain more of their traditional landscape than the downs, where at least four-fifths of the grassland has been lost or impoverished by changing agricultural practices. Just as once they were created by changing agricultural practices.

The natural tree cover was cleared relatively easily from the thin chalk soils so that these hills became early centres of settlement. Some of our oldest routeways, notably the Ridgeway, followed the crest of chalk hills, and the downs are rich in the remains of prehistoric forts and burial mounds. For a time the downs were cultivated, but by the Middle Ages they were devoted mainly to pasture. It is grazing that prevents a return to woodland; left to itself, the grass would become scrub from which trees would eventually emerge. Sheep ruled the downs and their grazing produced a short sward in which flowers flourished that do not exist amid the rougher grasses left by cattle grazing. Some ploughing of the

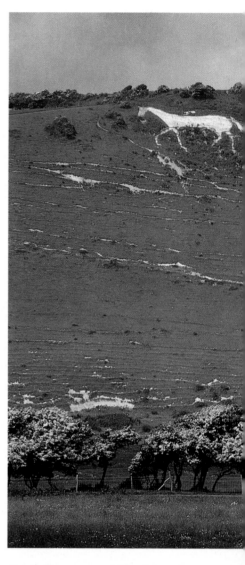

South Downs, near Litlington. Chalk forms the main hills of south-east England

Ditchling Beacon, South Downs. Much of downland is now under the plough

downlands began in the seventeenth century and continued fitfully through to the present century, spurred by wars and discouraged by falling corn prices when ploughed land would revert to grassland. Such reversion is virtually impossible today. Not only is there less uncultivated downland to act as a base for colonisation, but pesticides and new strains of grass-seed banish the wildlife associated with unimproved chalk grassland.

Twentieth-century changes have been greater in extent and more permanent. The emergency of the Second World War saw large tracts of downland ploughed, and the trend has continued, with new machines able to tackle slopes previously too steep for cultivation. Ploughing grants were withdrawn in 1972, but the profits from arable production enticed farmers to continue converting the open downs into fenced fields of wheat, barley or oil-seed rape. As farms became more specialised, arable enterprises tended to neglect pockets of grassland on the steepest slopes so that – ungrazed even by rabbits after myxamatosis – these reverted to scrubland. Conifer plantations have also taken their toll of the downs and are likely to increase as farmers seek alternative uses for their more marginal land.

Most of these changes occurred long after the wartime need for extra food had gone. The NCC has estimated that 25 per cent of the South Downs grasslands were lost between 1966 and 1980. Looking back over fifty years, the national rate of loss or damage is put at 80 per cent of all chalk and limestone grasslands. By 1985 only 6 per cent of the South Downs in East Sussex was still traditional chalk grassland. In 1976 a government survey of 660 known archaeological sites in Sussex found that 38 per cent were being damaged by ploughing. A decade later the figure was put at 50 per cent, with many completely destroyed. Among the casualties identified by the British Council for Archaeology are 6000-year-old Stone Age enclosures, 2500-year-old Iron Age hill forts and Roman villas.

Of the areas shortlisted as possible national parks in the 1940s, only the South Downs now lack this status. Ten of the twelve on the shortlist were designated during the 1950s and the eleventh, the Norfolk Broads, is promised similar status in 1988. The South Downs slipped from favour because of the large-scale conversion of grassland into arable fields. This has reduced the previously unfettered freedom (and satisfaction) of roaming open downland. It also means that the wildlife traditionally associated with chalk grassland is becoming increasingly rare. The varied and hummocky turf of unimproved downland is home to a pageant of colour which persists through the summer. The yellows of cowslip, horseshoe vetch, field fleawort and kidney vetch are usually the first to appear. Blues, pinks and whites follow with flowers such as squinancywort, viper's bugloss and rampion. In autumn, there is the purple of autumn gentian and the pink of common century. Above all, there are orchids, which thrive on the low nutrients of the thin chalk soils. The survival of some of these orchids, along with some birds and butterflies, is now threatened. An internal report compiled for East Sussex County Council in December 1985 said:

Plants such as the Early Spider Orchid and Burnt Tip Orchid are confined to only a few sites, and insects like the Adonis, Chalkhill and other Blue butterflies are similarly under threat. Birds and other fauna of the open downland have little habitat for their continued survival — what is left is threatened by the purely commercial interests of today's farming.

The fragmented nature of the surviving grassland intensifies the dangers, as a report published by Hampshire County Council's planning department explains:

The isolation of remaining chalk grasslands from each other puts their plants and animals in danger, because there is little likelihood of uncultivated sites being reinforced by the spread of seeds, plants and animals from other similar sites nearby. The picture is gloomy, and will get darker unless as many areas of chalk grassland as possible are retained.

Some areas of unimproved downland are theoretically protected as nature reserves or sites of special scientific interest

ABOVE: Fairfield Church, Romney Marsh

LEFT: Frensham Common near Hindhead – Surrey heathland

BELOW LEFT: Seven Sisters country park

(SSSIs). While neither designation is foolproof, the protection of SSSIs is particularly flawed. Landowners have to notify the NCC of any action which may damage the site, such as ploughing, aerial spraying of pesticides or afforestation. But the modest financial penalty of a £500 fine for failing to do so may not deter landowners from carrying out the work. Conversely, the NCC has to weigh the potentially high cost of compensation in deciding how far to push its objections. Away from the downs, on the north Kent marshes, in 1987 the NCC negotiated a £320,000 a year management agreement with a farmer in return for his conserving 1800 acres of grassland. More typically, landowners display a willingness to reach a compromise, yet lack access to any nationwide assistance to manage the land in ways that retain its landscape and wildlife features.

Chalk grassland has to be managed if it is to retain what we regard as its traditional qualities. So do virtually all English landscapes. In addition to ancient woodland and downland, country in south-east England which has been singled out for concern by the CPRE and the NCC includes water meadows (in Hampshire, Sussex and Oxfordshire), marshes (the Thames estuary and Romney Marsh) and heathland (Surrey and Hampshire). Marvellous examples of all these habitats still survive. Some are national nature reserves, as at North Meadow on the banks of the Thames at Cricklade. Some are Ministry of Defence training grounds, as on the Surrey heathlands. Some are preserved for public recreation, as at Seven Sisters near Eastbourne. But preserving pockets of countryside implicitly acknowledges the decline that has occurred outside these sanctuaries.

AONBs abound in southern England, yet assignation confers no powers and few sanctions against unwelcome development. However, several local authorities have adopted positive policies for the countryside which often anticipated subsequent national policies. Hertfordshire, Essex, East Sussex and Hampshire county councils are foremost in this respect.

In Hertfordshire, a management scheme run jointly with the London borough of Barnet and local district councils operates a countywide programme of developing footpaths, managing woods or heathland and generally liaising between farmers and the public. Hertfordshire County Council has also promoted a code of practice with the local National Farmers' Union (NFU) to try and protect features such as ancient woodland, hedgerows and ponds. In Essex, the county council encouraged the promotion of existing trees and helped to establish a demonstration farm at Bovingdon Hall near Braintree where conservation does not inhibit profitability. In East Sussex, job-creation teams have been used in a downland conservation scheme to help clear the scrub from slopes where grazing has been abandoned. All local authorities can tap the array of conservation and forestry grants introduced during the 1980s and several try to resolve disputes over access between landowners and leisure interests, inevitably common in a region that boasts so many

217

towns. But the most significant programmes have been a small woodlands project in East Sussex and a 'countryside heritage' policy in Hampshire.

Despite the loss of so much ancient semi-natural woodland, more remains in Sussex, Surrey and Hampshire than in any other counties. Fifteen per cent of East Sussex is wooded, with the proportion as high as 40 per cent in the Weald. From Roman to Tudor times, the Wealden woods were managed as a source of charcoal for early industry, thus limiting their destruction for agricultural purposes and adding the delights of 'hammer ponds' to the landscape. Woods continued to have an economic role long after industry

switched to water and steampower, generating timber for farm buildings, hedgerows, fireplaces and domestic furniture. By the Second World War much of the traditional market for hardwood timber was in decline, and so were the woodlands. Many were destroyed or converted to quicker-growing coni-fers, although enough remained to arouse protective concern among conservation groups.

The concern was amply justified by the findings of a study of farm woodlands in nine areas of England and Wales carried out for the Countryside Commission in 1979. The study, by the Dartington Amenity Research Trust, concluded that farm woodlands were 'a considerable asset which is badly used and whose value for a range of purposes is diminishing'. The survey was generally confined to woodlands smaller than 25 acres; most, in fact, were smaller than 3 acres. They were precisely the kind of woodlands which make England seem a wooded country, yet only 1 per cent of the farmers or

LEFT: Footpath near Radlett, Hertfordshire

ABOVE: Harewood Forest, near Andover

landowners knew how to manage them. Despite past neglect, the study argued, virtually all the woods had some value for their timber, game or contribution to the landscape; many were also ancient woodlands with 'incalculable value' for wildlife. One of the areas surveyed, in East Sussex, has since developed a new approach to managing farm woodlands.

In 1981 East Sussex County Council, the Countryside Commission and the British Trust for Conservation Volunteers joined together to help farmers manage their woodlands. The project's importance was reflected in the fact that the steering committee included representatives of the Ministry of Agriculture, Forestry Commission, NCC and NFU. It had two broad objectives: to advise landowners on how to manage woodlands (including sources of grants) and to provide practical assistance in the form of conservation volunteers or Manpower Services Commission (MSC) teams. 'My job is to devise schemes appropriate for individual owners,' says project officer David Saunders. 'Some may be looking for timber profits, some may be more interested in recreation, some in wildlife. You cannot impose one scheme on everyone. It's made-to-measure or bespoke forestry. Farmers had become specialist food producers and had neglected their woodland, often for years. They lacked the

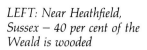

LEFT: Near Heathfield, Sussex – 40 per cent of the Weald is wooded

BELOW: Demonstration wood at Farley Farm, Chiddingly

BELOW RIGHT: Sawmills at Farley Farm

confidence, motivation, skills and usually the staff to manage their woodlands – for any objective. One consequence of this neglect was that woodland became more vulnerable to removal and conversion to agriculture.'

David Saunders has been singularly successful. The project began with a demonstration wood to show how coppicing can be reintroduced (and protected), woods thinned and new trees planted. Only broad-leaved trees native to the locality are used. It may not be entirely 'semi-natural', but the demonstration wood at Farley Farm near Chiddingly north-east of Lewes is still a place of beauty, sustaining hornbeam, alder, hazel and chestnut coppices, as well as mature oaks (known as 'coppice with standards') and 120 different species of flowers. It will also be a place of profit, thanks to David Saunders's ability to find timber markets as diverse as firewood and musical instruments. The project now covers the entire county and Farley Farm has established a sawmill in an adjoining yard. Here, too, craftsmen have set up a furniture workshop in a converted pig building.

Many farmers, accustomed to the rhythms of annual harvest and cash crops, find it difficult to adjust to the timescale involved in forestry. This is why they have often been attracted to faster-growing conifers. But the East Sussex project was fortuitously timed, catching not only a tide of public concern about trees after the loss of so many elms but, more relevantly, coinciding with the advent of new or increased grants for broad-leaved tree planting. The Countryside Commission, the NCC and the Ministry of Agriculture all offer woodland grants, sometimes through local authorities. But the most important is the Forestry Commission broad-

221

leaved grant scheme, introduced in 1985. Timber production is still a primary aim, but the importance of broad-leaved trees for landscape, wildlife and recreation is also acknowledged. In addition to higher grants for new broad-leaf planting, there is help for restocking existing woods through natural regeneration. Tighter controls on felling and management guidelines drawn up in consultation with the NCC are other elements in a package which marked a major departure from the Forestry Commission's apparent preoccupation with large-scale afforestation.

Conservationists had long complained that previous policies for woodland had been too destructive (afforestation), too negative (tree preservation orders) or too peripheral (shelter belts or field-corner copses). Now, at last, there was encouragement for broad-leaved trees, including an explicit recognition of the value of ancient semi-natural woodlands. The principles are fine, but groups such as the CPRE nevertheless have some reservations. Their doubts centre upon the exclusion of 'non-timber' species such as hazel, field maple and native shrubs, the lack of financial grants for coppicing, the insistence on strict planting plans and the limited advisory role of the NCC. Above all, perhaps, there has been worry about the emphasis on planting new woodlands rather than managing existing ancient woodland.

Broad-leaved woodlands were given a further boost, at least in theory, in 1987, when the government announced additional assistance for farm woodlands as part of its plans to divert farmland out of agriculture. Annual payments (initially envisaged as £50 an acre for the lowlands) will be paid to bridge the income gap between planting and felling, with payments over longer periods for wholly broad-leaved woodlands. Overall, the government is aiming to finance an additional 30,000 acres of woodland a year. This constitutes a substantial planting programme, with significant implications for the landscape, especially as it is likely to be mostly coniferous. Only one third of the new farm woodlands, according to government targets, would be broad-leaved. The NFU, while welcoming the principle of increased help for farm woodlands, want even fewer broad-leaved trees — and more money.

The fashion for farm forestry may thus fail to satisfy either farmers or conservationists. The NFU and the Country Landowners' Association fear that the financial help is inadequate, particularly as farmers on the whole lack any tradition or training in the management of woodlands. The conservationists fear that current policies will encourage the wrong types of trees in the wrong place. Despite new grants and new techniques to promote faster tree growth (such as the ubiquitous plastic 'Tuley tube' used to shelter and promote young trees), forestry still offers farmers a poor rate of return on their better land. In south-east England the NFU expects any increase in farm woodlands to be confined to marginal agricultural land. Yet this is the land — heathland, marshy areas, chalk escarpments — which is often the most important in terms of wildlife. Acknowledging this fear, the Ministry

Butterfly corner at Farley Farm

of Agriculture has said that the scheme will be targeted primarily on arable land and improved grassland. Welcome news but most new planting will still be coniferous.

The importance of the East Sussex woodlands project derives more from its support of existing woodlands than its assistance for new plantations. It is the existing woodlands, ancient and not-so-ancient, which are crucial for landscape and wildlife. In convincing a new generation of farmers and landowners that managing existing woodlands can reward the bank balance as well as the eye, the East Sussex project has offered a lifeline to many endangered woods. Although conversion to conifers remains a possibility, the tighter controls over clearing should help to avoid outright destruction. The government now says that felling will not normally be allowed if it is proposed to convert land to arable. It is also putting money into other woodland schemes which develop the ideas pioneered in East Sussex. By 1987 a dozen schemes were in existence, including one in the Chilterns and another

in Hampshire, where concern for woodland instigated a more comprehensive approach to conservation.

'In 1978 our councillors were worried by changes to the Hampshire countryside,' recalls Vernon Hazel, of the county council's planning department. 'We knew we were losing woodlands and we had a gut feeling that we were losing more than we realised in terms of scenic and wildlife value. All didn't seem to be well. There was a dearth of information about the countryside which was not designated as nature reserves, sites of special scientific interest or whatever, so we decided to take a look at what was happening.'

The results were published in nine detailed reports on specific topics. These delved into history before assessing the pressures of the present day. Phase two was to work out what to do with the information so impressively collated. The council's initial worry had sprung from the fact that, as

Chilbolton Common

one councillor put it, 'In my lifetime, so much of the excitement and beauty of the countryside has vanished with frightening speed.' But Hampshire is a county where farming interests are also strong. Although agriculture was singled out repeatedly in the detailed studies as the principal agent of damaging change, the county council had to move cautiously. And so, in 1984, Hampshire adopted a non-statutory policy — the first of its kind in the country — which would identify 'heritage sites' otherwise unprotected by any national designation. More than 150 sites were recorded in the first two and a half years. Many were woodland, but there were also meadows and chalk grassland; all were of scenic, ecological or historic value (perhaps all three) yet also scarce or vulnerable. Recording a site gives the council no additional powers, but enables the local authority to offer owners and farmers advice, help and possibly grants through management agreements to ensure the retention of its heritage value.

The council cannot compel compliance and farmers are free to spurn offers of help. Some do. Yet the existence of the scheme makes it more likely that more parts of countryside will be protected. One call to one council department can tap specialist conservation advice, pools of job-creation work teams or information about the dauntingly complex variety of conservation and forestry grants now available. All three services have been employed on Worthy Down, a triangle of chalk grassland north-east of Winchester. Much of the down was scrubland and the owner was planning to convert this and some neighbouring woodland to arable. For £1000 a year the farmer is keeping the down as grassland and cutting down only some of the woodland. MSC teams and volunteers cleared the scrub, and the council experts found sheep to graze the land and laid down policies for grazing intensity, fertilisers and pesticides. Elsewhere, landowners have been helped to restore ponds, reintroduce coppicing, reduce overgrazing and combat invasive bracken on heathland. Part of the work is educational, not only in schools as part of environmental education, but also in liaison with other local authorities. In the Test Valley, Hampshire County Council has sought the support of a parish council to stop plans for improved drainage on Chilbolton Common, a beautiful marshy area bordered by thatched cottages and enveloped by wooded hillsides, where cattle graze in and alongside the river which meanders sleepily across the common.

The Countryside Commission has been an enthusiastic supporter of the Hampshire initiative, which demonstrates its belief that farmers and conservationists can work together voluntarily. The Commission and the county council see heritage sites as complementary to the national policy of ESAs. David Lloyd, a member of Hampshire's countryside team, says that their efforts to protect unimproved grasslands in the Test Valley were aimed partly at holding the line until the region was designated as an ESA.

The Test Valley was one of eleven areas wholly or partly in south-east England which were in the forty-six named as

225

potential ESAs by the Countryside Commission and Nature Conservancy Council (see chapter 5, pages 177–80). Two made it into the shortlist of fourteen – the Test Valley and South Downs, and both were among the first eleven English ESAs to be chosen. Dedham Vale along the Essex–Suffolk border was included as part of the Suffolk River Valleys ESA, but excluded were the North Kent Marshes, the North Downs, Ashdown Forest, the Pevensey Levels, Surrey Heaths, the Itchen Valley, the New Forest and part of the North Wessex Downs.

The greater prosperity of some southern farmers (although far from universal) may make it more difficult for the Ministry of Agriculture to secure majority support for conservation in the south than in the uplands. Payment for maintaining chalk downs as grassland without reseeding, fertilisers or pesticides was initially a modest £14 an acre, while farmers willing to reconvert arable fields into grassland would reap roughly £65 an acre. The appeal of conservation-oriented farming will also depend upon other factors. How profitable is conventional farming? Are there other uses for potentially redundant farmland?

Threats to the countryside tend to obliterate success stories. Yet, if competing interests have been successfully reconciled, this can set precedents. The reclamation or redevelopment of disused mineral workings is another example of a positive approach to the future use of land. At Thurrock, just north of the Dartford Tunnel on the M25,

Devil's Dyke, South Downs. The South Downs was one of the first ESAs to be chosen

no fewer than twelve abandoned chalk quarries are being reclaimed. In one corner over 4000 homes are planned; elsewhere on the site, a lake will be the focal point for shops and sports facilities; a mile or so away, hypermarkets are being built and factories planned. None of these proposals is being opposed by conservationists because the developers are reclaiming land which otherwise would remain derelict. London, in fact, is ringed with active and disused gravel pits. Many which have gone out of production have been transformed into leisure parks – including the Thorpe Park theme park near Staines – and a few have even become nature reserves.

At Amwell quarry near Ware in Hertfordshire, nature coexists with the mineral workings. Whilst extraction continues on one part of the site, land already worked is being developed into a nature reserve. This does not mean simply leaving the land to take care of itself. With the advice of naturalists, a variety of bays, spits and islands have been created around a lake. Water depths and gradients of the banks have been adjusted, willows pollarded, marshland encouraged. The intention is to produce a wide variety of habitats for plant and animal communities. With the conservation project still incomplete, 169 species of birds and 266 species of flowers have been recorded at Amwell.

At the moment public access to Amwell is restricted, because quarrying is still in progress. A public path passes the site, but exploration is by invitation only and then with

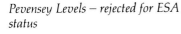

Pevensey Levels – rejected for ESA status

a compulsory hard hat. Plans exist for a path through the nature reserve in due course, not least because the industry is anxious to present a conservationist face to the world. Since 1970 the Sand and Gravel Association has given more than 250 awards to its members for restoration schemes. Just over half the prizes have been awarded for land restored to agriculture. Drainage can be a problem on restored land, along with underground gases from domestic refuse dumped into old pits, which limit soil fertility. Although techniques of restoration are improving, some loss in overall fertility is scarcely surprising given that the land has endured years of scavenging for its minerals.

However laudable (and imaginative) the attempts at restoration may be, they offer little comfort to people living near gravel pits which are still being worked. The noise, the dust and the traffic can blight the neighbourhood as well as scar the landscape. The same fears have been expressed about the prospect of oil and gas exploration. So far, the oil companies have gone to great lengths to minimise their impact upon local communities and the landscape. Conoco's appraisal well at Holmen's Grove near Haslemere in Surrey was fairly typical of fifty new wells being drilled in 1986. Meetings were held with local residents, conservation groups invited to the site, strict controls imposed on traffic (enforced by threats of instant dismissal), and the site was screened by trees. A hut on the site offered photographs, background explanation and leaflets for visitors, many of whom were given guided tours. Even where oil has been found, as at Humbly Grove near Alton in Hampshire, local conservationists acknowledge that the operations are far less obtrusive than they feared. None of this assures the oil

228

BELOW LEFT: A new route for the M40 extension will avoid Otmoor, near Oxford

BELOW: The A20 from Folkestone to Dover, where plans for road improvement have stirred strong opposition

RIGHT: Sussex Downs, threatened by a Brighton bypass

companies of a warm welcome when they alight upon sites in south-east England. Some sites, such as Fairlight Down near Hastings, may lack a protective screen of trees. Nevertheless the efforts of oil companies show a welcome awareness of public concern about the environment. Efforts to landscape new motorways are put in a similar category by government planners, although sometimes modifications are simply cosmetic.

The M40 extension from Oxford to Birmingham was the first motorway proposal which the CPRE opposed outright. Even the victory of a new route to avoid Otmoor did not dissuade Robin Grove-White, then CPRE's director, from his view that the motorway was unnecessary. Existing roads, he felt, should have been improved. Along the south coast, the opposition to the A20 improvement from Folkestone to Dover is backed by the Countryside Commission. Again, it is argued that a new motorway is unnecessary. A Brighton bypass, part of a notional M27 which the Department of Transport dreams one day will link Folkestone in Kent to Honiton in Devon, may well be needed. But its route across the downs has prompted considerable opposition. If it ever becomes the northern boundary of Brighton, much downland will be lost.

The coast generally will need careful planning if it is not to succumb totally to pressures for housing and recreation. Large stretches are already heavily developed. The longest stretch of heritage coast (see chapter 4, page 135) is off the mainland altogether, on the Isle of Wight, where just over 20 miles of the West Wight shoreline is protected. Elsewhere there are pockets of heritage coast – just over 8 miles near Dover and another 8 miles around Beachy Head near Eastbourne. However, Chichester Harbour is an AONB which provides a peaceful interlude between the busy south coast resorts. Harbour is an inappropriate word for this 29 square miles of dunes, mud flats and languid tidal waters which is now the preserve of yachtsmen rather than commercial craft. Large areas are mercifully undeveloped and it is still possible to enjoy a sense of solitude along its shore.

Chichester Harbour is one of several shorelines important for birdlife as well as human recreation. Several are threatened by development, according to the RSPB. These are the Blackwater estuary and Foulness in Essex, the Medway and Rye Harbour in Kent, and Langstone Harbour, between Chichester and Portsmouth. Foulness, Blackwater, the Medway and Langstone are all SSSIs and qualify for protection under an EEC birds directive. The development threats include not only several marinas but also barrages, holiday chalets and industrial expansion. Pollution from chemicals, sewage and power stations are other problems, along with the sheer numbers of visitors.

The density of population makes some difficulties inevitable throughout south-east England. It may be traffic jams on the roads back to London on a summer Sunday or the exposure of bare chalk on an over-visited chalk down. Local authorities and the Countryside Commission have sought to ease the pressures by creating country parks and special footpath routes, especially in the urban fringe and metro-

LEFT: Batemans—Rudyard Kipling's house at Burwash, Sussex

ABOVE: Langstone Harbour

politan green belt. Official long-distance routes traverse the downs and Chilterns, with another promised to follow the course of the Thames. Unofficial routes emphasise circular paths to entice families out of their cars. A circuit centring on Ditchling Beacon on the downs near Brighton was used by the Countryside Commission as a model of how such routes can be planned. Clearly signposted routes also lessen the likelihood of conflict with landowners, not that farmers should need such signs to maintain legal rights of way. However, as walkers increase in number and militancy, there have been disputes over paths ploughed up, planted over or fenced off. The Ramblers' Association has taken some landowners to court and launched campaigns to open up new areas for access. Among these is Wychwood Forest, a remnant of a royal hunting forest near Charlbury in Oxfordshire, partially open to the public for just one day a year.

Landowners often grumble about the litter and damage caused by the public. This undoubtedly happens and is no more forgivable in a country field than in an urban subway. But public recreation saves more country than it scars. The Seven Sisters country park near Eastbourne and the Queen Elizabeth country park near Petersfield contain some of the largest remaining tracts of chalk downland outside army training grounds. The National Trust not only safeguards but opens up for access some of the region's most beautiful and varied countryside – from downland, heathland, woodland and riversides to hammer ponds, windmills, gardens and exquisite half-timbered cottages. Access to national nature reserves is sometimes more restricted but in this lowland, supposedly town-dominated region, these reserves include chalk downland, semi-natural ancient woodland, seashore,

ABOVE LEFT: Rye Harbour caravan site

ABOVE: Ditchling Beacon

RIGHT: A clearly signposted circuit centring on Ditchling Beacon has been used by the Countryside Commission as a model of how such routes can be planned.

heathland, wetlands and Europe's oldest yew forest at Kingley Vale in Sussex.

Such variety is the essence of south-east England's charm. A day out in the country can mean hiking along the Ridgeway or angling in a Hampshire trout stream, sailing in the Blackwater estuary or visiting Winston Churchill's home in Kent. There are bustling seaside resorts, ancient market towns and sleepy villages. They survive, often altered, sometimes impaired, but how will they fare in the next century? The uncertainties afflicting agriculture could present unparalleled opportunities for a new alliance between farmer and conservationist, country and town. However difficult it will be to achieve an integrated approach in practice, there need be no conflict in principle. The protection of rural England is in everyone's interests. It preserves the countryside not only for agriculture but for recreation within reasonable reach of the nine in ten people who live in towns; it also prevents towns from sprawling into each other or submerging country lifestyles. Yet the dangers are at least as great as the opportunities; and nowhere is more vulnerable to destructive development than this most populous south-east corner of the British Isles.

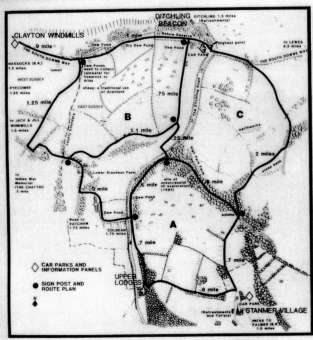

THE DOWNS WALK

These paths are suitable for inexperienced walkers. The network will take you to the top of the Downs with panoramic views, into tranquil valleys, through mature woodlands and past historic landmarks.

The Circular Walks are

A – 3.60 miles from Stanmer or Upper Lodges
B – 5.00 miles from Clayton Windmills
C – 3.80 miles from Ditchling Beacon

Combinations of these circuits provide longer walks. The outer circuit is 7.35 miles and takes about 3½ hours. Allow more time if it has been wet or you have children or inexperienced walkers with you.

Car Parks Each starting point has a car park. At peak periods (Bank Holidays and summer weekends, for instance) parking may be difficult at Ditchling and Clayton Windmills. Try Stanmer or use Public Transport.

Buses (May be subject to change)

At Stanmer Park Gates (18, 19, 21, 22, 28, 729, 799) – to Brighton and Lewes, minimum 2 per hour.
At Clayton* and Pyecombe Garage (770, 771) – To Brighton and Haywards Heath, 2 per hour. 1 per hour on Sundays
(773) – To Brighton and Crawley, 1 per hour, Monday to Saturday.

*Last bus to Brighton 6.30 p.m.
Last bus to Haywards Heath 7.15 p.m.

At Coldean (25a) – To Brighton, 4 per hour.
At Hollingbury (36a) – To Brighton, 4 per hour.
At Patcham (5, 5a, 5b) – To Brighton and Hove, 4 per hour.

Rambler No.23 and Open Top No.24 run on Sundays and bank holidays during summer. SEE TIMETABLE FOR DETAILS.

Trains

Falmer – To Brighton and Lewes minimum 2 per hour.
Hassocks – To Brighton and London minimum 2 per hour.

Be prepared for the weather
– Wear suitable clothing.

1. **FIND YOUR STARTING POINT ON THE MAP.**
2. **CHOOSE YOUR ROUTE.**
3. **FOLLOW THE BLUE OR YELLOW WAYMARK ARROWS CONTAINING THE "SOUTH DOWNS CIRCULAR WALKS" LOGO.**
4. **EACH CIRCULAR WALK JUNCTION HAS A SIGNPOST WITH A ROUTE PLAN SHOWING YOUR POSITION.**

Follow the Country Code ● Enjoy the countryside and respect its life and work ● Guard against all risk of fire ● Fasten all gates ● Keep dogs under close control ● Keep to public paths across farmland ● Use gates and stiles to cross fences, hedges and walls ● Leave livestock, crops and machinery alone ● Take your litter home ● Help to keep all water clean ● Protect wildlife, plants and trees ● Take special care on country roads ● Make no unnecessary noise

For further information and comments to the Director of Parks and Recreation, Brighton 602271 or South Downs Conservation Officer Lewes 475400 Ext 244

For general walking in the area: Ordnance Survey Map Sheet Brighton and the Sussex Vale Outdoor Leisure Map or Brighton and the Downs Landranger 198

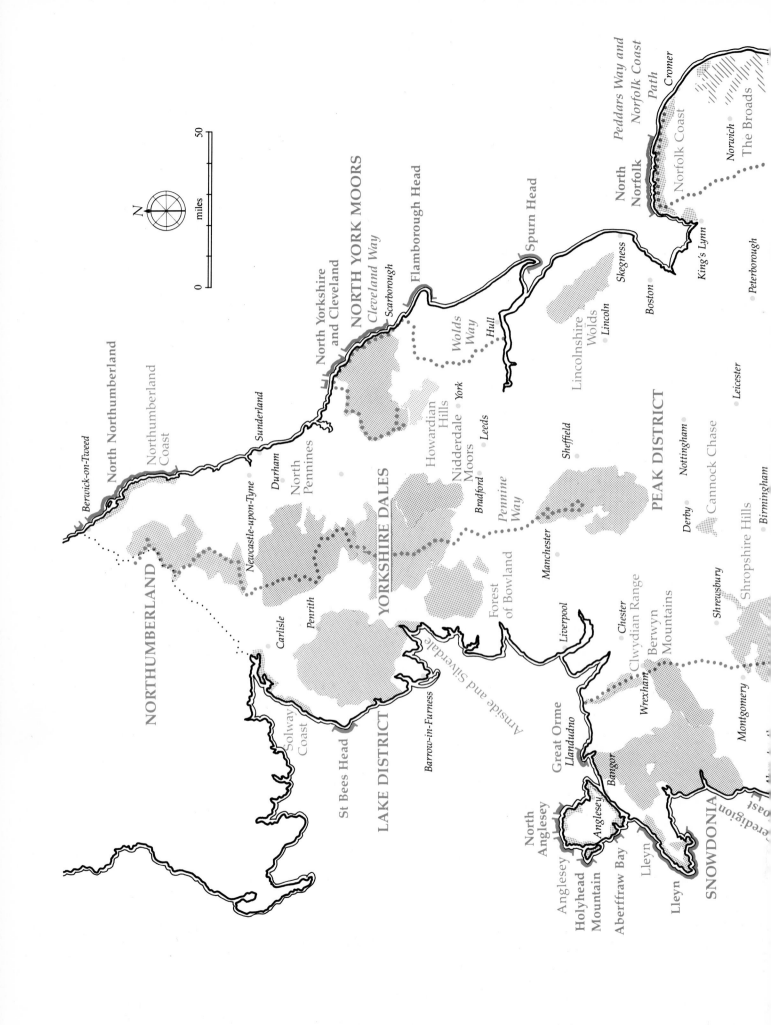

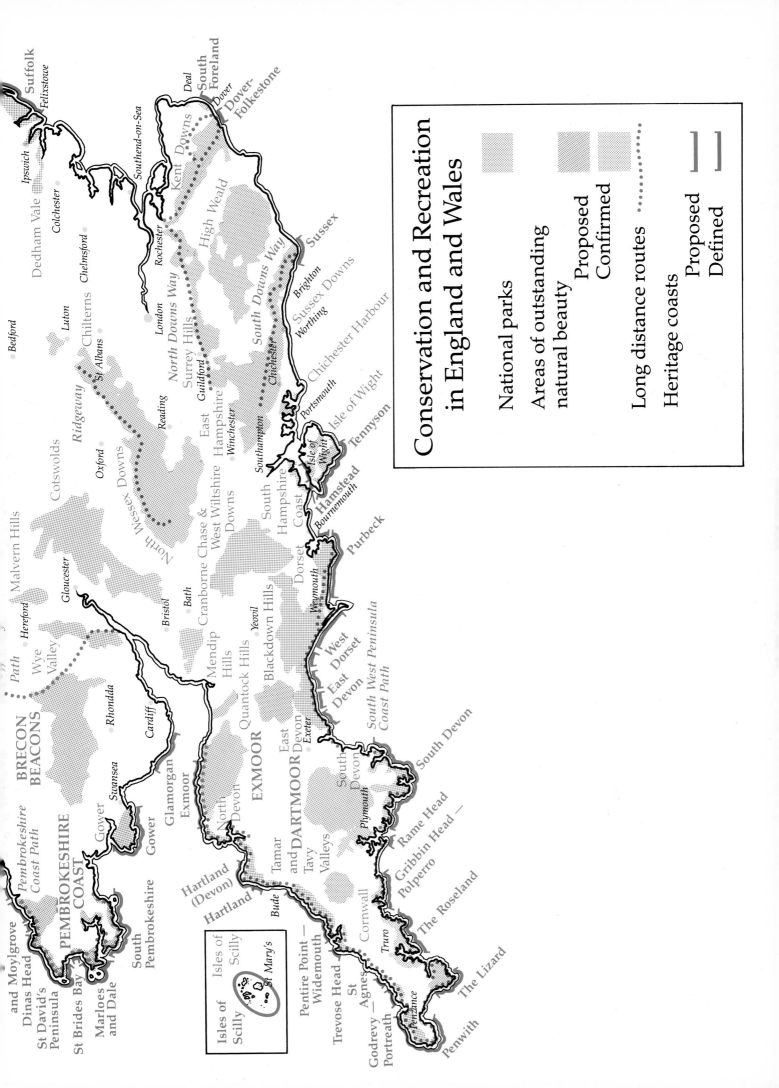

Conservation and Recreation
in England and Wales

National parks

Areas of outstanding
natural beauty
    Proposed   Confirmed

Long distance routes   ••••••••

Heritage coasts

    Proposed

    Defined

Suffolk
Felixstowe
Ipswich
Dedham Vale
Colchester
Chelmsford
Bedford
Luton
Chilterns
St Albans
Ridgeway
Cotswolds
Oxford
Reading
North Wessex Downs
Gloucester
Malvern Hills
Hereford
Wye Valley
Path
Bristol
Bath
Cranborne Chase &
West Wiltshire Downs
Mendip Hills
Yeovil
Quantock Hills
Blackdown Hills
Weymouth
Dorset
West Dorset
East Devon
South West Peninsula
Coast Path
South Devon
South Devon
Plymouth
Rame Head
Gribbin Head —
Polperro
The Roseland
South Devon
Exeter
East Devon
DARTMOOR
Tamar
and Tavy Valleys
EXMOOR
North Devon
Glamorgan
Exmoor
Gower
Gower
Swansea
Cardiff
Rhondda
BRECON
BEACONS
Pembrokeshire
Coast Path
PEMBROKESHIRE
COAST
South
Pembrokeshire
St Brides Bay
Marloes
and Dale
St David's
Peninsula
Dinas Head
and Moylgrove
Hartland
(Devon)
Hartland
Bude
Pentire Point —
Widemouth
Trevose Head —
St
Agnes
Godrevy —
Portreath
Cornwall
Truro
Penwith
Penzance
The Lizard

Isles of
Scilly
Isles of
Scilly
St Mary's

Deal
South Foreland
Dover
Dover-
Folkstone
Southend-on-Sea
Kent Downs
Rochester
High Weald
London
North Downs Way
Surrey Hills
Guildford
East
Hampshire
Winchester
South Downs Way
Chichester
Sussex
Brighton
Worthing
Sussex Downs
Chichester Harbour
Portsmouth
Southampton
Isle of Wight
Isle of
Wight
Tennyson
Hamstead
Bournemouth
South
Hampshire
Coast
Purbeck

AFTERWORD

A message from CPRE

Rural England is a compelling assessment of the issues facing our rural landscapes. As such, it charts the role of one of England's most impressive countryside pressure groups – the Council for the Protection of Rural England (CPRE) – in its unceasing fight over more than sixty years to protect and enhance England's most treasured national asset: our countryside.

CPRE was established in 1926, and has operated since then, as an independent charity free from any party affiliation, in the vanguard of countryside protection policies. In the 1930s CPRE helped secure that most effective of all safeguards against thoughtless, damaging change – the Town and Country Planning system. By constant diligence and effective use of its lobbying skills, CPRE turned the tide of ribbon development and obtrusive advertisements, and helped create irresistible pressure for establishing our National Parks. Down the years it has built on these early triumphs and constantly nurtured Parliament's understanding of the importance of our countryside to the nation as a whole.

Today, CPRE has 44 Country Branches and Associations – one in every English County, and over 30,000 individual members. It is very proud of its reputation for excellent research, diligence and persistence, and its ability to mobilise public opinion in defence of the countryside. Literally thousands of battles, local and national, up and down the country, have been won by CPRE's tireless efforts. Many are charted in this book.

This is not just a matter of saying 'No!' CPRE helps to channel local energies into solutions which positively enhance, rather than damage, the environment. It plays a key role in developing new policies for the future, for instance farm policies which encouraged the ripping out of local landscape features – hedgerows, ponds and heaths – have begun to be refocused as a result of CPRE pressure.

The challenges for tomorrow are as great as they have ever been in the past. *Rural England* ends with a metaphorical questionmark as uncertainties about key countryside policies abound in the late 1980s.

The first is fundamental, especially to CPRE. Planning has become an unfashionable word, as 'enterprise' and 'market forces' become, at least superficially, more attractive motivations for business and development. More explicitly, trends towards deregulation in the planning process and the threat to the future shape of strategic planning documents (especially County Structure Plans) are of deep concern to CPRE.

CPRE must help rebuild public confidence in a robust, creative planning system which is not incompatible with the notion of enterprise and is capable of guiding, in the wider public interest, the direction of market forces. And as development pressures in the prosperous parts of the country intensify, and creative new development is needed to revive vulnerable rural areas, the planning system has a unique role to play in delivering vibrant rural settlements and a green, protected and beautiful countryside.

The second major challenge for CPRE lies in the re-shaping of the European Community's agricultural policies as public outrage about the volume and cost of farm surpluses grows. There is, now, unanimity in Europe about the need to cut the cost of the CAP, but little about how it might be done without destroying the countryside, farmers' livelihoods and rural economies in the process.

Whatever the measures selected — and there are many proposed, including the troubling and negative prospect of land 'set-aside', CPRE will be in the forefront, arguing for agricultural policies which integrate the need for appropriate levels of food production with environmental protection, public enjoyment and jobs in the countryside.

And the local battles — a bypass here, intrusive housing development there, the devastation caused by opencast coal extraction, and so many other threats — will go inexorably on. A strong, effective CPRE voice for the countryside was never more important than now. Nor has CPRE ever been in more need of *your* support and involvement. Your backing — and those of thousands of others — is what we rely on to make our voice heard. Please help us, by making a donation or by joining CPRE. Without your support and CPRE's tireless efforts, tomorrow's rural England will be a poorer place.

Please help us!

CPRE
4 Hobart Place
London SW1W OHY

237

INDEX

INDEX

240